UNACCOUNTABLE

How the Accounting Profession Forfeited a Public Trust

Mike Brewster

WILEY

John Wiley & Sons, Inc.

Published by John Wiley & Sons, Inc., Hoboken, New Jersey.
Published simultaneously in Canada.

For general information on our other products and services, or technical support, please
contact our Customer Care Department within the United States at 800-762-2974, outside
the United States at 317-572-3993 or fax 317-572-4002.

Wiley also publishes its books in a variety of electronic formats. Some content that appears in
print may not be available in electronic books.

For more information about Wiley products, visit our web site at www.wiley.com.

Library of Congress Cataloging-in-Publication Data:

Brewster, Mike.
    Unaccountable : how the accounting profession forfeited a public trust / Mike Brewster.
        p.   cm.
    ISBN 0-471-42362-9 (cloth)
    1. Accounting—Moral and ethical aspects.   2. Public
interest.   3. Responsibility.   I. Title.
    HF5625.15 .B74 2003
    657'.09—dc21

                                                                                    2002156440

Printed in the United States of America.

10 9 8 7 6 5 4 3 2 1

For Bill,
who made work fun

ACKNOWLEDGMENTS

WO GOOD FRIENDS AND COLLEAGUES, PAUL ROGERS AND BILL Schwartzman, volunteered their time to read this manuscript. Their suggestions made the book much better. Robert Brewster, Michele Turk, and Amey Stone read parts of the manuscript and offered improvements.

Many people recommended sources or otherwise smoothed the way for interviews, including Jennifer Scardino, Lanier Stone, Frances Burke, Dana Hermanson, Lynn Turner, David Rogers, Denise Schmandt-Besserat, Jonathan Goldsmith, Sharon Roll, Courtney Rowe, Wayne Guay, Dwight Owsen, Will Shafer, and Seth Kaufman.

I'd like to give special thanks to Jean Ashton, Bernie Crystal, and the rest of the staff at the Columbia University Rare Book and Manuscript Library. Their help with the Robert Montgomery and PricewaterhouseCoopers collections was invaluable. The staff of the Thomas J. Watson Library at Columbia University Business School were gracious and helpful beyond my expectations.

My wife, Amey, not only made this book better, but also made the process fun, which was no small feat. After all, this book is about accounting.

Susan Barry, my agent, provided the voice of reason exactly when needed, time and again. My thanks to Jeanne Glasser and Wiley for seeing the value in this topic.

ACKNOWLEDGMENTS

Several excellent books about the history of accounting and auditing greatly helped my understanding of the profession, including *A History of Accountancy in the United States,* by Gary John Previts and Barbara Dubis Merino; *The Accounting Wars,* by Mark Stevens; *In the Public Interest,* by Harvey Kapnick; and *The Accounting Profession, Years of Trial: 1969–1980,* by Wallace E. Olson.

Much of the material for this book was based on approximately 45 interviews conducted between August 2002 and December 2002. All the people quoted directly, without a footnote, were interviewed by me. Several people interviewed asked not to be named or spoke to me only on background. My thanks to everyone who gave so generously of his or her time. Information for this book was also gathered from primary documents, including historic accounting papers and records, congressional testimony, court filings, and annual reports.

M. B.

CONTENTS

CONTENTS

MY INTRODUCTION
TO ACCOUNTING

I N THE SPRING OF 1993, FRESH OUT OF COLUMBIA'S GRADUATE School of Journalism, I responded to 20 or 30 classified advertisements for corporate communications jobs appearing in the *New York Times*. A few days later, I received a message from a man named Bill Sand, who was "calling from Peat Marwick about the writing job." Annoyed that Bill—obviously an incompetent lackey employed by some guy named "Pete"—hadn't even mentioned the name of the company that he and Pete worked for, I called back and left a noncommittal message. Later that day, Bill returned my call and started to fill me in about Peat Marwick and the world of the "Big Six" accounting firms. When I was still a bit slow on the uptake about the firm's place in the world, Bill employed an effective phrase that I, too, would use in the years ahead when confronted with someone who had not heard of Peat Marwick: "It's like Price Waterhouse."

Another thing Bill said stuck in my mind: "You might not know much about accountants, but, believe it or not, the good ones are some of the smartest and hardest-working people you'll ever meet." At the time, I knew even less about accountants than Bill suspected. I associated accountants with just three things: (1) good penmanship; (2) Ebenezer Scrooge; and (3) Ward Cleaver, of *Leave It to Beaver* (okay, Ward may have been an actuary).

MY INTRODUCTION TO ACCOUNTING

It didn't seem to matter to Bill that I knew little about accounting, and he hired me after our first interview. The purpose of Bill's small band of writers and graphic designers was to assist KPMG's partners win new audit, tax, and consulting clients by writing and designing marketing proposals. When a Fortune 500 company decides to switch auditors or to devise a plan to pay less in taxes, it often issues a request for proposal (RFP), which lists the requirements for the job and elicits information from potential firms about their qualifications. KPMG's partners and senior managers (senior managers are one rung below partners and are typically the hardest-working people at these firms) supplied the technical verbiage for the proposals, and Bill taught us how to edit their ungainly copy and to handle ourselves in strategy meetings with the firm's top partners (rule number one: You should "dummy up" for about a year, until you understood what was really going on).

By the time I joined Bill's group, it had become astonishingly adept at churning out winning proposals, which typically consisted of a pleasantly over-the-top brew of shameless flattery of the client, personal entreaties by the partners who so desperately wanted to win the contract, and dry accounting work plans. It was very clear that our firm was pitching to assist the client's management team, not to act as a watchdog over them.

At the time, this didn't strike me as a conflict in any way. During my career at KPMG, if you had asked me what the job of a Big Five accountant was, I would have said: "To understand a client's business and to help that client run its business better." That was the primary message conveyed in these proposals—that we understood our clients better than the other firms and could, therefore, better help them improve operations, pinpoint the risks facing their business, and so on. And our partners were very, very good at helping clients. In fact, I quickly found out that Bill was right in saying that a good accounting partner had to be both a superior intellect and a glutton for hard work. I always admired the tenacity, business acumen, organizational skills, and single-minded focus of KPMG's best partners. Many times, after working all day at a client, a partner I was working with would call me at 6 P.M. to say he was coming to the office to start

3

working on the proposal draft. Other times, after working for 70 hours during the week, a partner would rewrite the proposal draft on a weekend.

In retrospect, it's abundantly clear that unyielding devotion to client service can undermine the skepticism needed to perform a rigorous audit. Partners at many accounting firms were essentially leading dual professional lives in the late 1990s: independent auditor and expert business adviser. During my seven years in the industry, each of the global firms—KPMG, PricewaterhouseCoopers, Deloitte & Touche, Arthur Andersen, and Ernst & Young—shifted its focus from auditing to consulting. In fact, by 2001, the bulk of Big Five revenues came from consulting sales.

By the time I left KPMG in late 2000 to start a magazine for McGraw-Hill, I had been director of the New York group for two years, and Bill was in a national marketing job. Just as I was leaving, Securities and Exchange Commission (SEC) chairman Arthur Levitt was engaged in a showdown with the profession over consulting. Levitt wanted to introduce rules that would bar accounting firms from offering most consulting services to their audit clients, reasoning that it would be exceedingly difficult for an auditor to provide an independent opinion on a company's financial reports if his or her consulting colleagues were huddling with company management at the same time. I remember thinking at the time that Levitt was right. I also remember thinking that he didn't have a chance of succeeding.

That, as they say, was then.

Since the collapse of Enron in late 2001, the accounting profession has forfeited what was nearly unconditional respect from the public. It has lost its peer review system and the ability to self-regulate performance. The profession watched as one of its own—Andersen—was put out of its misery by the Justice Department with a June 2002 conviction for obstruction of justice. In addition, a comprehensive new law, the Sarbanes-Oxley Act, has created a powerful accounting oversight body, and the profession's last real friend—former SEC chairman Harvey Pitt—was forced to resign in November 2002 after he bungled the search for a leader of the new oversight board.

Back in 1993, I'm sure I wasn't alone in my stereotyping of accountants. And now, nearly 10 years later, most Americans still stereo-type accountants, though the general classifications have shifted slightly: good shredding skills, Ebenezer Scrooge (it's timeless), and Al Capone. These impressions have been formed over the previous two years as the once-sleepy profession has come to the fore. Here's what the public has learned: Something is clearly broken in the accounting industry. The disgraced and defunct Arthur Andersen abdicated at Enron just about every fiduciary responsibility it had and then invented some new ones to flout. Corporate restatements are increasing in number every year. Companies are cooking the books, and auditors are letting them get away with it.

While there is certainly much truth to the public perception that accounting is broken and needs to be fixed, something much more basic and profound has been missed. A profession that prided itself on technical skill, modest ambitions, and public service has turned into a profit-maximizing industry rooted in salesmanship, product development, and double-digit annual growth. Satiating this hunger for growth and profit—as became evident in 2001 and 2002—is not in sync with safeguarding the public trust.

None of this means that accountants are bad people. In fact, one of the great ironies is that accountants are often model citizens. Accounting firm partners are leaders in their communities, civic organizations, and schools. They volunteer their time and money for all sorts of causes. Many accounting firm partners have families they are devoted to and wish they could spend more time with. Part of my reason for writing this book is fascination with a profession that, though bulging with conscientious professionals who work 70, 80, or 90 hours a week, seems to have so little understanding today of what the public wants from it or how to go about fulfilling these expectations. For example, it was widely reported in late 2002 that accounting firms torpedoed the candidacy of John Biggs as head of a powerful new accounting oversight body, even though the public clearly wanted a reformer like Biggs in the position.

One of the most striking things about this shift to profit is that most accountants at the big firms don't even realize how different their profession was 100 years ago or even 30 years ago. One example is fraud. Today's auditors insist that searching for management fraud is not within their purview. But in the historical research I did for this book, much of it from original accounting documents hundreds of years old, I found that ferreting out management fraud was for hundreds of years one of the accountant's most important fuctions. The following is from a December 1909 memo to all Price Waterhouse offices in the United States from the firm's legendary senior partner, George May, often referred to as the "father of American accounting":

> The rate of client defalcations [cases of fraud] is unacceptable and review of inventory and vouchers by Price Waterhouse auditors is perfunctory and insufficient. This is bound in the long run to lead to an omission to discover some fraud which could have been discovered; or to the loss of credit for that discovery, which might have followed from the observance of the above precautions.[1]

The next excerpt is the text from a 1993 Price Waterhouse, New York–office, weekly newsletter regarding the firm's audit of AlliedSignal:

> [Our] five managers took on the challenging assignment with tremendous enthusiasm. Their observations and recommendations went far beyond management's expectations. The results of their work resulted in immediate direct savings for AlliedSignal and will enhance the company's competitive position going forward. Their work led directly to an additional consulting project in another automotive sector division and has enhanced and deepened our relationship throughout the organization. In addition, we have been asked to expand this approach within AlliedSignal as well as to assist in training the internal audit department in the process.[2]

The juxtaposition of these two very typical writings of their times, both Price Waterhouse documents, precisely captures the evolution of the audit over the past century. The first is concerned with the quality of the auditing work being done by partners, the disturbing possibility that client fraud was escaping the notice of Price Waterhouse partners, and the opportunities the firm missed to enhance its reputation by finding fraud. The second encapsulates the five essentials to auditing in the 1990s: (1) "exceed expectations," or show management how eager the audit team is to please; (2) find "cost savings" for the client throughout their operations, which will enhance the audit team's reputation as a trusted adviser; (3) structure the audit so that it inevitably leads to consulting services; (4) "deepen" the relationship with management, a phrase that implies shared goals and that should set off independence alarms with any decent auditor; and (5) take over the internal audit function, thus creating additional fees and perhaps cutting down on the hassle of dealing with internal auditors when doing the external audit work.

THE ACCOUNTANT AND THE PUBLIC TRUST

A zeal to safeguard the public trust began long before George May's Price Waterhouse. With the exception of accounting historians, however, almost no one realizes the tremendous public responsibility and respect that has been given throughout history to the people now referred to as "accountants." It's not an overstatement to say that modern society would have never developed without the people who brokered, sanctioned, recorded, and organized economic transactions. For thousands of years, those who controlled and monitored society's finances were often the most powerful, respected, and influential people in the community. From the collectors at communal granaries in the ancient Middle East to the scribes who monitored Queen Victoria's Exchequer, the accountant's role has been to preserve the integrity of financial systems.

The giants of early-twentieth-century U.S. accounting, from British import George May to a young accounting professor in Chicago named Arthur Andersen, essentially created an honorable profession in the United States from scratch. They forged their own standards, rules, and ethical norms, and relied on their own professional pride and ironclad integrity to guide their business in the public interest. Not only did early-twentieth-century U.S. accountants play a vital role in shaping the transparency of U.S. capital markets, but they also advised the Allies in World War I armistice negotiations, formulated the innovation of consolidated financial statements, advised Congress on the creation of the federal income tax law, and came up with the idea of a gross national product (GNP).

Consider this example: In 1966, Leon Kendall was the vice president and economist of the New York Stock Exchange (NYSE). A high-ranking priest from the Vatican on an official visit to Kendall happened to mention that he was very concerned about the corruption he saw in Brazil and other South American countries. The priest bemoaned the lack of honest record keeping in that part of the world, and he granted that U.S. accountants were the "secret weapons" behind the econonomic clout of the United States. He wanted help from the NYSE to "train" priests throughout South America in rudimentary accounting so they could become the "CPAs" (certified public accountants) of South America.[3]

The questions this book poses and attempts to answer are: Why did the profession squander this legacy of public service? What happened to the public accountants that presidents, senators, and captains of industry like J. P. Morgan ran to for advice with the toughest economic questions of the day? How has it come to be that this profession finds itself in its current unlikely and humiliating state? Some of the answers to these questions are, ironically, grounded in the profession's own astounding success.

A PUBLIC TRUST

Certified public accountants employed as auditors at accounting firms examine public company financial statements and vouch for their adherence to generally accepted accounting principles (GAAP). As then–SEC chairman Arthur Levitt said in a June 6, 1996, speech concerning the critical role of accountants: "They are highly sophisticated, knowledgeable professionals. And they serve one of the most valuable functions in a capitalist society. Their stock in trade is neither numbers, nor pencils, nor columns, nor spreadsheets, but *truth.* Accountants are the people who protect the truth."[4]

CPAs derive their independent auditing franchise from two pieces of landmark New Deal legislation: the Securities Act of 1933 and the Securities Exchange Act of 1934. The idea, however, that U.S. accountants *owe* their independent audit franchise to the generosity of the federal government is patently untrue. Before 1933, more than 80 percent of public companies listed on the NYSE had their financial statements audited by independent auditors. This was because companies needing capital or wanting their stock to be attractive to investors needed a competent third party to vouch for the accuracy of their financial statements. The government had nothing to do with it; and, in fact, during congressional debate over the acts of 1933 and 1934, the ignorance of the senators about the proliferation of independent audits was laughable. Congress, in fact, foolishly considered barring audits by private firms and, instead, hiring its own corps of government auditors. As Colonel Arthur Carter, senior partner of accounting firm Haskins & Sells, testifying before the assembled senators, said, "You had better plan on some more buildings in Washington to house [the auditors]."[5]

Eventually, Colonel Carter convinced Congress that audits should continue to be performed by CPAs. The period until 1950 can be summed up as a time when the ethos of the British-founded firm Price Waterhouse dominated. George May, though retired from Price Waterhouse, remained the voice of the profession; accountants themselves suggested accounting principles; there were few hard and fast reporting rules for companies; and auditors showed considerable backbone to management. But it was also true that financial statements were not prepared to be easily understood by the general public. While companies disclosed alternative accounting principles or methods used to come up with their numbers, they did not make any attempt to explain why they chose such principles and the impact that the choice had on the financial statements.[6]

After 1950, a man named Leonard Spacek, who succeeded Arthur Andersen as head of Andersen when the founder died in 1947, changed everything. Andersen himself had believed that the talented workforce of young auditors whom he had personally recruited from the colleges around Chicago could do all sorts of work for a client and that they could do it better than anyone else. He also thought it necessary to keep challenging his young professionals or they would move on to another line of work, due to the inherent drudgery of auditing financial statements. Spacek took this legacy and supercharged it with bravado, ambition, and a determination to make Andersen the leader in providing new nonaudit services, like installing computerized accounting systems for clients. Indeed, in the 1950s, when most people believed that computers were useful only for scientists and fantasy writers, Spacek's Andersen consultants installed in General Electric's Louisville, Kentucky, office an early vacuum tube computer that was designed to modernize the office's payroll system.[7]

Accounting firms soon realized that through the audit relationship forged with a company, they might easily have an inside track to various projects throughout the client's operations and administration. The auditor saw the company's finances across all lines of business, became well acquainted with the management team, and had front-row seats to operational problems at warehouses or far-flung locations.

Parlaying this advantage, the largest accounting firms, through sheer determination and good business sense, became the consultants of choice for hundreds of the best U.S. companies. Then, companies in the newly competitive 1980s raised the stakes again—increasingly wanting business advice, not just a stamp of approval on their books. As consulting revenues climbed, big accounting firms decided they could not survive with the audit as their marquee service. As firms downplayed traditional auditing services, the auditor's function became less and less valued, cutthroat com-petition pushed their profit margins lower and lower, and the selling of consulting services and the parrying of lawsuits became the most important business of the firms. CPAs had begun their transformation from trusted public watchdogs into fierce advocates for Corporate America.

The lack of interest in the audit within the big firms—the ramifications of which the public is just beginning to see today—was nudged along by reasons other than just higher profit margins in consulting. The everaccelerating pace of corporate mergers, for example, meant fewer public company audits to divvy up among the big firms. The explosion of shareholder lawsuits in the late 1960s and 1970s made auditing more risky than consulting engagements and caused the firms' litigation insurance to go sky-high. Global expansion meant that companies were more difficult and more expensive to audit. Audit professionals and prospective auditors still in college were increasingly attracted to the more glamorous and rough-and-tumble worlds of investment banking, securities trading, investor relations, and brokerage services.

By the 1990s, it was decided at the global accounting firms that the audit function had to morph into something new, something that the client valued—a business instrument that, instead of simply validating financial information, told companies something of value about their business. Incredibly, the firms took a service on behalf of the shareholder and turned it into an information-gathering tool for the client. This served two purposes: (1) to sell consulting services that would inevitably result from this new information, and (2) to rationalize higher fees. As the audit report itself became a tool for the client rather than for the public, so, too, did the auditing team become an extension of the management team rather than a representative of the shareholders.

THE SITUATION NOW

By June 2001, more than 70 percent of accounting firm revenues came from consulting, according to proxies filed by public companies. This number surprised even the SEC, which had mandated a year earlier that firms start reporting their revenue breakdowns. Then came more bad accounting news from Waste Management, Cendant, Rite Aid, Adelphia, Xerox, Tyco, and, of course, Enron and WorldCom. Early 2003 marks the public relations and, perhaps, technical auditing nadir of the professional accountant in the United States.

It will be a long road back for the profession to regain the confidence of the public. As Mike Cook, former chief executive officer (CEO) of Deloitte & Touche, said: "The profession's stock is at an all-time low. We have dropped a long way in public perception due to where we positioned ourselves in the last couple of years. This time, we are dealing from a much weaker position. The public has said: 'Number one, you don't audit very well; number two, you don't have a real commitment to the public trust.'"

It's easy for people who have never performed an audit to simply say that those who perform shoddy auditing get what they deserve in terms of litigation. As many auditors will attest, however, the workload, deadlines, and level of responsibility at a tier-one or tier-two accounting firm are harrowing. Florie Munroe, now an internal auditor at Greenwich (Connecticut) Hospital, worked at Price Waterhouse for nearly 10 years, where she rose to senior manager. She described an environment in which partners, juggling many client responsibilities, would come in to review the fieldwork that the audit staff had done. "You have this tremendous amount of sensitive work that needs to get done in a short amount of time," Munroe said. "Many, many times, this is where audit failures occur. A partner just has to give the thumbs up or thumbs down because of the deadline. The partner has to think, 'What is the likelihood that what I'm about to do will blow up?'"

In July 2002, the discovery that another former Andersen client, WorldCom, inflated its bottom line by billions of dollars by recording expenses as capital improvements—a simple sleight of hand in accounting terms—was a body blow to the profession. As Jon Madonna, former CEO at KPMG, put it: "I don't understand how you could miss WorldCom. When I heard that, I was just like everyone else in asking, where were the auditors?" Just prior to this revelation, it seemed that steam had run out on Capitol Hill for a major accounting bill that many wanted passed in response to the Enron crisis. The WorldCom debacle forced Congress's hand, leading to the Sarbanes-Oxley bill, which created a new oversight board with great power to regulate the profession.

"Before WorldCom, accounting legislation was basically going nowhere," said Lynn Turner, former SEC chief accountant under Arthur Levitt. "Then that weekend, after the WorldCom news broke, you saw new polls out that corporate corruption was the number one issue, and things got done." As Congress debated, the profession could only sit back and watch as their suggestions were brushed off. As one former CEO of a big accounting firm put it: "We had no credibility left. They didn't have to listen to us."

Despite this tumultuous year, many people who should have known better trotted out tired old cliches about the profession. A piece in the April 22, 2002, issue of *The New Yorker* on the crisis in accounting carried a lead sentence that spoke volumes about the reporter's attitude toward her subject: "Nothing, it is said, is duller than accounting."[8] The accountant's world is, of course, no duller than the supposedly rollicking worlds of corporate law, investment banking, or the brokerage business. In fact, auditing is a high-stakes, complicated art that cuts across the fault lines dividing government and the private sector.

One obstacle the profession faces now is that after losing its reputation for integrity, it will be difficult to get that reputation back. The biggest reservoir of value that big professional services firms have is their good name, and Andersen's fate made it devastatingly clear what happens when that good name is tarnished. When a big public company like Citigroup takes a few hits, as it did in late 2002 over its loans to Enron and the web of apparent conflicts personified by disgraced analyst Jack Grubman, it can boast of higher credit card issuances or more consumer lending. When Andersen's reputation was sullied, however, its clients ran faster than actuaries from a roulette wheel, because the expertise and integrity of its partners is *all* Andersen sold. There was nowhere for Andersen to hide, and there may be nowhere for the rest of the accounting profession to hide if audit failures keep materializing. There is no guarantee that another global firm won't go the way of Andersen. As accounting professor Wayne Guay of the Wharton School (University of Pennsylvania) put it, "We only have three big auto makers. Who is to say how many accounting firms we need?"

CLIENT SERVICE

Every incentive for auditors at big accounting firms motivates them to assist, to please, and to retain their all-important blue-chip clients. "The phrase 'client service' is one of those terms that has become very seductive," said Stephen Zeff, an eminent accounting historian at Rice University in Texas. "But what does that mean when these firms say they are proud of the service they provide their clients? It means they are advocating for them to the point where the auditors are not independent anymore."

Auditors have been paid by their clients since the inception of the CPA designation, making the notion of complete independence of auditors a fantasy. The Sarbanes-Oxley Act will not alter the fundamental power dynamic between the company management team and the accounting firm partner so desperate to show how energetic, helpful, and smart his or her team is. As Jon Madonna said, "If Andersen didn't get a dollar of consulting from Enron, David Duncan [Andersen's lead partner on the Enron account] still would have been under enormous pressure to keep a $25 million audit client."

Even after all that Andersen went through, the big accounting firms still believe that first and foremost they must create value for their client, not act as a public watchdog. For example, according to a source, when KPMG purchased the Andersen Dallas operation in May 2002, a presentation was given to KPMG staffers and their new colleagues from Andersen on how to transition Andersen audit clients to KPMG, how to target new clients, and how to get more consulting fees from clients. There wasn't anything in the presentation reminding Andersen that KPMG expected a higher level of performance than the one that had brought Andersen down.[9]

The accountant of the late twentieth century, in essence, managed to fumble thousands of years of trust and power. If that sounds like an exaggeration, it's only because accounting research has just started to discover how old and how important record keeping and the tracking of value of goods was in antiquity. Several scholars, in fact, are redefining accounting—along with the beginnings of agriculture—as one of the two watershed human developments that brought about organized society. It was from talking to one of these scholars, Dr. Denise Schmandt-Besserat of the University of Texas, about the history of accounting that I realized that other accounting professors would have interesting ideas about the *current* state of accounting.

WHISTLING PAST THE GRAVEYARD IN SAN ANTONIO

In August 2002, I headed to San Antonio, site of that year's annual meeting of the American Accounting Association (AAA), a group made up mostly of academic accountants. I arrived at the conference on Wednesday—before the heavy hitters—when the younger academic set signed up for continuing education courses and browsed the various trade show exhibits. As I wandered around the exhibits and tables of accounting literature, I was reminded that accounting is a profession of acronyms: Conference attendees talked about GAAP, GAAS, FASB, FMT, ROA, AICPA, IASB, LLC, LOB, to name just a few. In fact, I recently found an entire book dedicated to accounting acronyms—*The International Dictionary of Accounting Acronyms*. Despite its more than 2,000 entries, the book states in its preface that "this volume is not intended to be either authoritative or exhaustive."[10]

While poking my head into various research presentation sessions, I fully realized the huge gulf between auditing and accounting. Only a fraction of the research being presented at the conference had anything to do with auditing. All auditors are accountants, but less than 40 percent of the nation's 340,000 CPAs audit the financial statements of public companies. The rest work at companies or in government as chief financial officers, internal auditors, or controllers; provide tax services; or provide other types of business advice.[11]

The San Antonio conference was being held just when Arthur Andersen was going through its final death throes. Oddly enough, while debates about hundreds of arcane accounting subjects raged on, very few people wanted to talk about the elephant in the corner of the conference. At first, I assumed that, like a recent death in the family or an uncle who had absconded with the family fortune, the fate of Andersen was simply too tragic and raw for practitioners to discuss. I soon found that was not the case. The reticence had more to do with either repressed hostility toward the firm, a genuine belief that its demise did not signify anything significant in the big accounting picture, or sort of a dignified desire not to speak badly of the dead. "Well, what's the point of talking about Andersen," said Professor Felix Amenkhienan, chair of the accounting department at Radford University in Virginia. "They're history. They embarrassed the profession. And this particular group of people doesn't necessarily like to kick people when they're down."

One of the few events at the conference devoted to Andersen was the surprise, lightning-quick visit of Enron whistle-blower Sherron Watkins. Watkins had been contacted by organizers of the conference and asked if she could participate by phone in one of the sessions. Instead, Watkins hopped on a plane and flew to San Antonio on Thursday. Watkins, 42, grew up in Timbale, Texas, 45 minutes northwest of Houston. Her mother, Shirley Klein Harrington, taught accounting. Watkins was secreted into a ballroom to speak at a lunch for audit academics. She recalled her own days at Andersen, saying that "it wasn't about how good an auditor you were, it was about how much business you brought in."

One thing I did learn at the conference was that there was no consensus in the academic community that CPAs have abandoned their core purpose. Professor Guay believes that if accountants had not been doing their jobs over the past two decades, the U.S. financial system would have revealed it sooner. "You'd have to believe that, if auditors systematically stopped doing their jobs 20 years ago, the capital markets would reflect it by now," Guay said. "Yet we have the most liquid capital markets in the world." John Koeping, a Jesuit priest and accounting professor at the University of San Francisco (he jokes that he's the most unpopular man in the United States), said that there is something seriously wrong with the moral compass of the profession but that change is better made from within. He pointed not only to auditors in league with clients but also to accountants helping corporations duck U.S. and foreign tax obligations, as well as accounting firms making more money from consulting than from auditing.

SHARING THE BLAME

Auditors, of course, do not prepare a client's financial statements, and it is naïve to blame any accounting crisis solely on accountants. In his September 1998 "Numbers Game" speech at New York University, SEC commissioner Arthur Levitt, who had already been battling the accounting profession from his bully pulpit in Washington for several years, spread the blame for the erosion of financial reporting. Levitt described a "game of nods and winks" conducted by auditors, analysts, and corporate managers who colluded to create "a gray area where the accounting is perverted" and where "earnings reports reflect the desires of management rather than the underlying financial performance of the company."[12]

As Levitt pointed out, accountants could not have gone so far astray from tried-and-true auditing without the complicity of Wall Street analysts who demanded companies hit their quarterly estimates and corporate managers who wanted to paint the best face on earnings to meet these expectations. Hiding debt and writing off dubious expenses were techniques corporate managers and their outside accountants used together to inflate earnings and to satisfy Wall Street. Corporate officers also tacitly encouraged the accounting profession in its decision to concentrate on nonaudit services. Executives at major companies had to keep their organizations competitive, and they needed good ideas to do it. One handy choice to provide input was the outside auditors. They knew the business. They knew the industry. As Mike Cook of Deloitte & Touche put it: "I was recently talking to a partner at a big firm, and he told me his client has been upset with him because he's stopped pitching consulting projects. His client said, 'C'mon, you're in there every day looking around; I need some help.'"

There is also an ongoing debate concerning how much blame can be ascribed to auditors for failing to recognize and/or report management fraud and whether the historical and ethical underpinnings of accounting support a renewed push for accountants to ferret out fraud. For years, the American Institute of CPAs (AICPA) and the global firms have maintained that their purpose is not to root out fraud and that they are not trained to find fraud. Joe Wells, a former FBI agent who specialized in white-collar crime and founded the Association of Certified Fraud Examiners, believes that the complicated task of defining corporate disclosure standards distracted the accounting profession from focusing on fraud. This was the start of the modern preoccupation with financial reporting issues. "Until the early twentieth century, fraud detection was the main thing accountants did," Wells said. "But most of the twentieth century, with the power of stock exchanges and the SEC, has been devoted to figuring out reporting issues—what is an asset, how do we get a uniform system—those kinds of issues." Wells believes that auditors can and should reclaim a portion of their past fraud-detection role. He advocates fraud training for all auditors. "Auditors are smart people, they are well-trained, they are good at what they do," said Wells. "But right now they are neophytes when it comes to fraud. They are trained to understand how a system works; they are not trained in how that system can be abused."

Indeed, more and more, shareholders have been demanding that accountants sniff out upcoming and illegal corporate shenanigans. As Mark Cheffers, a former Price Waterhouse senior manager and president of accountingmalpractice.com, a web site that advises accountants on litigation-related issues, put it: "There is this huge expectations gap between what auditors believe accounting standards tell them they are supposed to do and that which the SEC and the public expects them to do. I think some of this dynamic has to do with the fact that CPAs have been very good at promoting themselves to the public as being business advisers. The guy in the jury box is saying, 'Hey, if you're there at the company and you're so smart, you should be able to spot this stuff.'"

THE FUTURE OF ACCOUNTING

Depending on who you listen to, the accounting profession is now entering either a renaissance of pure auditing or an unprecedented period of intellectual stagnation.

"I think the situation coming up is great for people that really want to audit," said Todd Walker, a former KPMG senior manager, now a single practitioner in Munford, Tennessee. "Prices for audits are going to go back up, and that means that the people who want to audit are going to get the work and get paid for it."

But given the legal costs of operating an accounting firm, the decline in public respect, the crushing workload, the client demands on partners, and an alleged lack of talented students going into the profession, there is a real question as to whether the accounting industry will survive as currently constituted. Jon Madonna believes that the heavy regulation of the accounting industry imposed by Sarbanes-Oxley may send the profession into a downward spiral, attracting only nominally qualified professionals. "My fear is that we are creating the IRS," said Madonna. "The IRS auditor—that's the type of person this profession is going to attract soon."

Wholesale changes in the way audits are done may be on the horizon if Sarbanes-Oxley doesn't do the job. Professors like Joshua Ronen of NYU's Stern School of Business and G. A. Swanson, accounting professor at Tennessee Technological University, believe that public companies should pay insurance companies "financial statement insurance" and that insurance companies should match up accounting firms and public companies. That way, accounting firms would be paid not by the company they are auditing but by the insurance companies. In addition, an incentive would be in place for companies to keep clean books, lest their premiums go sky-high.

"If we could go back to 1933, that would be one thing," said Swanson. "Back then we thought that public auditors would be a stronger force in the system. It didn't work out that way, so I, for one, think it's time for a change."

Given the disparity of opinions on the future of accounting, I was determined to gain my own understanding of where the profession is headed. I decided to start by going back to the beginning. By understanding the development of accounting, a clear picture is formed of how the profession ended up in its current predicament. The story begins in the Middle East with the first accountants.

CHAPTER 1

THE FIRST ACCOUNTANTS

LIKE ANY GOOD ARCHEOLOGIST, DR. DENISE SCHMANDT-BESSERAT loves raw data. After all, data—looked at the right way—contains the truth. Schmandt-Besserat, the world's leading expert on ancient accountants, has spent the past 35 years traveling the Middle East, gathering information from tiny clay spheres, disks, and cones. That information led Schmandt-Besserat to discover nothing less than the origins of accounting and the powerful societal role of the first accountants.

In 1964, Schmandt-Besserat had just completed her graduate studies at the Ecole du Louvre in Paris and had come to Cambridge, Massachusetts, with her husband and three children. Her husband was teaching at Harvard, and she was itching to get out in the field. Within a few months, Schmandt-Besserat announced she was heading to Iran for her first major archeological excavation. "It was very daring for a woman with a family to make that kind of decision," she said. "In my neighborhood, no one didn't have an opinion on what I was doing. Half of my neighbors thought it was great; the other half thought I was out of my mind."

After that first season in the field, Schmandt-Besserat took a position as a researcher at Harvard's Peabody Museum, long known as a training ground for talented young archeologists. She began cataloguing thousands of small clay "mystery objects" that were being found at sites all over the Middle East and being stored in museums like unneeded Christmas lights in an attic. Throughout the 1950s and 1960s, archeologists digging up ancient Sumerian cities (in present-day Iran and Iraq) had been finding tiny clay objects in a variety of geometric shapes, including cylinders, disks, cones, and spheres, at excavation layers dating as far back as 8000 B.C. Most Mesopotamian scholars didn't expect to find evidence of any formal record-keeping system at such layers, so often the clay objects weren't even mentioned in the report of the dig; they were just catalogued and stored in a museum somewhere.

The few clumsy attempts at identifying the objects included one professor's observation that on a dig in Iran he had encountered "five mysterious unbaked conical clay objects looking like nothing in the world but suppositories. What they were used for is anybody's guess."[1] Schmandt-Besserat became interested in these small clay artifacts, so different from the household pots and jars that clay was typically used for at the time. In her writing about the objects, she took to calling them "tokens."

"I became interested in the fact that these tokens were meant to symbolize something, and they were being found all over archeological sites in Iran and Iraq," Schmandt-Besserat said. "I would ask the excavator of certain sites, 6500 B.C. and before, and they didn't know what these things were. They just labeled them 'objects of uncertain purpose' and put them in drawers."

Like an auditor visiting a company's warehouse to count widgets, Schmandt-Besserat started systematically visiting museums to see how many and what kinds of tokens were there. Her search took her to Baghdad, where, equipped with a ladder from the museum curator so that the diminutive Schmandt-Besserat could reach even the highest cabinets, she became the first foreign scholar to roam freely and unattended throughout the labyrinthian Cultural Museum. "I opened every single drawer," Schmandt-Besserat said. "I needed to see for myself what tokens were being found in Iraq because the tokens many times weren't even catalogued. At this point, I was going crazy, I was seeing these things everywhere, seeing tokens in my sleep."

Schmandt-Besserat had an epiphany when she found that, throughout her broad survey of the tokens, the unmistakable presence of early agriculture was evident in the same excavation layers as well. "The tokens were found exactly when cereals were planted because cereal pollen was found all around," she said. "So it was clear that agriculture was coming in as well. It makes sense; if you were farming, you had to be able to count and record the crops. I was sure that the tokens were used to keep a record of the crops and other basic staples." The tokens, according to Schmandt-Besserat, were the world's earliest accounting records.

In the basement of the arts building at the University of Texas at Austin in August 2002, Schmandt-Besserat sat in her office lined with photos of acquaintances King Fahd of Saudi Arabia and King Hussein of Jordan, as well as posters of ancient figurines and artifacts. She was preparing to go to California for a symposium on accounting in antiquity. Even as she spoke with a visitor, President George W. Bush addressed a group of business executives in nearby Waco about the corporate accounting scandals that had rocked U.S. capitalism over the previous 12 months. "We see problems, but we're confident in the long-term health of this economy," Bush told his audience.[2]

The accounting scandals had gotten Schmandt-Besserat thinking, too. She couldn't help but offer her own opinion on the travails of the modern accountant. "When you look at the evolution of accounting, what is important is that you are dealing with the communication of economic data," said Schmandt-Besserat. "Today, there is an overexaggeration on numeration, and a lot of the important information people need is getting lost."

THE ANCIENTS AND GOOD INFORMATION

As Schmandt-Besserat implied—with words that curiously mirror those of today's corporate governance experts—accountants, both those working for companies and those at public accounting firms, need to supply U.S. investors with higher quality information. In fact, archeology and accounting have a good deal in common in this regard. The practitioners of both professions need raw data with which to work and then have the responsibility to extract useful information for the people who need it. The ancient practitioners of accounting, according to Schmandt-Besserat and other scholars, were extraordinarily adept at providing good information to their audience.

For thousands of years before the birth of accounting, humans did not need any more economic information than met the eye. Small groups of nomadic hunters and gatherers simply collected whatever they could and consumed it. Schmandt-Besserat contends that humans only started to count when it was clearly needed for survival. "Man did not count for a very long time. Nowadays, it's obviously one of the things that people teach children very early. It was not a question of survival, so it wasn't developed."

Even when counting did develop, humans didn't seem to need to count very high. Because humans have 10 fingers and 10 toes, it is often assumed that they pragmatically counted at least that high and that the Arabic numerical system was subsequently based on 10. But for millennia, humans could not count to more than three. After two, the word for "three" was the same as the word for "many." Even today, some isolated people in New Guinea and Indonesia don't use a 10-based counting method but still "body count," pointing to various parts of the body to represent particular numbers.

Early humans finally did begin to count items for the purpose of tracking and organizing, and that's when things began to get interesting. The ability to count, sort, and organize various staples, like grain and oils, in fact, was at the center of power in ancient kingdoms, a radical theory when Schmandt-Besserat first started publishing in the early 1970s. Her work shifted the traditional timetable for the beginnings of accounting from approximately 4000 B.C. to 8000 B.C.

Schmandt-Besserat's theories about the tokens and the origins of accounting have now come to be widely accepted, with many scholars building on her work, including McGuire Gibson, a professor at the University of Chicago; Miriam Balmuth, an archeologist at Tufts;

and Marvin Powell, a historian at Northern Illinois.[3] Schmandt-Besserat hasn't always been warmly received, however, by colleagues who theorize that true "accounting" didn't start until 4,000 years later than Schmandt-Besserat says. The 1996 accounting encyclopedia *The History of Accounting*, for example, makes no mention of the tokens and says that "knotted cord may be the world's oldest accounting device. . . . The knotted strings apparently predated the appearance of a written language about 3300 B.C."[4]

Despite the occasional dagger from colleagues, Schmandt-Besserat's theories have prompted some scholars to suggest that today's accounting practitioners need a much better understanding of the profession's underpinnings. "If you accept Denise's work—and I think just about everyone does now—you have to recognize that accounting is a fundamental, basic column of society," said G. A. Swanson, professor of accounting at Tennessee Tech. "Imparting the theoretical underpinnings to students does not happen much anymore. We've abolished theory. There are no theory questions on the CPA exam, and there is no theory being taught in the classroom; and that could be working to undermine the quality of audits today."

HOW THE FIRST ACCOUNTING WORKED

After Schmandt-Besserat connected the tokens to accounting, the next step was determining exactly how the tokens fit into recording the crops. One clue was that the only successful way for small groups of humans to move from hunting and gathering to agriculture was to pool their crops in some kind of communal way. "Near the tokens we often find big granary rooms," said Schmandt-Besserat. "They are too small to live or sleep in and too big for a private granary. Communal granaries were the trigger for that first accounting because you needed some way to keep track of what was coming in."

That is when some enterprising individuals devised the method of using the clay tokens to stand for a specific staple, like a sheep or a container of grain. The beauty of the tokens was their simplicity: Their shapes were striking, they were easily identifiable, and they were easy to replicate. The impact of the use of the tokens and the organizational ramifications of easy record keeping was immediate. Through agriculture and accounting, these early humans had transformed their economy over a few hundred years from strict hunting and gathering to established villages of about 300 people.

With the change in society came a change in the leadership of the society. "All of a sudden, skilled hunters were no longer the leaders," Schmandt-Besserat said. "The person in charge of the commercial resources, of collecting and dispensing the grain, was the most powerful, and this was the accountant using the tokens."

Because of field evidence yielded from hundreds of burial sites that have been excavated throughout Iraq, Syria, and the Arabian peninsula, it is clear that the individuals who practiced accounting were very important members of society. "Among the many graves dating from 8000 to 3000 B.C., only a few are known to have yielded tokens, and these tokens were found in the tombs of individuals of high status," Schmandt-Besserat said. Many of the tombs are filled with gold furniture and beads, obsidian, and other symbols of power.

The tokens may have been used not only to record what came into the granary, but also to recognize who gave it and how much should be dispensed to specific individuals. "It would be interesting to know if the tokens indicated how much each person had given to the communal granary, because then you would basically have a narrative, the start of recorded history," Schmandt-Besserat said.

Indeed, history is the accountant's stock in trade. As accounting professor Wayne Guay at the Wharton School put it: "Accountants are basically historians. The corporate finance people make the decisions, and the outside accountants look at the results months later." Accountants have always looked at the transactions and records over a period of time and made judgments based on that evidence. Some of the current troubles of the accounting industry, in fact, may have resulted from a desire to become more than just a historian commenting on past transactions, to become rather a big-time player in dealmaking and other "sexy" aspects of business. Schmandt-Besserat's accountants, though, *were* the players. More important than the hunter, more in control than the chief, the holder of the tokens and dispenser of the grain, cereals, animals, or oils was the most important figure in these first small villages because they served as "honest brokers" and controllers of the shared wealth.

Between 8000 B.C. and 3000 B.C., the tokens carried more and more accounting data. Soon, the tokens were filled with economic information for the user, perhaps more revealing—and certainly less confusing—than today's financial statements. The tokens grew much more elaborate, appearing in hundreds of different shapes and bearing all manner of surface markings. In about 3000 B.C., the state emerged, and the token in Mesopotamia was being supplanted by other accounting devices, such as tablets and seals. In addition, ancient Hawaiians and Chinese were using the *quipu* (the knotted cord) as an accounting tool. This system used strands of cord to count particular items, much as the Sumerians used the tokens. Just as the tokens had various shapes, the color of the cord and the placement of the knots had meaning. "It was close to the token system because each commodity was counted with a different type of string," Schmandt-Besserat said. But the cords were logistical nightmares. A person carrying many different strands of cord would have a hard time communicating the data. Like oblique financial statements, the cords could end up confusing the user of the information. "There's no doubt about it; the tokens were much better and easier to use," Schmandt-Besserat said.

ACCOUNTING AND ABSTRACTION

Whether through tokens 10,000 years ago, knotted cords 5,000 years ago, the pen and quill 200 years ago, or computers today, the communication of economic data has progressively become more abstract. The challenge thousands of years ago was to count something, like grain or sheep, without having to actually have the sheep or grain right there, and to then impart that representational tally with communal credibility. So two sheep were abstracted into two tokens.

Today's complex accounting represents staggering levels of abstraction. Included in every modern annual report are the results of thousands upon thousands of corporate transactions—very few of which auditors actually test. This abstraction of day-to-day business is one reason why it's so difficult to ascertain just how much of an accounting problem exists today. Accounting firms are not counting inventories in a factory anymore, at least not very often. Accountants randomly test very complicated financial information using highly abstract methods based on controls and risk avoidance. There is also a growing demand that today's accountants—both those who work at accounting firms and those who work at public companies—better capture the value of intangible assets like intellectual property, brand recognition, innovative culture, and human resources.

A general lack of understanding about what auditors actually do and how abstract their job has become is pervasive. Mark Cheffers, a former Price Waterhouse auditor who now runs his own web site on litigation, has seen firsthand many jury pools in accounting cases. "I remember one jury pool," Cheffers said. "One of the jurors said, 'I work in the accounting department of my company, and when the auditors come in, they look at everything.'" But as Cheffers pointed out, the juror was mistaken. "Anyone who has been in the profession knows that they barely look at anything," he said.

One interesting possibility is that, given the problems accounting faced in 2002, there may be a return by auditors to more detailed testing of data—a reversal of sorts of the path to accounting abstraction. "I think there will be more detailed sampling and testing than there has been," said John Koeping, an accounting professor at the University of San Francisco and a Jesuit priest who teaches accounting ethics. "But auditing is going to advance somehow. Business moves too fast, and we can't audit companies the way we did 20 or 30 years ago." The challenge for today's global accounting firms will be finding a way to perform the detailed tests needed to root out management fraud, while still keeping prices affordable for clients.

GREECE AND ROME

Egypt, China, and Greece simultaneously developed accounting methods from around 2000 B.C. on. Besides tracking and recording agricultural and other goods, accountants at that time added to their repertoires the duty of searching out fraud. This is an important fact for people who today believe that public accountants have strayed too far from a responsibility to find and report corporate fraud. "There is a 4,000-year history linking accounting and fraud detection," said Joe Wells, a former FBI agent and CPA who founded an association for certified fraud examiners. "Fraud detection was the primary thing they did."

The Greek philosopher Aristotle discussed accounting in several of his works, and his comments illustrate that by 1000 B.C. accountants had already become important professionals in society. In his book *Politics*, Aristotle focused on the role of the government auditor, who received all accounts of expenditures and subjected them to audit, a duty so important that these officials handled no other business. In his book *Constitution*, he distinguished between three boards of accountants, each of 10 men: (1) the council accountants, (2) the administrative accountants, and (3) the examiners. Clearly, in Ancient Greece the accounting profession was firmly established.

Rome especially had a very weak and static accounting system, when compared with its highly developed language, legal system, political system, and military capabilities. One of the reasons for this was that merchants were quite low in the social pecking order, and the business of well-known citizens was often conducted by proxy by educated slaves who were not encouraged to innovate. Another problem for the Romans was their numerical system. According to *The History of Accounting*, "the Romans never learned to express a number's value merely by the position of each of its digits in relation to the others. This lack of position value made arithmetic cumbersome and errors hard to find."[5] Clearly the Roman Empire had not built on Greek advances.

DOUBLE-ENTRY BOOKKEEPING

The roughly one thousand years between the end of the Roman Empire and the rise of great merchant houses in fourteenth-century Italy was known as a period of accounting stagnation. That all changed with Luca Pacioli's *Summa de Arithmetica, Geometria, Proportioni et Proportionalita*, published in Venice, the nexus of fourteenth-century Italian trade. Pacioli is sometimes referred to as the "father of accounting," but a more accurate description of Pacioli is that he was the most effective dabbler in accounting the world has ever seen. Pacioli was a Franciscan friar whose main areas of interest were mathematics and theology and who counted among his friends and colleagues fellow Renaissance man Leonardo da Vinci.

Pacioli's famous treatise on accounting, which also contained sections on geometry and physics, set forth the principles of double-entry bookkeeping in a section called "Particulars of Reckonings and Their Recordings." Double-entry bookkeeping, which seems intuitive today, simply means recording transactions in two different entries in order for a company to keep track of what it is owed and what has been paid. According to the *Dictionary of Accounting*, an example of double-entry bookkeeping is when "a debtor pays cash to a business for goods he has purchased, the cash held by the business is increased and the amount held by the debtor is decreased."[6] According to Professor Gary Littleton of the University of Illinois, seven conditions were necessary for double-entry bookkeeping, or, essentially, modern-day accounting, to take hold: (1) private property, (2) capital, (3) commerce, (4) credit, (5) writing, (6) money, and (7) arithmetic. All of these influences coalesced in fourteenth-century Italy.[7]

When popularized through Pacioli's text, double-entry bookkeeping—or "the Italian system," as it was known—was the accounting equivalent of the printing press in publishing. Its application was so significant in terms of the efficiency and the clarity it introduced that it became the standard throughout the West and is still the basic model for businesses today. More specifically, Pacioli's Venetian method, in which credits and debits were presented on adjacent pages, was especially popular up until the ninteenth century. According to *The History of Accounting*, "All of the accounting books published during the sixteenth century in other European countries presented descriptions of bookkeeping similar to that one by Pacioli."[8]

ENGLISH APPLICATIONS

Following Pacioli's landmark work, major developments in the practical application of accounting came in England, where hundreds of accountants were collecting taxes, figuring out interest, recording stock sales, and monitoring the finances of the Crown. Some of the most significant accounting advances came about directly because of the bureaucracy inherent in Britain's royal monarchy. Along with Scotch whiskey and golf, Scotland exported to England young men to fill the need for newly trained accountants.

The power of accounting to provide information to the user is forcefully illustrated by original accounting records from fourteenth- and fifteenth-century England. These show that the most powerful members of society invested enormous trust in the top accountants. In a 1350 account of Edward III's household expenses, for example, the royal accountant, Walter Wentworth, had the huge responsibility of properly recording all funds going into or out of the king's accounts.[9]

Wentworth may have had one of the toughest jobs any accountant has ever had. During his 50-year reign, Edward fought several wars against Scotland and France and demanded meticulous records of the costs of waging war. The king also wanted to know who was contributing how much to the war effort. Accordingly, Wentworth carefully noted the 1347 arrival of hundreds of noblemen in London to support the upcoming campaign against France and the prizes they brought for their king. For example, "John, Earl of Oxford," brought with him several knights, servants, and several hundred pounds to add to Edward III's literal war chest, for which Wentworth was also responsible. A few months later, Wentworth made several entries noting the costs of the ongoing siege of Calais, which ended in victory for Edward.

In the fifteenth century, the delineation between "accountants" and "auditors" emerged more clearly in England. Original records show that the "Royal auditor" played a far more prestigious role than the "accountant" did. Various accountants serving the Crown compiled endless figures about the salaries of household servants or the amount of livestock belonging to certain noblemen. The auditors wrote reports directly to various nobles, ministers, and members of the royal family.

Practicing accounting at the time could be very difficult in England, particularly because accountants employed by the royals and nobles were expected to travel widely and to report back on how various investments were faring. The accountants often failed and missed deadlines or, even worse, absconded with funds belonging to the Crown. More than 300 years before SEC chairman Arthur Levitt would make an issue out of the independence of CPAs in the United States, British officials were attempting to implement their own accounting reform. In the late 1600s, the royal family was upset because auditors were late in getting the total revenues of the Crown to the Exchequer (the royal treasury). The official in charge of the Exchequer at this time, Lord Treasurer Rochester, knew he needed to act to prevent more humiliation in front of the Crown. He proposed in 1685 a new set of accounting rules that were to solve, once and for all, the problems of the accounting profession.

One of Lord Rochester's proposals was that accountants be required once every year ("in the lent vacation if your Lordship think fit") to provide a certificate listing all outstanding accounts under their jurisdiction that were owed to the Crown. This is one of the first examples in British accounting records of an annual reporting requirement. Lord Rochester hoped to sufficiently spotlight and embarrass accountants who were chronically late in delivering monies to the Exchequer or who simply kept the money and reported it as delinquent. If the problem really was with the debtor and not with the accountant, Lord Rochester hoped to ascertain this as well. He explained all of this in a letter to several noblemen, in which he wrote that he hoped to keep them "informed of the true state of all accounts, by whose neglect (if there be any) accountants are delayed."[10]

Foreshadowing modern circumstances, it seems that accountants were already an influential group with plenty of political power. Lord Rochester's reforms were met with chronic resistance on the part of many of the official auditors. He was further stymied because several other bodies criticized him for acting imprudently.

By the late seventeenth century, England had created a formal body—called the commissioner of accounts—that monitored government spending and operated mostly apart from the accountants for the royal family. It served much the same role as today's Government Accounting Office (GAO) in the United States. In August 1668, the commissioners sent a letter addressed to William Legge, lieutenant-general of the ordinance, which basically amounted to a threat: "Sir: Upon sorting your accounts remaining with us, and comparing your vouchers, we find that very many . . . are wanting, and therefore wee [sic] urge you, with as much speed as may be, to . . . adjust your said accounts, and so wee rest."[11]

Along with fighting accounting reform and forming unwieldy commissions, other modern corporate accounting practices claim roots in British aristocracy. For example, the British royal auditors perfected the accounting treatment of expense reimbursement in order to monitor the island's growing diplomatic corps. Alexander Stanhope, England's envoy to the king of Spain in 1697 and 1698, put in for hundreds of pounds in expenses for each of his years at the Spanish court, for everything from "entertainment to luminaries three days successively for the Emperours victory in Hungary" to clothing he purchased for "English, Irish, and Scotch deserters from the French," to "stationary ware, newspapers, copying papers, and intelligence." Unfortunately for Stanhope, the royal auditors were quite hard on him, and he was denied the £50 in reimbursement for his newspapers.[12]

ACCOUNTING AT THE FIRST JOINT STOCK CORPORATIONS

Sometime around the second half of the seventeenth century, the joint stock company emerged in England, and accounting was used for the first time to ensure that the interests of investors were fairly represented. The best example of this was used by the East India Company, the original charter of which was granted by Queen Elizabeth on December 31, 1600.[13] The shareholders of the East India Company enjoyed many of the same privileges as the modern company, including the right to sue and to use a common brand. Indeed, the East India Company seemed to try to exert just as much control over its corporate image—its logo (a circle with a sailor's cap on the top) appeared on every invoice in the 1600s—as a modern corporation or a professional services firm does.

Original records from the East India Company indicate that although it was already keeping very detailed accounting records, there was little headway made in the area of annual financial statements that reflected the overall financial health of the company. The records were geared toward individual journeys because that was exactly how capital at the company was raised—voyage by voyage. In page after page of records from the company, long lists of investors are presented, with how much (in pounds, shillings, and pence) each person invested.[14] Subsequently, there was no demand from investors for annual or biannual summations; the timetable of voyages to the East Indies dictated the financial reporting schedule.

At the end of the expedition, the stockholders were paid in accordance with their investment, and then the next voyage would be capitalized. On July 8, 1685, for example, the East India Company officially recorded that a recent voyage's goods had sold for a total of £122,343. The top payouts went to a William Atwill (£30,000, nearly 25 percent of the entire sum) and an alms house (£4,000; why an alms house was investing in overseas trade is anyone's guess). It was not until the later 1600s that the company established a permanent capital base. Hundreds of years later, the legendary George May of Price Waterhouse defined accounting for impermanent circumstances, such as a single voyage, as "venture accounting"; he pointed to the transition from venture accounting to regular income reporting—which supplied investors with information about a company at fixed intervals—as one of the greatest triumphs of English accounting.[15]

The East India Company often got into trouble with its royal sponsors in its later years as it became a merchant bank of sorts and started to fund other companies and lend money to individuals. Money owed to the East India Company, according to company records, went under the column heading "Debts, Desporata, Bad and Dubious Owing to the Honorable East India Company." In 1816, in fact, the company made a loan of £1,200 to General Napoleon Bonaparte, who had been exiled to St. Helena following his defeat at Waterloo. The East India Company itself met its Waterloo in 1858 as public companies not affiliated with the Crown came to the forefront.

Accounting wasn't just for British royalty and nobles and wasn't practiced only by specialized individuals. A respect for fiscal order permeated society and stretched to the common man. Even the taverns and blacksmiths in seventeenth-century rural England used solid and sophisticated accounting practices. At Robert Fox's inn in Canterbury, records show that even on the busiest of nights, accounts were kept with good double-entry bookkeeping methods, with the credits on one page and the debits on the facing page.[16] Tavern owners and blacksmiths themselves kept the books as the pace of business permitted. These entries had to be detailed enough to differentiate between transactions. For example, "Mr. Woolet of Elham" had several big nights at Mr. Fox's tavern in January 1628. One evening, he spent "20 pounds on wine with Mr. Gamman and his brother in the further parlor."[17] By the seventeenth and eighteenth centuries, clerks and bookkeepers realized that in order to charge a premium price and to obtain the choicest assignments, they had to set themselves apart. They formed professional associations and established standards that could be enforced through certification.

ACCOUNTING IN THE COLONIES

Meanwhile, as English colonists journeyed to the New World, so did their accounting standards. The several villages that comprised the Plymouth Colony provide some of the best early accounting records of colonial America. Like the Jamestown Colony in 1607 and the Massachusetts Bay Colony in 1629, Plymouth, founded in 1620, was established on the strength of a British joint stock company. Just a few years after the *Mayflower*'s 102 colonists settled into their harsh life, history shows a primary concern arising that the colony's treasurer, a Mr. Martin, was not particularly able. Shareholders of the Plymouth Bay Company in London demanded "accounts as perticulerly as you can how our moneys were laid out."[18]

In fact, accounting was fairly advanced within the Plymouth Colony, with ample evidence of double-entry bookkeeping, because of the demands of the shareholders. The colony even hired teachers to tutor children how "to read and write and cast up accounts."[19] The Massachusetts Bay Company, too, recognized the importance of keeping track of the finances of its colonists. The official records of the governor of the colony show that the company did not skimp when it came to hiring auditors: "Auditors appointed for auditing the accompts, via Mr. Symon Whetcombe, Mr. Nathaniel Wright, Mr. Noell, Mr. Perry, Mr. Crane, Mr. Clark, Mr. Eaton, and Mr. Andrewes; these 8, or any 4 or more of them, to meete at a convenient time and place to audit the accompts."[20]

EARLY ACCOUNTING EDUCATION IN ENGLAND

In the early eighteenth century, it was clear that accounting was a skill that required a degree of specialization and training. One of the first texts devoted purely to teaching accounting skills in England was *An Essay upon the Italian Method of Bookkeeping*, which addressed the pros and cons of using Pacioli's double-entry bookkeeping method rather than simple single-entry bookkeeping.[21]

This book discussed the three critical accounting record-keeping books that any accountant must have: (1) the memorandum book (also called the waste book or the daybook), (2) the journal, and (3) the ledger. The accountant transferred the raw data in the daybook (daily sales of grain, for example) into the journal. Eventually, the information would be entered into the all-important ledger, meant to be a permanent record of the business. The instructional text included this short verse to remind readers how double-entry accounting worked, namely, that accounts received went on the left-hand page and payments going out went on the right-hand page:

The owner or the owing thing
Or whatsoever comes to thee
Upon the left hand see thou bring
For there the same must place be
But they unto whom thou dost owe
Upon ye right let them be set
or what so ere doth from ye go
to place them there do not forget.

Although books like this helped popularize good accounting, the best accounting records were still kept where the most resources and the greatest need to be authoritative coexisted—with the British government. In the 1700s, royal auditors often knew more about their "clients" than anyone else did. In April 1735, esquire John Selnyn, the Queen's treasurer and auditor general at the time of Queen Caroline's death, listed £24,814 in cash in her account; and it seems he had the authority to disburse it. One of his first duties was to pay out salaries to the attorney general, cup bearers, carvers, gentlemen ushers, page of the robes, secretary keeper of the privy seal, and the extraordinary number of other palace employees.[22] Royal accounting wasn't this meticulous without reason. The nation needed money to maintain its empire around the globe and needed an accurate system to keep fiscal order. Sometimes, however, the system was used to make unwise public policy decisions.

ROYAL ACCOUNTING AND PUBLIC POLICY

In a 1740 account of the annual income of the public revenues of the Crown, it is clear just how this accounting report—which was intended for high-ranking ministers—was used to justify several public policy decisions. The last page of the report had a column for "A state of the national debt with the annual charges thereupon."[23] The national debt was over £100 million. The rest of the income statement is basically a record of the numerous taxes that were being levied on the American colonies. In the report, tax revenues were pouring into the royal coffers from taxes placed on, among other items, brandy, spices, sailcloth, silk, and—of course—tea.

Accounting can provide valuable economic information, but no one ever said that the information leads to wise policy making. Much like any science, its power can be turned to the public good or to its detriment. This 1740 income statement showed how desperately England was relying on taxes on the American colonies, and the document might have helped convince British authorities that the only way to reduce the national deficit was to continue taxing the colonies to the utmost. But these taxes were actually sowing the seeds of the American revolution, still 35 years away. In fact, even as Britain was using accounting as a tool to try to hold its empire together, the American colonists were attempting to harness this same knowledge to make their own lives better.

CHAPTER 2

THE BIRTH OF AN AMERICAN PROFESSION

I F THE BRITISH SET THE DIRECTION FOR MODERN ACCOUNTING by starting the first joint stock companies, defining auditing and accounting, and creating the first accounting standards, it was the American colonists who, before long, gave further definition to the field. George Washington, for one, had he not been destined to become one of the greatest generals and politicians in history, would have made a fine accountant. From the day Washington became commander in chief of the Continental Army in 1775 through to the end of the Revolutionary War in 1783, Washington kept two copies of all his expenses down to the smallest detail.[1] He wrote the entries himself (with an occasional entry from his wife, Martha), whether he was at a tavern in Schenectady, New York, a printing house in New York City, or in Valley Forge with his troops.[2]

Although Washington did ask Congress for the occasional loan, he used his own money for many personal items, such as horse saddles and writing instruments. At the end of his eight-year command, Washington sent his account books to the Treasury to be audited, where it was found that Washington's calculations were off—he shortchanged himself by a little less than one dollar. James Milligan, then comptroller of the Treasury, was astounded by Washington's wartime record keeping and wrote Washington that "your excellency having in your accounts clearly displayed the degree of candor and truth, and that attention you have constantly paid to every denomination of civil establishments, which invariably distinguish all your actions."[3]

His expense logs and their treatment by the government revealed more than a meticulously organized General Washington. The fact that a heroic general, addressed as "your excellency" by the nation's comptroller, would have his expenses examined so closely speaks volumes about the role of accounting and auditing in the fledgling United States. Long before the private-sector accountant fully emerged, U.S. government auditors and comptrollers held posts throughout federal and state government to act as a check on fraudulent and illegal activities by government figures. Preventing and discovering abuse by public officials was the most important function of these early government auditors, as there was no central banking system, no income tax system, and no stock exchanges to oversee. The comptroller of the United States himself often closely monitored transactions between the federal government and important businesspeople, politicians, and military officers. This government-based auditing, a legacy from the royal accountant tradition in England, created a culture of fraud detection that lives on today in the U.S. General Accounting Office (GAO), the investigative arm of Congress that examines the use of public funds and ensures the executive branch's accountability to the American people. Washington, in fact, went on to legitimize the importance of government accounting posts when he included the comptroller general office, the job Milligan held, in his first cabinet.[4]

FORGING A PROFESSION

Private-sector accounting, meanwhile, developed much more slowly than government auditing in the young republic, but its historical mandate to search out fraud is still apparent. The first American book to contain a section on bookkeeping for merchants was *The Secretary's Guide, or Young Man's Companion*, published in 1737, 350 years after Pacioli's seminal work on double-entry bookkeeping. In the eighteenth century, the specialized bookkeeper started to emerge in the American colonies. The earliest known American accountant was a man named Browne Tymms, who advertised in Boston newspapers in 1718, saying he kept shopkeepers' and merchants' books. But the role of an accountant varied from city to city and job to job. The designation "accountant and auctioneer" started to appear in Boston and New York newspapers (a professional duality the SEC just might frown on today). Another burgeoning business for accountants was the collection of debts and rents for clients.

The first public company in the United States wasn't founded until 1814, when Boston merchant Francis Cabot Lowell started a textile mill called the Boston Manufacturing Company in Waltham, Massachusetts.[5] But even then, there still wasn't much need for professional accountants. For one thing, there was no requirement for companies to have their books independently examined. For another, business in the late eighteenth and early nineteenth centuries generally wasn't on a scale that needed great attention to accounting. In some cases, however, people engaged in business saw the need for a trusted outside party to deter fraud by company officers, to mediate a dispute, or to take on sophisticated accounting issues. Such was the case with the Mill Creek Marsh Company in Wilmington, Delaware.

TROUBLE ON MILL CREEK

On the night of February 12, 1827, four of the biggest investors in the Mill Creek Marsh Company gathered at the Black House Tavern for an emergency meeting. Convening at their favorite public house was not unusual for the group. Taverns were often the best place to conduct business in the early-nineteenth-century United States because most houses weren't big enough to comfortably host a meeting, and places where work was done—like a mill or a blacksmith shop—weren't built with meeting space in mind. The problem that had brought the four men together was a recurring one: The floodgates that controlled the amount of water that flowed downstream from the upper reaches of Mill Creek had malfunctioned again, threatening to flood their mill. If heavy rains came before the floodgates were repaired, the milling operation could be destroyed.[6]

The fact that the Mill Creek Marsh Company was located in Wilmington—the future tax-friendly home of many U.S. corporations—is somewhat ironic. As it turned out, the company taxed itself more shamelessly than any twentieth-century government agency would have had the audacity to do. At each annual meeting, the biggest shareholders voted on whether to levy any new charges on themselves and their fellow investors; and during the late 1820s, the company repeatedly required further investments from shareholders to address the malfunctioning floodgates.[7]

Several of the shareholders, however, refused to pay, arguing that the company was not using the taxes it collected wisely if Mill Creek still had not been restrained by a working floodgate. Things looked bleak until the Mill Creek Marsh Company saw another opportunity to get the money it needed to repair the floodgates. Two nearby mills were afraid that Mill Creek would sweep away their operations as well and wanted to know whether they could work with the Mill Creek Marsh Company to jointly address the problem. At the February 12 meeting, the Mill Creek Marsh investors enthusiastically decided to pool resources with the other companies. To seal the deal, the men decided to bring in an outside accountant "whose duty it shall be to pay all orders, drawn by the joint committee, and keep a true account of all the receipts and payments of money by him."[8] The man hired was named Jeremiah Woolston.

During the following nine years, the Mill Creek Marsh Company books show that Jeremiah Woolston became a trusted proxy for all three companies. He performed many of the duties that would later be enshrined under the dominion of the certified public accountant (CPA): balancing books using the double-entry method, verifying balance sheets and financial statements, keeping track of the number of shares and shareholders, accounting for expenses, and generally getting involved in the broader business decisions. Woolston also acted as a check on all three companies, ensuring that all the accounts were "true" and that expensed items actually existed. This is just one episode in accounting history that illustrates the growing need for the accountant in the young United States. This example also shows that contrary to the spirit of recent SEC and congressional reforms seeking to limit nonaudit services to audit clients, U.S. accountants have historically performed a number of related financial and administrative services for a client. It also supports the notion that nineteenth-century accountants did, in fact, search for management impropriety.

The managers of the Mill Creek Marsh Company typified many nineteenth-century U.S. company owners. They needed skilled guidance in their financial affairs. The idea of the "company" had been transferred to the United States from England; but in the United States there was a huge, unfilled demand for someone—anyone—familiar with accounting to help with the books and to give business advice. The practice of accounting had not yet given birth to a profession, and it was a struggle finding financially literate people to assist small businesses.

Records indicate that the large plantations in the South also demanded precise bookkeeping and accounting. These plantations, which supplied tobacco and cotton to the northern states and Europe and had hundreds of slaves working seven days a week, needed far more accounting detail than most businesses in the Northeast. The records of the Mounthope Plantation in South Carolina, for example, show a self-sustaining economy made up of hundreds of people with 20 to 30 recorded transactions every day. The plantation account book lists that all accounts were kept by the master of the house and that the account book entries were made by "Emily."

Through the plantation's meticulous accounting, it is clear that slavery was the major engine for the plantation, and several ledger entries are all the more disturbing due to their banality. For example, the entries on Thursday, August 20, 1801, show that the plantation purchased, among other things, "one flint of molasses; one hand file; one dozen buttons; one bottle Turlingtons; 100 fish hooks, and three bowskin whips."[9] Every several weeks, in fact, the plantation purchased one or two new bowskin whips.

The master of the plantation may have required some help in keeping the books besides "Emily"; but there is no sign, such as a signature on a page, of a professional accountant being employed by the plantation. About this time, however, some businesses started to hire full-time accountants. For example, financial statements from the Pajaro and Salinas Ranch in California covering the years 1853 to 1858 were certified and signed by "F. N. Massa, accountant."[10]

DISCLOSURE IN EARLY AMERICAN ACCOUNTING

Even when a relatively large company was involved, nineteenth-century American accounting was far more informal than its British counterpart. Many account books and ledgers from this period are rife with pictures, doodles, and poems; and some early bookkeepers even stuck recipes into the books. In the Continental Railroad account books, for example, almost every page contains a two- or three-stanza poem in beautiful, cursive handwriting. Apparently, keeping Continental Railroad's books brought mordant thoughts to mind. The poems had such titles as "The Dying Boy," "The Blind Girl to Her Father," and "Who Will Care When I Am Gone?"[11]

This creative flair with companies' books illustrates that many businesses knew that no one from outside the company would ever be looking at the doodles and limericks that passed for their financial records. Unlike in England, where the English Companies Act of 1855–1856 introduced a standardized balance sheet intended to prod companies to disclose financial information, company management in the United States maintained ironclad control over their information. Whatever they wanted to disclose to present the best possible picture to lenders and investors, they did. If they didn't want to present anything, they didn't.

One agent acting to change this trend of nondisclosure was the New York Stock Exchange (NYSE). In 1853, the NYSE mandated that every listed company provide the number of shares outstanding and a sourcing of their capital resources.[12] This requirement was essentially ignored, however. In 1866, the NYSE attempted to extract financial statements from companies. The only companies that complied with these regulations were those that heavily depended on outside sources of capital. Even the managers of those cutting-edge companies didn't agree with the concept of disclosure. In a complaint often cited today, they felt it gave their competitors too much information about their operations.

In addition to the English Companies Act, the English Parliament passed laws in the 1850s that required independent examination of a company's financial statements. These laws spurred a critical spasm of growth in English accounting because they created an insatiable demand for qualified accountants to sign off on the books—a dynamic that would be repeated 80 years later in the United States. Future industry titans such as Price Waterhouse and the forebears of Deloitte & Touche emerged during this time of growth in England.

Meanwhile, in the United States, there wasn't much the accounting profession could do about lack of disclosure in financial statements, although late in the nineteenth century it tried. The first nationwide society of U.S. accountants was founded in 1887 and tried to use its limited clout to push the standardization of corporate reporting. It didn't get very far.

TRANSPORTATION: AN ENGINE FOR ACCOUNTING GROWTH

The burgeoning westward movement and ocean trade in the mid-nineteenth century in the United States proved another engine for robust accounting. Before railroads, steamboat travel was the primary means of transport for Americans.[13] Steamboat owners needed people to keep their books—people who knew double-entry bookkeeping and who could keep the books current with the intense pace of the transportation business, with frequent updating of schedules, adding and dropping routes, compiling passenger lists, and so on.

Railroads, too, were pioneers in providing financial statement disclosure because they relied so heavily on raising outside capital. For example, the Pacific Railroad published financial statements starting in the 1880s for the examination of Poor's Manual, the rating agency (the forerunner to Standard & Poor's).[14] As early as the 1850s, railroads developed the idea of the internal auditor, and they occasionally brought in outside accountants to investigate fraud. The first paragraph of an 1855 memo from internal auditor William Ritchie of the Western Rail Road to the company's president and board of directors gives a good idea of Ritchie's duties as auditor:

> In discharge of my duties as Auditor, I have once each month during the past year, thoroughly examined the books of the treasurer, ascertained that the amount of moneys received and paid out, were correctly entered upon his books from the proper vouchers in his possession, and that the balance represented to be on hand by his cash book, was actually on deposit at various Banks, as shown on the first day of each month by their account current and books of deposit.[15]

Ritchie's role was clearly as an independent witness to the activities of the Western Rail Road's treasurer. Performing tasks like confirming that reported cash holdings were on deposit at a bank was common for auditors then, but unfortunately this kind of detailed testing has gone the way of the horse and buggy.

Some of the biggest advances in accounting in the United States arose out of the data-intensive shipping industry, as insuring the nation's cargo required detailed accounting to make sense of the wealth of information. The account books for Atlantic Mutual Insurance Company, for example, were loaded with information about shipping cargo, including date of entry, date of landing, name of vessel, destination, amount of bill, and date of approval. Again, however, this was primarily internal information. Like other companies at this time, Atlantic Mutual did not publish financial statements that gave lenders or investors a clear picture of the financial health of the company. Over in England, it was a different story.

A GOLDEN AGE OF ACCOUNTING IN ENGLAND

British accounting in the last quarter of the nineteenth century was by far the most developed in the world. In France, for example, the idea of understandable financial statements and open corporate disclosure was relatively undeveloped, while in Germany accounting was dictated by big, government-operated central banks. In the 40-year lag between the birth of British laws mandating auditing of public companies and the 1897 New York State law creating the first U.S. CPA designation, accounting firms in England aggressively audited the books of public companies. They also performed "consulting services" for these same clients. For example, the London accounting firm Oscar Berry & Carr was hired in 1883 by a literary agency to ascertain the number of books one of their authors had sold in order to ensure the author received his full royalties.[16]

During the last third of the nineteenth century, a series of English court decisions helped clarify, in both England and the United States, the scope of audit work and the responsibilities of auditors. In a case involving Kingston Cotton Mills, the court ruled that an auditor, having no reason to suspect dishonesty, had no duty to verify inventory figures given him by a company official who had himself certified the inventory. This was an important step toward outlining the duties of the modern auditor, who is required not to find fraud but to certify that books have been prepared under recognized standards.

In the middle and late 1800s, many of the firms that would drive the public accounting profession for the next hundred years were springing up in London. At the time, of course, no one knew they would come to dominate their industry; they started out just like other firms, with a few founding partners and perhaps several employees.

Samuel Lowell Price, who saw the great need that British companies had for reputable auditors to examine their financial statements as British law required, founded Price Waterhouse in 1850. British Price Waterhouse partners went to the United States in the late 1800s to open offices to serve important clients who were increasingly doing business there.

Another pioneering firm, Coopers Brothers, was founded in London by William Cooper in 1861. Coopers Brothers soon became known as experts in bankruptcy, liquidation, and receivership cases. A common joke about the firm was that one could find one or more of the Cooper brothers at the tavern nearest to the bankruptcy court on any given day. Ernest Cooper told a gathering of the Institute of Chartered Accountants in England and Wales in 1921 that "to be seen talking to or having your office entered by an accountant was to be avoided, particularly in the stressful times of 1866," when England was in the middle of a severe recession.

Peat Marwick, the root firm of what would one day become KPMG, was the product of a chance meeting on an ocean liner. The English branch of Peat Marwick was founded by Sir William Peat shortly after Price Waterhouse, in 1867. James Marwick and Roger Mitchell established the U.S. firm in 1897. Marwick met Peat during an ocean crossing from London to New York in 1911. For the next 14 years, the firm operated in the United States as Marwick, Mitchell, Peat & Co., before changing its name to Peat Marwick.

Deloitte, Haskins & Sells, like Price Waterhouse, has its roots in the mid-1800s laws passed by Parliament requiring the certifying of company financial statements. Touche Ross, the firm that combined with Deloitte, Haskins & Sells to create Deloitte & Touche, began in 1899. Although there were no big firms in the United States, the profession was about to get a major boost. Arthur Young founded his namesake firm in Kansas City in 1895 after leaving another firm in which he was a partner, and Ernst & Ernst was founded in Cleveland by brothers Alwins and Theodore.

IN THE UNITED STATES, A PROFESSION AT LAST

Together with the increasing drive for more disclosure and the proliferation of accounting firms like the ones previously mentioned, the timing was perfect for accounting to gain recognition as a formal profession. It did so when the New York State legislature created the CPA designation in 1897. This essentially ensured that New York City would become the home of pubic accounting in the United States. With a professional designation backed by an officially sanctioned body of knowledge that had to be mastered, the CPA had made an important leap. By the turn of the century, over 70 percent of companies hired outside CPAs to audit their books. "One of the things a lot of people don't understand is that companies were getting audited long before the securities laws of the 1930s required it," said Wayne Guay, a professor of accounting at the Wharton School. "In order to get capital from banks and other lenders, you had to have your books certified."

Despite New York State's CPA designation (which was quickly followed by many other states) and U.S. practitioners' desire for business, the big English firms in the United States received most of the choice jobs. First, there were still not nearly enough U.S.–trained accountants to handle the work. Second, U.S. businesspeople knew that the best-trained accountants were from England. U.S. investors were happy to have experienced British accountants securing their statements, because these firms had logged 25, 50, or 75 years in business, as opposed to young, inexperienced U.S. firms that had one or two years in business.[17] In fact, it would be some time before U.S. colleges developed serious curriculums for accountants, such as the one at NYU's School of Commerce and Accounts.

THE CPA MOVEMENT IN THE UNITED STATES GAINS STRENGTH

In 1904, the CPA movement spread throughout the country in earnest. The profession pushed state CPA legislation throughout the country, emphasizing that standards should be uniform nationwide. Meanwhile, the comparatively worldly chartered accountants from England continued to stream in to New York, Chicago, and Philadelphia to watch over British investments in U.S. railroads and other industrial companies.

One of these accountants was George May. Born in 1875 in Teignmouth, England, to a family with a long history of lawyers and chartered accountants, May had become a chartered accountant on the insistence of his lawyer father, George England May, through the traditional five-year British apprenticeship. May's apprenticeship agreement stated that if the young May lasted four years and did not at any time "cancel, obliterate, spoil, destroy, waste, embezzle, spend, or make away" with any of the accountant's books or papers, he would start drawing a salary of 10 shillings per week.[18] After successfully learning his trade, May immediately joined Price Waterhouse. Just months later, he jumped at the chance to go to the United States to join Price Waterhouse's U.S. affiliate. As May was about to leave England, he was told by one of Price Waterhouse's London partners that the secret to the improvement of U.S. business in the late 1890s was the British character of its accounting. May was told to act "as aggressively British as possible" in his new position.[19]

May enjoyed a meteoric rise at Price Waterhouse. One reason was that he was unabashedly unafraid of the client. One of May's first assignments in the United States was the audit of the Louisville & Nashville Railroad in 1897. Thanks in large part to the efforts of the NYSE as well as to pressure from British investors, many of the biggest U.S. companies viewed outside audits as necessary evils that weren't going to go away. In the 1897 Louisville & Nashville annual report, Chairman August Belmont wrote in a note to shareholders, "It is now being adopted by a number of leading railroads, to have their annual statements audited by public accountants. This is a very prevalent custom in England, and as the English public is largely interested both in the bonds and stock of the company, it was deemed for the best interests of the corporation to have its accounts audited annually."[20]

Price Waterhouse landed the job of auditing Louisville & Nashville's books. Railroad auditing was one of the firm's specialties. In those days, Price Waterhouse went much further in vouching for Louisville & Nashville than auditors do today. The auditor's certificate—which wasn't standardized across firms at the time—virtually guaranteed the accuracy of the railroad's financial statements: "We have examined the books of the Company for the year ended June 30, 1897, and we certify that subject to the remarks which follow, the above balance sheet, of which a summary will be found on pages 22 and 23, is correct. Before arriving at the balance of profit and loss, operating expenses have been charged with improvements and betterments amounting to $546,570.87."[21]

May, however, noticed that the company had not taken a charge for about $80,000 worth of operating expenses for the year. He insisted that a qualifying statement be put in the report. Belmont was outraged; but May, backed by his Price Waterhouse superiors, wouldn't budge. Throughout his career, May would often tell this story to Price Waterhouse auditors whose backbones needed strengthening. And he wouldn't leave out the fact that Price Waterhouse retained the client. This is the kind of dedication to high standards and integrity that the auditing profession has lost today in the pursuit of growth and profit. May and his contemporaries understood that quality work would be consistently rewarded by the marketplace. Today's accountants, conversely, jeopardized their long-term reputation for short-sighted goals.

THE WORLD CONGRESS OF ACCOUNTANTS

The Federated Society of Public Accountants of the United States was the fledgling profession's governing body in the United States at the turn of the twentieth century, and under its umbrella were the state accounting societies, including the New York State Society of Certified Public Accountants. But the U.S. professional bodies were already splintering into various factions with different ideas of just what the responsibilities of professional auditors were. The then dean of accountants in the United States and George May's boss, Arthur Dickinson of Price Waterhouse, decided to gather prominent accountants from around the country to streamline the proliferating number of professional organizations, as well as to lay the technical foundation for the future of the profession.

The World Congress of Accountants was held in St. Louis in 1904 concurrently with the World's Fair, the better to draw accountants from near and far. In essence, it was the first major accounting conference in the United States. The conference literature said that the purpose of the Congress was "to establish in all states a uniformly high standard of efficiency and to disseminate throughout the United States a general knowledge of the utility of the public accountant in the industrial and financial development of the country."[22]

The World Congress of Accountants is largely ignored in the history of accounting; but, in fact, it marked the first and most important meeting among the men who would become the giants of the U.S. profession and would give accountants the jolt they needed to become serious professionals worthy of public respect. If the specially chartered train carrying accounting luminaries from New York to St. Louis for the conference had derailed—resulting in the untimely demise of its carful of auditors—every global accounting firm today would likely have a different name. The attendees of the conference, most of them in their thirties or early forties, included May, who would become senior partner of Price Waterhouse for a quarter century; James Marwick and Roger Mitchell, two of the founders of Peat Marwick; Elijah Sells, one of the founders of Haskins & Sells, which eventually became Deloitte & Touche; William Lybrand, Edward Ross, and Robert Montgomery, three founders of Lybrand, Ross Bros. & Montgomery, which eventually became Coopers & Lybrand; and Arthur Young, founder of the firm that became half of Ernst & Young.

May's view that accounting was really for the financial statement user (lenders and shareholders, for example) was enthusiastically shared by Lybrand and Edward Ross, and the three started a lifelong friendship.[23] In fact, the three could have saved everyone a lot of trouble if they had simply decided to join forces right then and there, because 93 years later, in 1997, Price Waterhouse's 102,000 employees joined Coopers & Lybrand's 105,000 employees to form the biggest accounting firm in the world, PricewaterhouseCoopers.

The story of Lybrand, Ross Bros. & Montgomery was an interesting one that showed how the best young U.S. firms formed. Lybrand and Edward Ross, along with Adam Ross and Montgomery, had all trained together at a firm in Philadelphia before pooling their resources to start the firm. Each would contribute over the years to making accounting a stronger profession. The firm led the movement to gain state certification of public accountants in Pennsylvania. Montgomery also authored one of the first U.S. accounting textbooks, published in 1905. Lybrand, Ross Bros. & Montgomery would eventually play a role in crafting the 1913 federal income tax law.

The World Congress of Accountants also marked the creation of the first official definition of the accounting profession in the United States. Actually, the definition had quite a bit more in common with that of today's accounting establishment than it did with the definition that would presumably be used by well-known modern reformers like Arthur Levitt. For example, the definition stated that "[the public accountant's] wide experience and varied practice peculiarly fit him as a *business adviser* and enable him to assist the financier, the merchant, and the manufacturer in the development of the country." (italics added)[24]

Despite the success of the world accounting conference in establishing parameters for the profession, May and his fellow expatriates watched in the years that immediately followed—mostly with empathy but also with a little humor—as new U.S. accountants floundered, trying to figure out what the difference between a bookkeeper and an accountant was or what an audit report was supposed to consist of. In England, there existed hundreds of years of court decisions and common law that set formal precedent. Accounting in the United States was still not a profession that appealed to the better educated. Most colleges still didn't offer a single course in accounting. In fact, U.S. accountancy attracted no small number of traveling hucksters and charlatans ready to perform an "audit."

A U.S. PRACTITIONER AT WORK

An early example of a traveling U.S. accountant comes from 1905 records from the Philadelphia office of Price Waterhouse, which periodically sent the firm's partners out to pay formal visits to prospective clients. One of these potential clients was Mahlon W. Newton, the proprietor of Green's Hotel in Philadelphia, a well-known inn at Eighth and Chestnut Streets. According to a Price Waterhouse write-up of the interview with Newton, a U.S. accountant named W. Scott Patmore had stopped by the hotel a few months earlier to offer his services.[25] Patmore suggested to Newton that he could audit the company's books, but Newton explained that most of the hotel's business was conducted on a cash basis and, besides, he watched everything so carefully that he knew that the books were correct. But Patmore went on to tell the hotel owner and his manager/bookkeeper, D. B. Olmstead, that he was a veritable magician in devising a bookkeeping system that could save the hotel money on labor and other expenses. The pair agreed to provide Mr. Patmore with room and board and an undetermined payment for his services.

For the next three weeks, Patmore busied himself, as the Price Waterhouse report termed it, "giving ample cause for dissatisfaction, and grave apprehension regarding the consequences of his lawless and unprincipled methods." Patmore apparently spent much of his time at the hotel bar, passing bad checks and borrowing money for drinks from hotel guests. Not all U.S. accountants were as bad as Patmore. And soon, with the emergence of a midwestern accountant named Arthur Andersen, they would have their very own U.S. role model.

THE ANDERSEN WAY

Since the 2002 demise of Arthur Andersen, it has gone virtually unremarked that the firm's namesake founded it to be different from other accounting firms—one that offered all manner of business advice, not just accounting skills. An accomplished academic, businessman, author, and philosopher, Andersen challenged every accepted axiom of accounting in the early part of the twentieth century. He insisted that auditors were the only professionals with an objective perspective and detailed knowledge of every nook and cranny of a company, due to their privileged vantage point at the nexus of all operations. He envisioned a much wider role for auditors as their client's most important advisers.

Andersen became a CPA in Illinois in 1908 and was appointed an assistant professor of accounting at the School of Commerce at Northwestern University in 1912. Andersen eventually became head of the university's accounting department, but most of his energies were focused on the firm he started, Arthur Andersen & Co. From the beginning, Andersen saw his firm as being different from both other local Chicago accounting firms and the British firms that were already serving some of the biggest clients in Chicago. As he said in a speech before the National Association of Cost Accountants in 1924: "Some ten years ago I had the idea that accounting was not in itself an end, and that the sooner public accountants developed that bigger and broader viewpoint, the sooner they would place their services on a professional basis."

A few months later, before the American Association of University Instructors, he set an even more radical course for the profession: "An accountant cannot remain merely a high-grade technician if he is to occupy his rightful place in the field of modern business. Business itself has changed and is still changing at a tremendous rate."[26] Andersen saw his young accountants not as bookkeepers or auditors but as good businessmen who could help Andersen's clients solve their problems.

Andersen used his position as head of the accounting department at Northwestern University to develop a feeder system for his downtown Chicago firm. He founded "Arthur Andersen University" for new recruits around the country to get initiated into the Andersen way of accounting. As Paul Knight, former student of Andersen who went on to become an Andersen & Co. partner, wrote about Andersen in 1946: "He looked behind the figures to ascertain the factors that contribute to the operating results and form a business judgment as to how to improve the good factors and eliminate the bad. He gave us a new and broader picture of the function of the corporate and the public accountant and showed that with a constructive approach accounting and auditing can be a dynamic, aggressive factor in business management."[27]

By recruiting aggressive young men and training them in the Andersen way, Arthur Andersen believed that his accountants could do much more than audit financial statements or figure out corporate taxes. He wanted his young hires—all of whom were expected to be on call on weekends and to work late into the evening—to think about their customer's business and how it could be improved. Andersen understood that his accountants could end up knowing more about the overall company than most of its employees. It's no surprise that Andersen & Co. became the most aggressive and successful pursuer of consulting services in the years ahead, given Arthur Andersen's penchant for looking *Behind the Figures*, as a collection of his speeches is known.

Part of Andersen's motivation was that he wanted to distinguish his firm. But much like the leaders of some of the other prominent firms, he understood that the purpose of the firm had to transcend profit. Andersen recognized that in the early 1900s investors needed some protection from unscrupulous businesspeople and that banks needed assurance that the companies to which they were lending money were, in fact, going concerns. Andersen was also a deep thinker and had very strong ideas about how accounting could contribute to the might of the United States. His writings, prodigious and wide-ranging, were not constrained by the lingua franca of accounting. In a commencement speech at St. Olaf College in Minnesota on the eve of World War II, Andersen sounded like anything but an accountant when he said in reference to the rampaging German armies in Europe: "It is easy, far too easy, to take a cynical view; but, once again, hope and life will conquer fear and despair. One must endeavor in addressing young persons, particularly on the eve of their graduation, to present views which are at least intellectually honest."[28]

FULFILLING THE PUBLIC TRUST

The introduction of the CPA into the financial world helped stabilize what was, in the early 1900s, a time of rampant stock speculation and corporate secrecy. This was a time during which accounting firms established their reputation for integrity and public service that lasted for many years to come. Price Waterhouse quickly became a leader in breaking new technical ground. For example, the accepted method for auditing financial statements for a company with many subsidiaries was to evaluate each set of statements separately. Price Waterhouse began consolidating company's subsidiaries' financial statements, and it proved a very effective way of presenting the financial health of a big client like U.S. Steel. Price Waterhouse was also successful in lobbying its clients to publish financial data on a quarterly basis, a major win for disclosure advocates.

Peat Marwick, too, came to the aid of U.S. investors. Its claim to fame in its early years was its role in helping J. P. Morgan, the legendary investment banker, salvage the Knickerbocker Trust Company during the panic of 1907, when banks and businesses were falling like dominos and the nation's investors were lining up at the Knickerbocker to yank out their deposits. In 1906, rumors abounded that President Theodore Roosevelt, already well known as a trust buster and a champion of the little guy, was planning to move against the monopolistic railroad industry. According to Jean Strouse's *American Financier*, Morgan "planned to leave for Europe in mid-March 1907, but the combination of monetary shrinkage (largely due to financing of the Boer and Russo-Japanese Wars) and a rumor that Roosevelt would make some dramatic new move against the railroads called him out of his 'Up-Town Branch.' He went to Washington on March 12 and spent two hours discussing 'the present business situation' with the President. As he left the White House, he told the press that Roosevelt would soon meet with the heads of leading railroads to see what might be done to 'allay public anxiety.'"[29]

As it turned out, there was plenty for the public to be anxious about. In the summer of 1907, several large companies went bankrupt. Depositors at the New York Knickerbocker Trust Company started a run on the bank on October 22, 1907, when $8 million was withdrawn in three hours. At one point, the New York Stock Exchange was in danger of failing until Morgan pledged $25 million to keep it afloat.[30] The panic of 1907 not only led to the federal regulation of banking with the creation of the Federal Reserve Board, but it helped open up a whole new set of activities for the CPA. Peat Marwick, which already was well known as a specialist in bank auditing, was asked by Morgan to assess the solvency of Knickerbocker Trust.

Deloitte, Haskins & Sells helped solve the problem of how to depreciate fixed assets. At the time, if a shipping company bought a new cargo ship, for example, it was thought the company could increase its balance sheet assets by the same amount it paid for the ship, disregarding the concept of depreciation. Deloitte's firm insisted that this practice change; and its work led to the British Joint Stock Banking Act, which required firms to provide balance sheets and income statements that showed fair value and reflected depreciation and other such ideas.

It was George May, however, whose actions and speeches best caught the spirit of this new field as it took on the most vexing business challenges of the day. In 1911, May became the leader of the profession in the United States when Arthur Dickinson, his predecessor at Price Waterhouse, stepped down. Through his writings for journals and his correspondence, it is clear that May loved his new country and the seemingly limitless business growth it offered. He displayed a philosopher's wonderment at the mysterious nature of accounting, in that perfection in representing a company's financial position was never attainable. May often emphasized the profession's unique quasi-public nature during this period. In one speech he gave before a gathering of accountants, May said: "The high-minded accountant who undertakes to practice in this field assumes high ethical obligations, and it is the assumption of such obligations that makes what might otherwise be a business, a profession. Of all the groups of professions which are closely allied with business, there is none in which the practitioner is under a greater ethical obligation to persons who are not his immediate clients."[31]

It was this ability to think about the larger ramifications of the profession that prompted May to aggressively spread his philosophy that it was the absentee owners—the shareholders—who were auditors' real clients and that management had to be both educated as to what good accounting was and challenged when necessary. Confronting management took courage in the early 1900s. Despite the activism of the big firms, accountants did not have a lot of power. Companies could fire an auditor; furthermore, they were not required to commission an independent audit at all. At a partners' dinner at the Union League Club in New York City on April 13, 1914, May was already cautioning his colleagues against losing their independence when auditing: "One caution in particular I would like to reiterate, and that is against allowing ourselves to lend our name to any enterprise or to say more in a certificate than we feel entirely warranted in saying for the sake of retaining an old or making a new connection."

THE EARLY FIGHT FOR AUDITOR INDEPENDENCE

Auditor independence also became an issue because of the increasing tendency at the time for clients to hire the partner on their engagement as their comptroller. Firms soon found it difficult to certify the books of these companies when their employees were crawling all over the finance department. One founder of a midsized accounting firm said this problem was overcome: "If one of my employees became the controller, let's say, and we audited the books of which he was in charge, we simply had to be more careful. If he were honest, it wouldn't hurt to be more careful."[32]

Robert Montgomery of Lybrand, Ross Bros. & Montgomery, was one of the most ardent advocates of the duty of the auditor to be totally, brutally honest about his client's financial condition. Later in life, he described the attitude of the public accountants who audited the nation's books in the years prior to World War I:

> Then, they were fearless seekers for the truth. Poor as they were, no power on earth could have swerved them from their search. . . . [O]ur profession always has had a vision—this urge to find and tell the truth—and we should cling to it and continue to strive for its accomplishment. I do not want to see our growth depend on anything else than that which has made us what we are today. We shall retain our strength just as long as we retain our independence—no longer.[33]

The accounting profession flourished in the early 1900s because of men like Arthur Andersen, George May, and Robert Montgomery. Indeed, it turned out that the firms that thrived were the ones that were led by executives who were much more public minded than their contemporaries. During times of crisis, such as war, financial panics, and the coming Great Depression, it was the firms that had a commitment to the public welfare that were rewarded with crucial assignments. That is one of the great ironies of the modern state of accounting, in which the big firms have led the charge *away* from auditing. Each of the biggest firms in accounting today had great and proud moments, like Peat Marwick's efforts to help J. P. Morgan stop the panic of 1907 or the consolidation of financial statements innovated by Price Waterhouse. The early 1900s were a time when the big firms were distinguishing themselves by solving some of the most vexing problems in business. In contrast, for example, during the 1990s the accounting firms all joined as one to oppose stock options expensing, a position that is today almost universally seen as shortsighted and incorrect from a pure accounting standpoint.

Even at this early juncture, however, the traits that would come to define the big accounting firms in future decades were already taking root. Geographic diversity became a key to success. For example, to serve the railways, the firms needed offices in cities into which the railways were expanding. As the firms grew, occasional accusations of accounting negligence cropped up.

One of the biggest scandals of the time involved Ernst & Ernst. Essentially, the firm turned a blind eye to the adventures of a pyramid scheme of a company called International Match Company. International Match, led by a Swede named Ivar Kreuger, reported phony financial statement profits from the sales of matches. The money investors received that they thought was interest and dividends—and on which they paid taxes—was really money received from the public and partially paid back to the public, a revolving loan that gave the impression money was being made. There actually were no profits at all. When Kreuger was caught, he killed himself. Many thought colossal frauds like Krueger's would be impossible to replicate. Ernst & Ernst took much of the blame. The consensus was that this kind of fraud couldn't be perpetrated without some careless auditing.

OTHER CONTRIBUTIONS TO THE PROFESSION

It wasn't just the big firms that helped solidify the accounting profession in the United States. Various individuals brought the profession along through their own efforts. One of these people was Dr. Joseph Klein. Klein was one of the most connected accountants in early-twentieth-century New York. When Klein was admitted as CPA number 526 in New York State, he asked the head of the New York Society of CPAs, "Is there any fee scale?" "Yes, sir," the man answered. "You can't be a CPA unless you charge at least $20 a day." Klein quickly found out that even though accounting was now a "profession," it still was quite difficult to secure clients who were willing to pay $20 a day. At that point, a non-CPA could be paid much less and still produce a statement that was perfectly acceptable for getting loans from a bank.[34]

Klein soon founded the firm of Klein, Hinds, and Fink, which lasted until it was gobbled up by another firm in the 1970s. He became chairman of the New York State CPA Society and of the Ethics Committee of the American Accounting Association. But first and foremost, Klein was an extraordinary teacher. He gave the first-ever course in municipal accounting, focusing specifically on keeping the books and records for the city of New York. In this way, Klein ended up teaching an entire generation of future New York City auditors and employees of the comptroller's department.

An anecdote Klein told for an oral history project illustrates how he and his students saw accounting—not as a financial reporting compliance function or a business advisory role, but as an exercise in truth telling. One day at City College in New York City, Klein was teaching one of his accounting courses. He mentioned to his students that he was thinking of switching and teaching a discipline other than accounting. One of the students spoke up.

"Please don't do that. I'd like you to continue telling us more about the accounting."
"Why's that?" asked Dr. Klein.

"I find it so interesting," the student said. "It's the most important subject in the curriculum."

"Why do you say that?"

"Oh," she said, "If you learn to take the work seriously you learn to tell the truth."[35]

Before Klein and other early-twentieth-century educators, accounting instruction in the United States had been spotty at best, and advanced teaching of the profession had been nearly nonexistent. Early U.S. accounting education emphasized mathematics. For college students interested in bookkeeping, there weren't even many books on the subject until the twentieth century. British accountants, however, were solidly grounded in bookkeeping accounting procedure, which was undoubtedly another reason that they were dominant for so long into the twentieth century. Furthermore, because there were few academic programs in the United States, it was very difficult to get the training to pass the CPA exam, even then known to be a difficult test. The British accountant enjoyed a well-worn and clearly marked career path, with the right training readily available for anyone with the aptitude.

By the mid-1910s, accounting was firmly established as a profession in the United States and had distinguished itself by playing a major role in the public and political life of the country. Still, it had no real mandate. A company could still audit its own books with an internal auditor or bookkeeper. Also brewing were some troublesome notions (to accountants anyway) that corporate accounting and auditing could be guided solely by a set of strict rules, rather than by professional judgment. The profession was soon to encounter powerful external challenges to the way it conducted its duties.

CHAPTER 3

ACCOUNTANTS EARN
A PUBLIC TRUST

GEORGE MAY HAD A SAYING THAT PEPPERED HIS PERSONAL AND business correspondence: Accounting would be "indefensible were it not indispensable." May understood better than any of his contemporaries that accounting was an imperfect art, based on artificial constructs of time that bore little resemblance to how companies made money. The necessity of applying arbitrary parameters to financial reporting, using tools such as quarterly or annual earnings reports, made men like May very reluctant to judge any financial information as "true" or not. To May, financial information was only as reliable as the integrity of the people releasing it.

It is not surprising that May's accounting writings had a way of flipping conventional wisdom on its head. In a letter he wrote to J. M. B. Hoxsey, an attorney at the New York Stock Exchange (NYSE) with whom May worked closely during the late 1920s and early 1930s, May discussed operating expenses versus capital in a way that might interest the defense team representing ex-WorldCom chief financial officer (CFO) Scott Sullivan: "The distinction between capital and operating expenditures turns wholly on the time unit. In an accounting in which the time unit was a day, a paintbrush lasting a month would be a capital asset. Conversely, if the time unit were a generation, heavy machinery would become an operating expense."[1]

May's strikingly original thinking also extended to matters of accounting ethics and propriety. He understood that accountants were no less susceptible to temptation than anybody else. That's why, for example, May insisted on complete financial independence from clients roughly 30 years before the idea occurred to accounting's professional bodies.[2] It's why May avoided conflicts of interest by not socializing with clients or joining the many clubs clamoring for his membership. May was trying, in his own small way, to make sure he could say to his clients, just at that moment when he needed to: "No."

May said no all the time. He said no to joining boards. He said no to dinner with important clients. He said no to George Eastman when the legendary tycoon offered him a job.[3] He said no to a very good friend and president of a company who was engaged in a dispute with another accounting firm. May sided with the rival accounting firm over his friend.[4] It was this duality of May's thinking—intellectual creativity combined with personal probity—that defined his singular role in the accounting debates of the 1920s and 1930s. But May wasn't alone. Men like Arthur Andersen, Robert Montgomery, and Arthur Bowman (of Peat Marwick), while not as deep thinking as May nor as interested in the future of the profession as a whole (as opposed to their own firms), built the underlying structure to public accounting that still exists today. It was the sterling legacy of these early leaders that created the public trust that has today been squandered.

And yet there exists a supreme irony to May's stature as the most incorruptible and visionary modern accountant. His insistence that there were no absolutes in accounting—no "truth," if you will—helped nudge the profession away from judging accounts by what was tangible and verifiable (e.g., company X has 1,000 widgets) to judging accounts by how effectively a company's financial reporting systems and processes worked. It follows that if accountants were not reporting truth, how could they be expected to find and report fraud? Today's public accountant, who insists that finding fraud is not part of his or her job, owes a good part of his or her job description to May and the reforms he spearheaded in the late 1920s and the 1930s.

WORLD WAR I AND THE 1920s:
AN AGE OF PUBLIC SERVICE

The responsibility to the public shareholder that British accountants instilled in their U.S. brethren during the years leading up to World War I soon manifested itself in a more general notion of public service to the nation. In fact, from 1913 through 1929, few professions embodied public service like accounting did.

One area where the skills of talented accountants were needed was federal income tax legislation. In 1913, the states ratified the Sixteenth Amendment, which gave Congress the authority to enact an income tax. The United States had long been ambivalent about the personal income tax. Congress created the office of the Commissioner of Internal Revenue in 1861, at the request of President Lincoln, to help pay for the Civil War. The income tax was repealed 10 years later and then reinstated in 1894, only to be ruled unconstitutional in 1895. After the panic of 1907, support for another form of income for the government finally resulted six years later in the passage of the Sixteenth Amendment. Robert Montgomery from Lybrand, Ross Bros. & Montgomery took the lead for the accounting profession in helping structure the law, acting as a consultant to the Ways and Means Committee as Congress deliberated the particulars of the legislation. Congress eventually levied a 1 percent tax on those with incomes more than $3,000 and a 6 percent surtax on incomes more than $500,000.

In 1917, Montgomery took on another public challenge. He and May joined forces, along with the municipal accounting expert Harvey S. Chase, in writing out a set of audit procedures for the Federal Reserve Board. Both Montgomery's and May's respective firms would play roles assisting the Allies during World War I. One wartime-related consulting job performed by May's Price Waterhouse showed how the firm and the profession could be a positive force in U.S. public life and illustrated how solid accounting could defuse a potentially explosive situation.

Sears Roebuck chairman Julian Rosenwald was appointed to head the Council of Defense—a liaison of sorts between the private sector and the Defense Department—at the start of World War I. A prominent congressman, John McKeller, charged Rosenwald with using his defense position to encourage the Army to buy Sears Roebuck goods. McKeller vowed to haul Rosenwald before Congress and grill him about the abuse of his government position. The U.S. government hired Price Waterhouse to determine whether Rosenwald had pressured military brass into mass orders of Sears Roebuck clothes or other items. The accounting firm soon reported that since the time of declaration of war several years earlier, Sears Roebuck's business from soldiers had actually dramatically *fallen*. It turned out that young men about to go to war, unsure of when they would have to report to the front, found it useless to order items by mail. They wouldn't know what address to put down on the order form because they could ship out any day. Congressman McKeller cancelled the hearings.[5]

During World War I, May was brought into the Treasury Department to advise the government on tax matters. The government heavily promoted the idea of contributing to the war effort by purchasing Liberty bonds. Unfortunately, this enthusiastic entry into investing by many Americans resulted in a rapid increase of charlatans peddling fake bonds and stocks to an unsuspecting public. On December 2, 1918, just days after the end of World War I, the Capital Issues Committee of the federal government said: "At no time has the obligation been so definitely placed upon the government to protect its public from financial exploitations by reckless or unscrupulous promoters. The field has been greatly enlarged by the wide distribution of Liberty bonds, and the purveyor of stocks and bonds is no longer put to the necessity of seeking out a select list of prospective purchasers with money to invest. He now has the entire American public."[6]

May, Montgomery, and their colleagues did their best to thwart this practice by encouraging stock exchanges to require independent audits of their listees. Even with independent audits increasing in the mid-1920s, as newcomers entered the stock market, securities fraud skyrocketed. Securities legislation had been proposed several times since the end of World War I, as it became clear that con artists issuing worthless stock had proliferated to a never-before-seen degree. The legislation, though, repeatedly went nowhere.

In the 13 years from 1919 to 1931, $50 billion worth of new stocks and bonds were issued in the United States, of which nearly $20 billion was stocks. The only significant securities legislation was at the state level, the series of so-called "blue-sky" laws, which got their name from an early lawsuit in which a judge referred to "speculative schemes that have no more basis than so many feet of blue sky."[7] Kansas enacted the first blue-sky laws in 1911, followed in quick succession by West Virginia, Iowa, South Dakota, Ohio, and so forth until, by 1923, only Nevada and Delaware did not have some type of state regulation of securities.

Though somewhat ineffective in dealing with companies that did business across state lines because of interstate squabbles over jurisdiction, one effect the blue-sky laws had was to encourage independent audits. Indeed, accountants saw their stature rise in the 1920s as they were seen, particularly in the latter stages of the decade, as the only class of professionals that attempted to reign in Wall Street speculation.

In the mid-1920s, as the U.S. economy boomed and accountants continued their ascendence in the minds of their fellow citizens, accountants also continued their civic leadership. In 1926, May traveled back to England to assist the British government in framing accounting for the Reparations Committee, in charge of ensuring that a defeated Germany kept its payment schedule. Also in 1926, May was appointed as a member of an advisory committee to a joint congressional committee on taxation, which participated in the preparation of the tax law of 1926. The year 1926 also saw a push for defining accounting principles that would improve corporate governance. The principles developed during this period would prove the accounting profession's salvation a few years later when the newly formed SEC threatened to exercise its power to set accounting standards. The profession made a beachhead for their argument that "true" financial statements were not guaranteed to be correct in the layman's sense, but true in that they were rendered with honest judgment and reasonable accounting principles. In the end, according to writers like Montgomery and May, auditors were issuing an opinion.

Although some literature asserts that accountants became caught up in the speculative frenzy that partly defined the 1920s and became cheerleaders for corporate management, the truth is that from 1926 to 1930 the number of audited companies climbed dramatically and that the quality of financial reports improved.[8]

Still, even as audits proliferated, the accountant's ability to fight management lessened. One problem was that with their coffers filled with profits, corporations didn't need to borrow as much money. Therefore, they didn't need independent audits to wow the creditors; there really were no creditors to impress. When a bank did get the chance to lend some money at interest, it wasn't likely to turn a borrower down because of one or two questions raised by the auditors.[9]

One of the most significant contributions any accountant has ever made to the fiscal health of the United States was May's push to establish accounting principles general enough that they would be relevant across industries. Starting in 1927, May became head of the American Institute of Accountants (AIA) special committee on cooperation with stock exchanges. The committee's job, when it started out, was to develop ways that the NYSE could instill better accounting in the companies listed on its exchange. For example, there were many reporting inconsistencies that plagued the NYSE: unreported sales figures, failure to account for asset depreciation, arbitrary asset revaluations, and failure to distinguish between expenses and capital expenditures (much like the WorldCom case). The result of the committee's work was the concept of generally accepted accounting principles (GAAP), still the standards to which U.S. companies must adhere when issuing financial statements.

For five years, May's committee and the NYSE struggled with such issues as the future of independent auditing, the folly of mandated monthly statements, and the impossibility of standard accounting principles for all industries. The market crash in October 1929, however, was about to provide added urgency to the battle for transparent financial reporting.

1929—ACCOUNTANTS AND THE DEPRESSION

In 1929, Price Waterhouse's office at 56 Pine Street in New York City harkened back to the days of London counting houses and scriveners. May allowed no newfangled adding machines; everything had to be calculated and checked by hand. Ink was the standard for working papers, although if paper became too damp for ink in the summer months, a pencil might be allowed. Depending on the time of the year, the "available room"—a large space, which took up nearly an entire floor, where young accountants waited for their assignments—would be bustling with activity. The phone would ring, and a few junior accountants would be called to a job that had just opened up.[11]

In 1929, U.S. business believed it was operating in a new economic era, where the old rules didn't apply and healthy annual economic growth was a given.[12] The language of business at the time was remarkably similar to the "New Economy" talk of the late 1990s. When the market crashed on October 29, 1929, and the subsequent Great Depression settled in, it was mostly bankers, corporate executives, and stock speculators who received the brunt of the public wrath. Accountants' reputations survived intact, but their economic viability didn't.

Like the rest of society, the accounting profession was devastated by the Great Depression. Thousands of CPAs lost their jobs, and the lack of new business formation meant there was literally no new audit or consulting work. However, the number of business failures during the first two years of the Depression illustrated a need for independent, detailed audits by outsiders. Even well-known holdouts such as Standard Oil, which had deemed itself unauditable due to its complexity and international nature, felt pressure to obtain outside verification of its numbers.[13] The ravages of the Depression, then, proved a critical building block in the independent audit franchise that would soon be awarded to the accounting profession.

"TRUTH" VERSUS "FAIRLY PRESENTED"

One way that May's committee recommended that the NYSE achieve the goal of educating the public on financial statements was by eliminating the "truth" aspect of audit certificates and replacing it with the "fairly presented" clause. The special committee felt that the auditor certificates currently in vogue misled investors because, typically, they pronounced that the company's financial statements were "true."[14] The committee recommended that, instead, the certificate should state that the financial statements were "fairly presented, in accordance with the accepted principles of accounting." To combat the view that this language was a way for accountants to get themselves "off the hook," it was in this report that May first outlined certain broad, stated, general principles of accounting that companies should use in the compilation of their reports. The idea was that companies could pick and choose the principles that they would use, as long as they disclosed their methods and used them consistently.

The movement away from "truth" to "fairly presented" was a watershed change in U.S. accounting. Although England's accounting had been superior in process to any other for many years, it contained a particular bias toward auditing the *numbers,* as opposed to auditing the *business.* The British accounting that was exported to U.S. shores through George May and his contemporaries mostly eschewed costly and time-eating activities like checking physical inventory and incoming shipments of accounts receivable. The reason was simple: The truth to which such checks would lead—while laudable—would take so much time and be so costly that clients would not be able to pay for it.[15] So, the big British firms checked the methods and practices that companies used, which one could examine simply by going through a company's ledgers. This movement, the kernel of what has become today GAAP, moved the simple, check-the-drawers U.S. accounting to the next level. But it also would open up the door to fraud by unscrupulous businesspeople who were adept at conjuring up fake warehouses and accounts receivable that they knew the auditors would never check—a scenario that would put a huge dent in Price Waterhouse's reputation a few years down the road.

The NYSE acted on May's recommendations and discreetly told companies applying for listing that starting in 1933, they would be expected to hire independent auditors to conduct periodic audits of their financial statements. May and his committee even recommended the form of audit report that should be used.

The NYSE also wanted to know what May thought of audited quarterly statements. Given the business failures during the Great Depression, public opinion at the time favored audited reports every quarter. May called his Price Waterhouse teams in England and Continental Europe. None of his partners could name one client in Europe that issued quarterly statements, much less quarterly statements certified by an independent auditor.[16] May articulated his belief that more frequent reporting did not necessarily translate into a better snapshot of a company when he wrote to the NYSE on September 22, 1932:

> Accounts are essentially continuous historical records and, as is true of history in general, correct interpretations and sound forecasts for the future cannot be reached upon a hurried survey of temporary conditions, but only by longer retrospect and a careful distinction between permanent tendencies and transitory influences.[17]

May eventually lost that battle when companies gave in to shareholder demand for quarterly statements. He was more prescient when it came to establishing guidelines for avoiding conflicts of interest. With auditor professionalism, both in appearance and in fact, bound to be under scrutiny under the new independent audit rules at the NYSE, leaders of the profession moved to eliminate any potential conflicts. So, more than 60 years before PricewaterhouseCoopers (PwC) was hit with a major independence scandal—in which the SEC cited 8,000 independence violations by PwC for investing in their clients—May decided for himself that he should not have any financial interests in his clients, even though it would certainly cost him a healthy profit. In a January 27, 1933, letter to a Price Waterhouse partner, May wrote:

A discussion of the Royal Bank of Canada case had led me to wonder whether it is altogether wise for me to continue to hold stocks in banks of which we are the auditors, and I have about come to the conclusion that it would be better for me for this reason to dispose of my holdings in the Bank of Toronto (200 shares) at a convenient opportunity before the next audit comes around. In many ways I am reluctant to reach this decision, because I feel that the bank is one of the strongest, if not the strongest, in Canada, and should prove a satisfactory lock-up investment.[18]

Early in 1933, it appeared as if the NYSE's decision to insist that companies applying for listing have their books independently audited would prove a watershed for the profession. It put enormous pressure on those CPAs whose work was largely with companies listed on the NYSE. If these professionals succeeded in doing respected, first-class work, the accounting profession would be seen as the profession doing the most to safeguard the interests of the country's investors. If they failed, not only would the NYSE and other stock exchanges be forced to consider other means of auditing, such as hiring government auditors, but private-sector auditors might not be considered an option in the event of any national securities legislation. The noble experiment at the NYSE, however, was about to be usurped by Congress and a new administration in Washington.[19]

A "NEW DEAL" FOR ACCOUNTANTS

One of the last things likely on President Franklin Roosevelt's mind early in 1933 was the fate of the nation's 15,000 or so CPAs. His worries included a deepening depression, hundreds of failing banks, sinking stocks, and Republican opponents decrying the president's "New Deal" legislation.

Once the banks were reopened in mid-March, proposed legislation poured out of the Roosevelt administration, addressing everything from farms to public works. It was inevitable that securities legislation would also be on the agenda. May and the rest of the Stock Exchange Committee obviously felt conflicted by the securities legislation when it was proposed in late March.[20] The Federal Securities Act of 1933 mandated the disclosure in registration statements and prospectuses of all material facts, as well as the *elimination* of nonessential information that would confuse investors. Soon, all of May's work with the special committee and the NYSE to ensure independent audits would be overshadowed by the all-encompassing securities legislation. If May and the other leaders of the accounting profession played their hands right, it would largely be their work on which Congress would base the new legislation. Besides, May's Price Waterhouse and the rest of the big audit firms were sure to thrive if independent audits were mandated for all public companies.

In a letter to Price Waterhouse's U.S. and Canadian offices in 1933, May highlighted the importance of remaining independent of client pressure throughout this period. In part, May was worried that Congress, during debate over the inevitable securities legislation, would question whether independent auditors hired by the client were too beholden to client management. Whatever his motives, however, May encouraged an adversarial stance toward management— even pledging his willingness to drop important clients—a stance that one has a hard time imagining a modern-day accounting firm CEO taking. May wrote to his partners:

> We wish to impress on all offices the importance of insisting on sound methods of accounting and presentation of facts, however difficult the circumstances may be and however important may be the client with whom the questions are raised. We are perfectly satisfied to sacrifice present business and profits to maintain the position of the firm and discharge our obligations to the profession, and have no doubt that such a policy will also prove ultimately the most profitable.[21]

The question of which accountant or accountants had the most impact on the Federal Securities Act of 1933 and its awarding of the independent audit franchise to CPAs is uncertain. The historical literature gives most of the credit to May, citing his groundbreaking work with Hoxsey of the NYSE. It was not May, however, but Colonel Arthur A. Carter (his World War I service earned him the military title he liked to freely use), Haskins & Sells' senior partner and head of the New York State Society of Certified Public Accountants, who represented the accounting industry before the Senate banking and currency committee during hearings on the legislation.

Carter appeared before the Senate on April 1, 1933. Unbeknownst to Carter, the Senate had already developed potential guidelines for a national corps of government auditors who would audit registrant certificates using not-yet-developed statutory bookkeeping rules. Many of the senators believed that government auditors would need to check the books of the companies once the private-sector auditors were through anyhow, so why not just skip a step? From the testimony, it is clear that most of the senators had little or no knowledge of the movement toward independent audits that market forces had wrought in the previous few years. Carter, at various times, was asked what auditors did, how many there were in the country, what kind of training they had, how many public companies had them, and so on.[22]

Given the lack of knowledge of the senators concerning the accounting profession, it was by no means certain that CPAs would win the right to exclusively audit public companies. Carter, however, explained in his testimony that independent, professional auditors were already in place at most big companies, successfully using various general accounting principles that had developed over the years and that May and the special committee had developed even further. The senators laid various traps for Carter that would have made him overplay his hand. For example, Senator Robert Reynolds of North Carolina tried to get Carter to say that the independent auditors would provide to shareholders an opinion on the value of the company's securities and the condition of the company. Carter responded that an accountant could only issue an opinion on whether the company's finances were being fairly presented.[23]

The senators also wanted to know who would audit the auditors. This exchange between Senator Alben Barkley of Kentucky and Carter allowed Carter to state the crux of where auditor independence is rooted. Carter had just explained how auditors act as watchdogs on company controllers.

> **Senator Barkley**: Is there any relationship between your organization with 2,000 members and the organization of controllers represented here yesterday with 2,000 members?
> **Colonel Carter**: None at all. We audit the controllers.
> **Senator Barkley**: You audit the controllers?
> **Colonel Carter**: Yes; the public accountant audits the controller's account.
> **Senator Barkley**: Who audits you?
> **Colonel Carter**: Our conscience.

The Securities Act was passed in April 1933, with independent CPAs winning the franchise to audit public companies. According to G. A. Swanson, an accounting professor from Tennessee Tech, the final decision to leave auditing of financial statements to private-sector auditors was due to the fact that despite the Senate's initial stance calling for a corps of national auditors, neither government nor industry really wanted to collectivize auditing. "People didn't want to accelerate the centralization of power," Swanson said, "because what happens with the centralization of power is you get corruption and stagnation. Nobody wanted that."

As with any legislation, the final language used in the Securities Act was critical to how the provisions of the law would be enforced. In the end, the word *accountant* was used instead of *auditor* because *accountant* was used in the English statutes on which the Acts were partly based. The word *independent* was used to ensure that a CPA in the employ of the government or the client itself would not be used to attempt an audit.

After the passage of the legislation, the Federal Trade Commission (the SEC would not be created until the following year) directed accountants in the fall of 1933 in formalizing a general series of accounting regulations that would govern the independent audits. They had to codify an entire body of accounting rules and practices in just a few weeks. What made matters even more complicated is that the profession had only just begun to agree on accounting terminology, accounting principles, responsibilities of auditors, and so forth. It is a testament to the accountants of the day and their appetite for public service that they so ably advised the FTC.

In late 1933, May and Colonel Carter conferred about a concern each had about the duties given to CPAs by the Act. The Act never explicitly laid out who was to prepare a company's financial statements—the company itself or the auditor. In England, it had long been the case that a company's officers had full responsibility for its financial statements, while the auditor issued an opinion on these statements. Throughout the 1920s at some companies in the United States, however, the auditor prepared the statements from raw data provided by company management. May was amazed that the accounting profession in the United States allowed itself to be coopted in this manner. One problem with the practice was that the accountants would be assuming the ultimate responsibility for the financial statements, opening themselves and their firms up to scrutiny, criticism, and litigation. Another issue was independence: How could an auditor issue an opinion on financial statements he or she largely prepared?

On November 14, 1933, Carter wrote a letter to May suggesting that auditor certificates should contain the sentence, "We have made an examination of your accounts for the purpose of expressing an opinion in connection with such statements, which have been prepared by you." Carter wanted to be explicit because he believed that the public did not understand that accountants did not produce financial statements for a company. He also believed that such a clear separation of responsibilities—the company issuing the financial statements and the auditor issuing an opinion on them—would give the auditor a free hand to criticize management's assertions. He wrote that a sharp dividing line between responsibilities meant that an accountant "has the responsibility of using his certificate for the purpose of calling attention to the defects and deficiencies."

May and Carter further refined the concept, and today the notion that accountants should never prepare a company's financial statements is gospel. But, again, May's influence contributed in some ways to the chaos in which the profession finds itself today. By setting itself apart as an independent judge that issues an impartial opinion, the profession raised the public's expectations that it would rigorously oversee company management. In fact, auditors typically work very closely with management to produce a company's financial statements. By disavowing any ownership of a company's financial statements, the profession ultimately misled the public.

When the Securities Act passed, it was, in terms of pure economics, no doubt the most important step forward for the profession since the reestablishment of the federal income tax in 1913. New work related to the legislation poured in for accountants almost right away, and soon audited reports for 1933 were coming in to the FTC. Because the format of the report had been left to the companies and the accounting firms, it was unclear how close they would mirror the report format May and his team had suggested for the NYSE. When the audit reports starting coming in, it became clear that the NYSE–style reports were being used as a model.

One thing the Act had not dealt with was uniform accounting standards. In his years of working with the NYSE on the issue, May had always been reluctant to recommend that the NYSE require listed companies to report their income and expenses or to figure out asset depreciation in a certain mandatory, prescribed way. Now that legislation mandating independent audits had been passed, however, it seemed that everyone suddenly wanted fixed rules or principles that would govern corporate financial reporting and the scope of the audits. It seemed that Congress wanted guarantees on how both the controller ("chief financial officer" was not part of the standard business vernacular at the time) and the auditor would operate. The problem was that much like business today, reality did not cooperate. As Lewis Ashman, a colleague of May on another AIA panel, the accounting principles committee, wrote to May on January 22, 1934:

It is rather appalling to contemplate the number of statements which in due course may be promulgated by our committee as accounting principles. Would it not be possible to describe as principles only the very bases of sound accounting? On these bases, or principles, we could build rules, to be observed by such methods as may be adapted and consistently followed. Two very basic principles are conservatism and consistency. I can think of no recognized accounting procedure or rule which is not based upon one or both of these principles.[24]

It is hard to overstate how differently the two sides saw things. Legislators and the Roosevelt administration wanted results; and they wanted to show the public that results were on their way, so they needed fixed standards. The accounting profession argued that revenue and profit did not emerge in a fixed instant in time; thus, there were many different ways that management teams could calculate such figures.[25] This same debate rages today, incidentally. Then as now, part of the accounting profession's dilemma was how far accountants should go to try to satisfy what all experience has taught them is unattainable.

May told anyone who would listen at the time that he understood that the great majority of people had a craving for certainty and for rules that they could follow and be safe. Still, his core beliefs and years of experience framing profits and losses in predetermined time periods would not allow him to simply cave in to an idea he thought was wrong. As he wrote to professor W. A. Paton in late 1934, "Financial accounting is a constant process of doing violence to fact by attributing profits to short periods which are, in fact, the results of operations extending over much longer periods of time."[26]

May felt that any gain for investors in terms of ease of comparison between companies would be outweighed by how misleading he felt uniform reporting would be. May felt, for example, that the painstakingly specific accounting standards on which the Interstate Commerce Commission insisted for railroads and utilities had led investors astray about the strength of these companies.[27]

Uniform reporting was about the only thing that wasn't required of companies under the Act, however. For the most part, industry felt that the amount of detail it had to provide about its business and securities was much too onerous. The FTC was also overwhelmed with its new duties under the Act. Late in 1933, people were already saying that the Act needed amending and that a new body overseeing securities regulation should be formed.

Despite the Act's provision giving them the sole right to audit public companies, accountants, too, began to criticize the legislation harshly, suggesting that the Act was highly punitive, that its provisions were harsh, and that it would have disastrous effects on business.[28] In addition, the legislation called for auditor's reports to verify the truth of the statements, despite Colonel Carter's testimony that it was not the job of the auditor to guarantee the truthfulness of a company's books.

If accountants were of two minds and somewhat disheartened at the passage of the Act, May and Carter, to their credit, at least recognized that the Act had been forged out of heinous abuses and betrayals of capitalism. The business community at large, however, was outraged and ready for armed battle. In the months immediately after the Act passed, major corporations and their attorneys kept a low profile, mulling over their options in private.

One option was to fight for an outright appeal, which most big law firms discouraged their clients from pushing for, as the public had clearly supported the legislation.[29] Instead, through these law firms, the country's major companies began a systematic campaign to undermine the essentials of the Act by saying that the Act's restrictions were halting capital investment. In a letter from Supreme Court Justice Felix Frankfurter to George Brownell on December 1, 1933, Frankfurter told Brownell:

> [T]hat charge against the Act is what we used to call, in our days at Harvard, "hogwash," and what Al Smith now is fond of calling "baloney." Not only is there a very active campaign of charging the Act with the continuance of the Depression, but there isn't a particle of doubt that lawyers of respon-

sibility and high standing infused clients with fears and worse than that—I know what I am talking about—actually discouraged clients, at times, from doing any financing for the present, so that the campaign against the Act, when Congress next meets, should show that the Act had prevented financing.[30]

The clamor led to the Securities Exchange Act of 1934, which established the Securities and Exchange Commission and gave the new body enormous influence over the markets, public companies, and accounting firms. The far-ranging power of the SEC is capsulated in Section 19(a), which gives the commission the power to make accounting rules and regulations, to mandate the form in which corporations must provide their accounting data, and to define the periods of time into which corporations must divide their earning periods.

Although the idea had been to strengthen the previous year's Act and to remove some of the gratuitous burdens on industry, the new legislation placed enormous new burdens on both industry and public accounting firms. The new bill, at one point, included the mistake that the NYSE had almost made two years earlier: requiring quarterly audits. When he appeared before the Senate in March 1934 to testify on the ramifications of the new legislation, May pointed out that even aside from the expense of companies hiring auditors to perform four audits every year, there was no way investors could possibly trust the constant churn of audited statements that would be rushed out every quarter:

> It follows from what I have said that there is room for error or difference of opinion in regard to the earnings of a business corporation for any period; and broadly speaking, the shorter the period, the greater the possible margin of error. The extent will vary with different businesses; it will be wide in any case in which inventories are large in proportion to profits, particularly if the inventory consists mainly of commodities which fluctuate in value. Thus monthly or quarterly statements of earnings of a packing house or a leather company are of

little value and probably as likely as not to be misleading unless accompanied by very full explanations.[31]

May successfully recommended the elimination of the quarterly audit, although quarterly statements of earnings eventually became standard. The Securities Exchange Act established a bipartisan Securities and Exchange Commission of five members, appointed by the president with Senate consent, to administer the Act and also to take over from the FTC administration of the Securities Act of 1933. The Act required the licensing of all stock exchanges and the registration of all listed securities with the new SEC. In addition, it was reaffirmed that corporations with registered securities were required to file periodic reports certified by independent public accountants. The Act of 1934 also carried several amendments that undid some of the highly criticized, onerous regulations that were in the Act of 1933, including the provision saying accountants had to vouch for the truthfulness of the financial statements.

Whatever the pros and cons for the accounting profession, the pair of Acts in 1933 and 1934 marked a huge victory for corporate disclosure. According to professor G. A. Swanson of Tennessee Tech, the securities laws cemented the idea of transparent corporate disclosure to shareholders. "What the Securities Act did was to create this new kind of information," Swanson said, "which was disclosure. It started out as adequate disclosure, and eventually the wording became full disclosure."

For hundreds of years, regulation—basically, looking over the shoulder of company management—was the accountant's purview. But now, the accountant's job was to facilitate the disclosure of information and to make sure that the information disclosed accurately reflected the situation of the company. This, incidentally, is where some of today's confusion about whether auditors should be fraud detectors is rooted. The Securities Acts essentially confirmed George May's premise that auditing was not about whether basic economic data was factual or fraudulent, but whether the principles used to arrive at the data were sound.

It quickly became apparent that Congress had done its job too well. Many believed there was too much disclosure mandated in the Acts of 1933 and 1934, in that mountains of information would soon be released to shareholders. For one thing, starting in fiscal year 1935, a company's prospectus had to include much more information than before. May, for one, believed that investment analyst lobbying in 1933 had unduly influenced the SEC.[32] John Landis, however, one of the principal authors of the 1933 Act and future head of the SEC, believed at the time that exhaustive information should be filed by companies.

Neither the 1933 Act nor the 1934 Act sets out exactly what the independent auditor was supposed to verify; the Acts just said that companies' financial statements must be certified by an independent auditor and that the SEC was to enforce this practice. What followed next was the very first volley in a long history of battles between the accounting profession and the SEC. The early rules coming out of the SEC revealed that certain of its members held the notion that the accountant's report should provide an opinion on the actual current values of all the assets, including fixed assets.[33]

May, of course, felt that the members of the SEC were trying to enforce by edict what the accountants had defeated in debate over the legislation. He wrote to one of the members of the SEC, Judge John Burns: "Personally, I believe that the regulations to be issued regarding the accounting reports should state that there are to be simply accounting reports, rendered in accordance with accepted accounting principles, and are understood not to represent current valuations or appraisals of the assets unless they specifically so indicate."[34]

Accountants also worried that the new SEC would try to remove professional judgment from accounting in the interest of trying to ensure that companies would not break accounting rules. In a letter to George Armistead on December 26, 1934, May wrote: "To my mind, two things are clear: first, that to be effective, principles which we seek to establish must have the concurrence of some independent body like the SEC, and, secondly, that it is not in the interests of the profession to encourage the belief that judgment can be eliminated from accounting and that it can be made a matter of rules and regulations enforced by unthinking subordinates in a bureaucracy. 'What is income?' is not an easy question; and 'When is income?' is a much harder one."[35]

Simply put, the Acts created a paradoxical situation, from the point of view of accounting firms. On the one hand, through the independent audit mandate, the Acts guaranteed that accounting firms would have plenty of growth over the foreseeable future. On the other hand, they created an oversight body that was already trying to establish standard accounting procedures and to force auditors to say whether financial statements were correct or not.[36] To establishment accountants like May, the Acts seemed to call for a rigorous reexamination of the fundamental tenets of the profession. Generally accepted principles had grown out of precedent and experience, and the profession now feared the new SEC would hand them down by bureaucratic edict.

JOSEPH P. KENNEDY'S SEC

Oddly enough, it was one of the premier rapscallions of U.S. business who insisted on getting even tougher on accountants in 1934. The first chairman of the SEC was Joseph P. Kennedy, a safe choice for business because he was viewed as "one of the club," but a controversial choice for the rest of the United States for just that reason. Kennedy, in his 18 months as head of the SEC, insisted that accountants live up to Colonel Carter's vision of the profession being the conscience of U.S. industry. Kennedy repeatedly called on accountants to get tougher with their clients.

Kennedy was such a polarizing choice to lead the SEC that Ferdinand Pecora, the Senate counsel who had grilled bank executives in February 1933, initially refused to take his seat as one of the five commissioners. Pecora was sure he was going to get the SEC commissioner post and eventually accepted his seat only because the leadership position of the SEC was supposed to rotate annually among the five commissioners. It never worked out that way, and Kennedy was eventually reappointed the following year.

In the nascent days of the SEC, Kennedy wanted to take the pulse of the accounting establishment and their leaders. On the morning of July 18, 1934, Kennedy met with May and other representatives of the accounting profession. With May were some of his allies from various professional organizations, including Paul Grady, Louis Reen of the New York State Society of CPA, and John Carey from the AIA. At the meeting with Kennedy were his four commissioners, including Landis and Pecora.[37]

From the official minutes of the meeting, one can presume that Kennedy left the gathering believing (correctly) that this group of crack accountants would not be easy to work with. Kennedy started the meeting by saying he wanted to form a permanent committee of accountants that would guide the SEC. So far, so good. Kennedy then asked for the accounting group's opinion as to the possibility of standardizing accounting methods for purposes of registering statements required under the Securities Exchange Act—one of May's pet peeves, of course. May told Kennedy that his special committee from the AIA had already dealt with this issue years before when it worked with the NYSE and had come to the conclusion that standardizing accounting methods across industries was ineffective. Pecora then pressed the issue, asking May if it would be feasible to achieve general uniformity of accounting principles and methods *within* particular industries. May ducked the issue, basically saying, "Eventually."

Landis then asked whether the SEC should prepare different forms of accounting statements for listing and registration purposes applicable to particular industries. The accountants stuck to their guns, saying it would be better not to mandate exactly the form in which the information should be submitted. Kennedy then brought up the desirability of requiring quarterly statements of companies registered with the SEC, which the accountants said was not feasible.[38]

Needless to say, Kennedy could not have left the get-to-know-you meeting in a positive frame of mind. It would not be long before he took the initiative in challenging the leaders of the profession. For one thing, there was tremendous pressure on everybody: the new SEC staff; the accountants, who had hundreds of new companies to audit; and the companies themselves, which in early 1935 were having so many problems complying with the provisions of the law that many of the reports due to the SEC were delayed in getting ready for the auditors.[39]

Emboldened by its hard line in the meeting with Kennedy, the accounting profession attempted to add further caveats to the recommended style of auditor certificates. One form that started circulating among the accounting firms contained the usual boilerplate about the company's financial statement adhering to GAAP and then included this sentence: "But we did not make a detailed account of the transactions." The decidedly negative statement not only smacked of dodging responsibility, but also gave the impression that critical audit steps had been omitted.

Kennedy saw these problems with the accountants' certificates right away. He raised the issue of deficient accountants' certificates with all the big firms, including Price Waterhouse, in a June 28, 1935, letter. Kennedy said that he was dissatisfied with many of the certificates that had been received because they were too full of "hedge clauses" and threatened punishing regulation from the SEC that would demand auditors take a stand on their clients' books. For example, he said that the SEC frequently received certificates that, after a long explanation of audit scope, stated the audit opinion was "subject to the notes on this page, the statement set forth on that page, etc., etc."[40] Kennedy said that, if necessary, the SEC would use any means it could to force the accountants to express clearly their opinions. He pointed out that such a step, in reality, would be a help to the accountants, as it would give them a good reason to settle any disputed points with his client.

The AIA wrote back to Kennedy that over the past several months the institute had already taken steps to deal with the problem, as representatives of all the large accounting firms had been studying all the forms of auditor certificates in order to make improvements. Also, Kennedy was told, the AIA had already put out one memo to its members on the subject of too-mushy auditor certificates.

The profession, of course, was the prime culprit in mushy auditor certificates. Kennedy might have been savvy enough to make millions in the market, land a top government job at the SEC, and later launch his son to the presidency and begin a political dynasty; but he was not clever enough to beat the accounting profession at its own game. By 1934, the profession's strategy of negotiating with regulators to retain self-governance was well developed, and one even feels a certain twinge of pity for Kennedy as he attempted to rein in the accountants and treat them like any other constituency.

In mid-1936, Kennedy left the SEC and sailed for England as U.S. ambassador, taking his son and future president, John F. Kennedy, with him to attend the London School of Economics. His successor, James Landis, continued to follow the precedent set by Kennedy to be somewhat critical of the profession in public but cordial and generous to accounting leaders like May and Arthur Andersen.

In May 1936, Landis had to fend off the first veiled threat of the SEC's extinction, and it came from a fellow government official. The Business Advisory Council, an arm of the Commerce Department, proposed that a Commerce Department commission be appointed to study the Acts, with the goal being their amending, consolidation, and simplification.[41] When Hamilton Katz of the SEC received word of the plan, he told the Business Advisory Council that Chairman Landis would never support a challenge of the law that created the SEC in the first place. It would not be the first time that the SEC's existence would be threatened, though this was a unique salvo because it actually came from the federal government.

May had a cordial relationship with Landis but was disturbed by the chairman's December 4, 1936, speech decrying the dual loyalties of auditors to company management first and the public second. Just three days after the speech, May sent off a letter to Landis: "No one feeling any sense of responsibility in the accounting profession could fail to take serious note of the comment contained in your address. . . . [Y]our comments on conflicting loyalties surprise me because in my own firm's experience up to now we have very little occasion for any such conflict."[42]

When Landis continued to make statements denigrating the accounting profession, May became one of the most severe critics of the SEC. In an April 20, 1936, letter to a former Price Waterhouse partner whose new firm was being investigated by the SEC, May wrote:

"I am in receipt of your letter of April 20, which certainly puts a materially different complexion on the case from that which would be gathered from a mere reading of the security commission release. It is a great pity that such bodies are so little concerned with fairness to the individual, and so much concerned with magnifying their own accomplishments."[43]

May's antipathy toward the SEC spilled over into his feelings about other policies put forward by President Franklin Roosevelt, whom May never met. When Roosevelt tried to push through the Undistributed Profits Tax Bill of 1936, Roosevelt and Treasury Secretary Morganthau turned to various eminent accountants to support the legislation, including Arthur Andersen, who assigned his best tax partner to discredit May's outspoken criticism of the tax legislation. A few years later, Senator Daniel Hastings of Delaware saw May at a party and told him, "You are about the only man I can remember who ever changed the Senate vote on a bill."[44]

THE SEC AND THE ACCOUNTING PROFESSION

The accounting establishment, from the get-go, took every chance it could to criticize the Acts. From complaining that the information required by the SEC in registration statements and annual reports would give false security to individual investors, to advancing the notion that companies were required to give away information competitors could use, it was clear the profession bristled under the authority given to the SEC.

Part of this resentment was rooted in the fact that prior to the Acts, accountants and auditors had recognized their public watchdog role—in fact, had forged the role themselves—and handed down this special responsibility to succeeding generations of auditors. After the Acts, the auditor had suddenly become part of the mechanism of government bureaucracy, doing the bidding for an aloof government agency in Washington, D.C. Even more galling was that the accounting profession's role in forging its own niche as independent auditors in the years prior to passage of the Securities Acts was scarcely recognized by Congress.[45]

It is not surprising, then, that well-known thinkers in the late 1930s considered SEC authority over the accounting industry an ill-advised measure. According to A. A. Berle, a respected professor at Columbia Law School, the SEC was an alien, administrative body that shared none of the accounting profession's interest in the development of healthy accounting rules but simply had an agenda that it needed to achieve. In a New Jersey speech to the accounting profession, Berle said: "Every administrative body has a specific job to do and serves a special interest. Its views on accounting, accordingly, are conditioned by its desire to reach that result, rather than by an interest in the healthy growth of accounting as a whole. . . . There is always danger, where accounting rules are made by specialized administrative tribunals, that the resulting body of doctrine may be lopsided, if not positively dangerous, however conscientiously the rulings have been made from the point of view of the administrators making them."[46]

The new agency, in practice, started to give its critics like Berle more ammunition. Its accounting weapon of choice was the deficiency letter, sent to companies whose application to register securities for sale contained problems or ambiguities. The registrant could comply with the suggestions—such compliance being often expensive and time-consuming—or could go to Washington to appeal the matter with SEC examiners. If agreement on what needed to be done to fix the application still was not reached, the company could either comply, withdraw the registration application and forget the idea of going public, or stand its ground and request an SEC hearing. But there was the rub. If the company lost the hearing, a stop-order would be issued on the securities, meaning that the company would stand accused of selling securities under a fraudulent set of representations. As Berle said in his speech: "Only if he is a merely irresponsible swindler will he, or can he afford to, try out an issue of accounting in the form of a hearing to determine whether or not he is about to commit a fraud. Businessmen who have any reputation do not put themselves in the position of putative swindler merely to determine matters of accounting. Now this, it is submitted, is not a satisfactory state of affairs."

In 1936, there were still several dozen administrative agencies that passed rules and regulations on accounting matters. Besides the SEC, there was the NYSE, which used its powers to list and delist to effect change; the Interstate Commerce Commission (ICC), with jurisdiction over railway accounting; the Federal Communication Commission (FCC), which held sway over telegraph and telephone regulation; the Federal Power Commission, which weighed in on matters concerning the utilities; and the Federal Reserve Board, which exercised power in relation to the banking industry. And then there was state regulation, such as the blue-sky laws, thrown into the mix.

But it was the SEC with which accountants had their real problem. During World War II, with the United States concerned with other matters, the accounting profession accused the SEC of extending its authority far beyond the limits contemplated in the law.[47]

The profession also believed that the rules set down by the SEC resulted in the early beginnings of litigation against accountants. The authority given to the SEC was perceived as resulting in many claims against accountants, though these tended to be made not directly under provisions of the Act but usually on more general law, with reliance on SEC rules or opinions as evidence of negligence. SEC rules, accountants said, also resulted in enormous and unnecessary extension of the amount of work done by auditors and, consequently, in the cost of audits, wasting millions of dollars on corporate audits.

Indeed, before the Securities Acts passed, a claim against an accountant would often hinge on the testimony of other accountants. After the SEC came into existence, that body became the primary issuer of accounting rules and regulations. As May wrote in a 1944 letter to Arthur Goodhar, "[T]he standard of adequacy is set by the SEC, and the employees who have charge of this work are theorists with no practical experience. The freedom with which charges of negligence are lodged makes partnership in an accounting firm definitely less attractive."[48] The profession also belatedly blamed the Securities Acts for losing prospective employees to law firms. Following the passage of the Acts, the profession was much more likely to lose talented employees to executive positions with corporations, to which no personal liability attaches.

THE McKESSON-ROBBINS CASE CHANGES PRICE WATERHOUSE AND AUDITING

On February 3, 1939, a sheepish and humiliated George May wrote to his old friend from the NYSE, J. M. B. Hoxsey. It was the first time he had been able to write Hoxsey in months, as he had been embroiled in an accounting scandal that threatened Price Waterhouse's existence. Earlier that day, the final Price Waterhouse witness had testified before Congress about the firm's role in the McKesson-Robbins affair.[49] The case would become the first real test of the public trust placed in accounting firms because it involved the firm the public trusted the most.

McKesson-Robbins was a drug company with, supposedly, both U.S. and Canadian operations. It came out in 1938, however, that company president Philip Coster was an ex-convict who had fabricated the entire international operation of McKesson-Robbins. The scheme went on for over 10 years and was built on a house of forged invoices, purchase orders, shipping notices, debit and credit memos, and forged contracts.[50] It was clear, though not quite to May, that accounting had swung too far toward the British methods of auditing accounts instead of auditing actual business transactions. Hoxsey took the case much harder than May and partly blamed himself for not insisting that auditor's certificates state whether inventories and receivables had been checked.[51] May, however, wrote to Hoxsey defending his Price Waterhouse auditors: "When I first looked at these figures I felt that they would have raised a question in my own mind, but when I went further into the matter I found that the figures stood out prominently in a three-year report which was sent to directors, banks, etc., in 1930 and elicited no questions or criticisms."[52]

In January 1939, the American Institute of Accountants recommended that auditors randomly test inventories and accounts receivable; if they cannot, they should explain why in the auditor's certificate.[53] Ultimately, the McKesson-Robbins case may have been the best thing that ever happened to Price Waterhouse. The firm, with the best clients and its preeminent senior partner in May, was satisfied with itself at that point, and the case made the firm pay very close attention to the auditing for a number of years after. The case also triggered the reform requiring confirmation of receivables and inspections of inventories. The rules were adopted by the institute and became mandatory for all the firms. This extension of auditing procedures was a small crack in the profession's avowed "no fraud" job description because physically checking inventories was, in a way, ferreting out fraud.

When World War II started, the accounting firms again did their best for the public good. For example, the English firm Coopers Brothers volunteered to run the financial affairs of the whole of the Belgian shipping fleet that had been commandeered by the Belgian government in exile. Generally, the firms played a major role in the wartime controls that were necessary to increasing industrial production for the wartime fighting effort. The profession was adrift, however. The McKesson-Robbins case had given investors reason to question what exactly a clean audit opinion was worth. Many accountants felt that they had lost professional ground because of the Acts, that they had become coopted by the SEC as government auditors, with little else to do besides whatever the SEC wanted them to do.

A crucial watershed for the profession had been reached. Even as the profession perceived that the SEC was trying to shrink its duties to what the commission deemed fit for it, other forces were demanding more from accountants. Certainly, more McKesson-Robbins cases had to be avoided. But there were also opportunities: the growing field of tax-minimization services and requests from companies for help in setting up accounting systems.

WOMEN ACCOUNTANTS DURING WORLD WAR II

There were forces acting on the profession other than the SEC, and the tantalizing possibility of a wealth of new services. With the shortage of trained accountants during World War II, it was obvious that a lot of work would have to be done by younger practitioners without a lot of experience. At the same time, the big firms realized they had been ignoring a ready-made reservoir of accounting talent: women.

In 1942 the first woman accountants came to the fore. At Lybrand, Ross Bros. & Montgomery (LRB&M), for example, they hired Dorothy Bertine, who in short order became the seventh woman CPA in Texas. The only woman in her accountancy class at Oklahoma State University, Bertine quickly became responsible for a number of accounts at LRB&M, as well as for filing tax-service bulletins.

During Bertine's time at LRB&M, the firm had a phrase: "doing things right the first time." Indeed, the firm, using as an example Robert Montgomery's uncompromising view of the auditor's right to challenge management, became known as the auditor's audit shop. The firm put a premium on preparation prior to going to the client, knowledge of the client, always establishing a way to prove your answers, knowledge of the law, proofreading, and reviewing for accuracy.

To Bertine and other auditors at LRB&M, production of an audit report could actually be "beautiful." As she told a Coopers & Lybrand interviewer years later for an internal oral history, "Good working papers was the firm's major innovation—a set anyone could read and use another year. . . . Even today, when I look at a financial report of a company, I turn to see who prepared it and usually know when I am looking at a Lybrand report, regardless of the name changes during the years. There is just a better presentation of the facts in a Lybrand report."[54]

In 1944 May wrote a spirited defense of accounting as a critical social pillar, *Accounting as a Social Force*. Reaction was swift and visceral among both friends and foes of May in the profession: They loved it. They loved that it gave the profession credit for reshaping U.S. business, and they loved it for saying that accounting could continue to thrive, despite regulatory straitjackets. Arthur Andersen, a frequent opponent of May through the years, dropped May a note saying that the book was "a most interesting summary with a great deal of sound philosophy."

This colorful note to May from former Price Waterhouse partner F. W. Thorton captured the general reaction to May's book and the regulatory bodies by which accountants felt threatened:

I thank you for *Accounting as a Social Force*. If accountants can do what you think they have an opportunity of doing, it would indeed be valuable work. The ICC, SEC, Supreme Court, and some other bodies need to either be rubbed out or manned with members who have both feet on the ground. . . . [A]t present they are manned largely by men who have four feet on the ground and have two long ears and a tail which covers the seat of their mentality.[55]

It is fitting that it was George May who gave the profession a much-needed shot in the arm just as he was about to leave the scene as a major player. His mantle would have to be picked up by someone; and to the consternation of May, the person who seemed most enthusiastic to represent the profession was Arthur Andersen's new leader, the bombastic and brilliant Leonard Spacek.

CHAPTER 4

THE QUEST FOR GROWTH

THE STORY OF THE 1950s AND 1960s FOR THE ACCOUNTING PRO-fession was one of transition. As the U.S. economy expanded and the country became the world's greatest industrial power, accounting firms evolved from relatively small, manageable partnerships to larger and more profitable businesses with an accompanying erosion of focus, social responsibility, camaraderie, and personality. If Price Waterhouse and its senior partner, George May, embodied the best of the accounting profession when it was struggling to establish itself in the 1920s, 1930s, and 1940s, it was Arthur Andersen and its chairman, Leonard Spacek, who defined the 1950s and 1960s, largely through the introduction of information systems consulting and a battle to supplement generally accepted accounting principles (GAAP) with strict accounting rules.

Until the end of World War II, accounting partners were generalists. There were no specialized tax, consulting, or auditing partners. Doing a little extra work with a company's taxes or payroll had always been the accountant's purview, so there was little call for specialization. Before the late 1940s, if a client had a particularly vexing tax problem, for example, the firm would just assign the matter to an audit partner who had done a lot of this type of work before for other clients. All the big firms, however, established tax and consulting practices after World War II, both to respond to clients' growing requests for various consulting projects and to strike back against the perceived SEC desire to limit the scope of the firm's work. At this point, most of the consultants were recruited from the ranks of auditors believed to possess the sales skills and business savvy to make the switch to consulting.

There were still huge unresolved issues in auditing itself, the growing severity of which was at least partly responsible for the big accounting firms' enthusiastic embrace of the no-strings-attached nature of consulting. Auditing under the aegis of the SEC was difficult enough, but the profession began to suffer fissures because of infighting over auditing standards. Those who were disciples of the George May school believed that uniform standards—for example, the idea that there should be only one way to measure the value of an aging piece of equipment—necessarily meant low standards. This group feared that uniform standards would replace independent judgment with bureaucratic rules.

An opposing faction of accountants, led by Andersen's Spacek, pushed for strict accounting rules. Spacek and other critics of GAAP, which gave a company and its outside auditor wide latitude in financial reporting, still clung to the notion that certain "absolutes" could yet save accounting.[1] Specifically, they wanted clear rules regarding annual income measurement, which by the late 1940s was firmly established as the most important statistic that financial reporting could produce. Both sides savaged the SEC because it was granted the power to prescribe accounting principles and methods but had, since its inception, been reluctant to insert itself into the murky waters of accounting rule making. In a way, Congress had granted the SEC too much power. In Britain, the English Companies Act dealt mostly with corporate disclosure, making it clear that British government bodies had no standing when it came to formulating accounting rules.

The upshot of all this was that corporate financial reporting in 1950 was weathering a barrage of criticism not seen since before passage of the Securities Acts. In 1950 a critic could have made the following general observations: Little or no progress had been made since the Securities Acts on broad authoritative accounting principles; infighting between the accounting experts over basic issues was on the upswing; a lexicon that the layperson had no chance of understanding was only getting more obtuse; there was still too much flexibility in the form and content of financial statements; there existed no minimum standards of disclosure in the financial statements. *Controller Magazine* said in 1948 that "it would not take much effort or ingenuity to present the essential features of a corporation's income statements in simple, understandable terms so that it would click with the man on the street."[2] To the public, it appeared as if the nation's controllers and public accountants did not care if financial reports were understandable. The truth was that the deep schism between those who wanted strict rules and those who wanted companies to retain the freedom to use their own judgment had paralyzed corporate finance.

The inability of the accounting profession to demand financial statements that were understandable and informative to the general public in the second half of the twentieth century has perhaps been its most significant failure. One of the root causes of this dereliction was the endless battle concerning principles-based accounting versus rules-based accounting. The debate still rages on today. In 2002, in the aftermath of two years of accounting failures, the Financial Accounting Standards Boards (FASB) announced that it would encourage a return to principles-based auditing. Unfortunately for the public accounting profession, its part in any new standard setting would be minimal. By then, a new Public Accountability Oversight Board had the power to set auditing guidelines.

The result of different standards in 1950 was a growing expectation gap between what auditors traditionally issued an opinion on and what some regulators, academics, and members of the public now believed their job to be. It was almost universally acknowledged in the United States in the 1950s, for example, that there had been a major shift on the part of Wall Street, banks, and individual investors about what defined a good company. The new emphasis was not on mere solvency but on income-earning potential. This evolution had begun in the mid-1920s, a natural result of businesses getting bigger and more complicated. An enterprise that was loaded down with debt but that had good potential for earnings growth had a future; the company with plenty of cash on hand but no plans for growth had little chance of attracting more capital and interest from investors. This line of thinking had a major impact on the auditing industry, as some believed that the profession's audit reports ought to emphasize earning capacity and not the rather dull matter of the previous year's balance sheet.[3] A similar gap still exists today. Many auditors and investors believe that the auditor must assist company management in providing financial information that is much more timely than quarterly or annual reports, lest the auditor become irrelevant. The audit scandals of 2001 and 2002, however, have led others to question auditors' basic accounting skills, to say nothing of their ability to provide quality real-time information. This school of thought maintains that auditors should forget about more timely financial reporting and just ensure that a company's books fairly represent its current financial condition.

THE DAWN OF CONSULTING

The prevailing attitude in the early 1950s was that there was no need for computers in the business world. Were it not for Arthur Andersen's pioneering role in the development of computers for business use, the age of the computer would have come later for many companies.

It is important to distinguish between systems consulting and other kinds of consulting, and it is hard to overstate the importance of their differences. The accountant was always a natural to do other kinds of consulting because he knew his client's internal controls, accounting methods, and tax philosophy. To Andersen senior partner Spacek, however, doing a client's personal taxes or telling a client how to reorganize inventory was the kind of consulting Andersen had been doing 30 years earlier. Spacek's idea was visionary: Leave the low-tech, low-growth consulting work behind, and use the computer as a revolutionary tool to solve the many nagging operational problems bedeviling Andersen's clients. Spacek found a perfect client when General Electric's Louisville, Kentucky, office wanted help redesigning its payroll system.

The payroll system was a hit, and Andersen was soon in demand to install systems at other clients. Andersen sold most of its systems consulting work, not surprisingly, to its audit clients. Typically, the audit partner controlled the engagement as lead partner, and the consulting partner would run a separate team for the systems project. In this way, the audit work itself was insulated from the consulting contract. This arrangement could occasionally lead to friction, though, as many consulting projects inevitably run into snafus and delays.

This sense of tension between information technology consulting and auditing would eventually have shattering implications for Andersen, cleaving the business into two parts in 1988 and creating the dysfunctional auditing/consulting relationship that doomed the firm in 2002.

Price Waterhouse soon followed Andersen in aggressively pursuing systems work. On February 28 and March 1, 1957, for example, Price Waterhouse held a national pep rally of sorts at the Downtown Athletic Club in New York City for its management advisory services (its name for "consulting") group. In his welcome talk, Price Waterhouse senior partner John Inglis addressed independence and ethics. He said the ethics of the profession should be strictly observed in all of the consulting work and stressed that the consultants should bend over backward to ensure that their work at audit clients did not in any way interfere with the audit work being done.[4] As early as 1957, then, Price Waterhouse executives understood the need to emphasize a clear demarcation between consultants and auditors. Not only would this avoid some of the turf problems Andersen was experiencing, but it would also take care of troublesome independence issues by ensuring that audits were properly insulated from consulting projects.

One of the very significant changes in accounting firms that facilitated the loss of the public trust was a shifting emphasis from raw numbers toward the marketing skills and "creativity" of consulting. For example, the 1957 Price Waterhouse pep rally was highlighted by a presentation on a radical new communications technique geared to help the firm's consultants come up with new, creative ideas to impress the client: brainstorming. One of the partners had studied the emerging research on this new way of generating ideas for a group and made a presentation to the other consultants. The partner said that brainstorming would help the firm's consulting teams come up with new ideas and would free them from the "tendency to substitute experience for creative thinking."

The partner said that brainstorming had three characteristics: (1) the free association of ideas; (2) an emphasis on quality rather than quantity; and (3) evaluation of the ideas at a later date so as not to inhibit creative thinking.[5] Brainstorming sessions, the partner said, should involve about 10 people, last an hour, and generate a minimum of 50 ideas. The partner ended his presentation with some sobering news, however. After trial tests with Price Waterhouse consultants in the field, there emerged several faults in the system. Brainstorming tended to generate superficial and stupid ideas (less than 10 percent of the ideas were helpful); the evaluation of the 50 or 75 ideas was tedious and time-consuming; and brainstorming tended to encourage lazy thinking and discourage individual thinking. Brainstorming, as it turned out, would not afflict the business world for another generation.

Systems implementation was next on the agenda at the Price Waterhouse consulting meeting. The session was meant simply to familiarize the partners with computers. Like many accountants who had for years viewed the computer as a scientific research tool and not a business tool, the Price Waterhouse consultants were not very sophisticated about computers. Up until 1957, in fact, Price Waterhouse classified different types of computers by their physical size: small, medium, and large. At this meeting, the firm's consultants were briefed on the development of two types of computers: those with "decentralized data processors," such as the Bizmac and the Elecam 125, which actually had separate pieces of equipment for merging and sorting data; and "centralized" computers, such as the UNIVAC, in which the tape units were connected to the mainframe. Another breakthrough was soon to be unveiled by IBM: a computer with "a printer capable of searching the tape to print selected items."[6] The partners also received updates on specific computers out in the business world—not specific *brands* of computers, but specific, custom-built machines. For example, they were told that the UNIVAC computer in use at Westinghouse Corporation in Pittsburgh actually appeared to be paying for itself. The point is that accounting firms did not come to dominate information technology consulting by divine right. They knew as little about computers in the mid-1950s as any other profession. Pushed by Spacek and Andersen, the other big firms realized that their knowledge of their audit clients gave them the inside track on installing new computer systems.

Each firm went at its own pace. However rudimentary were Price Waterhouse's ideas concerning systems implementation at this time, it at least had an organized approach to this kind of consulting. Other firms were not as quick as Arthur Andersen and Price Waterhouse to see the value in systems consulting.

FEAR AND LOATHING OF ANDERSEN

Throughout the 1950s and 1960s, the profession was obsessed with the innovative and aggressive Arthur Andersen. Besides being devoted to systems consulting, Andersen established a rigorous, comprehensive training program in Chicago, which every manager, regardless of where he or she was based, was required to attend. Conversely, the other big firms were essentially separate fiefdoms in each big city around the country that managed their own work, hired their own employees, paid for their own office space and supplies, and entertained their own clients.

Price Waterhouse, in particular, couldn't quite come to grips with

Andersen's philosophy, as the younger firm gobbled up markets and clients through aggressive marketing and salesmanship that tested the limits of what was allowed by the professional organizations. There was also a prevalent line of thinking at Price Waterhouse that the Andersen people, while great salespeople and technicians, did not have Price Waterhouse–level management skills and quality control throughout their organization.[7] Herman Bevis, Price Waterhouse's senior partner from 1961 to 1969, in an unpublished, internal Price Waterhouse oral history explained: "We considered ourselves the epitome of professionals, and the only promotion we would do would be through articles and speeches and good service, which would generate word-of-mouth promotion, whereas [Andersen was] openly soliciting in a way that we felt was not professional at all. As a matter of fact, they were headed by people who seemed to think that they were more businessmen than professional people."

It is telling that back in the mid-1960s, competitors were already characterizing Andersen, despite—or perhaps partly because of—its industry leadership, as a firm with lax management controls. Although envy of Andersen's consulting success can never be discounted as a reason for criticism of Andersen over the years, the facts do indicate that there was a flip side to the aggressively entrepreneurial nature of Andersen. For example, some of the roots of Andersen's problems at Enron and other companies between 2000 and 2002 might be traced to the 1960s. Andersen's tremendous growth during this period necessitated that the lead partner on a big audit client exercise enormous power. The partner had to sign off on new consulting contracts, make tough calls on clients' financial statements, and so on. At Andersen, this resulted in a lionization of the lead partner. By the time of Andersen's 2002 criminal trial, when it came out that Andersen's lead partner on the Enron account had not followed the advice of the firm's technical gurus, it was clear that this culture of the all-important lead partner had run amok.

Many businesspeople understood Andersen's full-throttle ambition in the 1960s a lot better than they did the competitive recalcitrance of the other firms.[8] Andersen was viewed, correctly, as a firm that unabashedly wanted to grow. The other firms, embodied in Price Waterhouse's half-hearted attempt at building its systems consulting group, confused clients with a clumsy combination of recalcitrance and ambition. They wanted to expand their scope of services, yet they did not want to promote these new services. They wanted growth, but they didn't want to grow *too* fast. What made Andersen so different was its ambition and personality. And Andersen's ambition and personality could not be separated from Leonard Spacek's ambition and personality.

Spacek took on the accounting establishment from the inside as no one ever had. According to Bevis, who was the Price Waterhouse senior partner at the time, Spacek started "giving speeches deriding . . . well, everybody. Their motives, their actions, the judgments."[9] While Spacek was a Cassandra in a sense, calling for changes in accounting principles lest the world end, he said many things the profession needed to hear. He criticized the SEC for allowing the proliferation of lax accounting standards; he criticized the other firms for not calling clients on dubious accounting methods. In a larger sense, it was a question of worldview. Spacek maintained an outlook that Herman Bevis likened to Gresham's Law, the maxim put forward by sixteenth-century businessman Sir Thomas Gresham stating that good money drives bad money out of circulation. Similarly, Spacek believed that the temptations for bad accounting within corporations drove out the incentives and rewards for good accounting. Certainly, one could characterize the excesses of the New Economy in the late 1990s as a time when bad accounting drove out good accounting. But it wasn't just the differences in opinion that forged a wedge between Spacek and the old accounting establishment. Spacek's abrasive style also angered the other firms, particularly the buttoned-down Price Waterhouse. "He was out shouting from the housetops, which Price Waterhouse considered very unprofessional," Bevis said. "Yes, he stirred up Price Waterhouse no end."[10]

Men like Price Waterhouse's Bevis and George May believed the opposite of what Spacek did. Their view was that business leaders had very real, fundamentally sound incentives to report fairly and accurately to their investors. May's belief in this concept was so thorough, in fact, that the McKesson-Robbins case, which happened under his watch, became in his mind nothing more than an aberration. To combat Spacek, Bevis busied himself writing and speaking before industry groups to push the Price Waterhouse approach of principles-based financial reporting.

The antirules contingent at Price Waterhouse and other firms was on the outside looking in. Spacek had successfully tapped into a vein of thinking (wishful thinking, George May would have called it) that wanted clear-cut accounting rules. Even May, though he had officially retired at this point, tried to take on Spacek when the former Price Waterhouse senior partner didn't think the leaders at his old firm were fighting the fight the right way. Spacek told May that accounting without hard-and-fast rules wasn't accounting at all, but was worthless.[11] "I do not want to see accounting principles laid down that are not binding on the accountant," Spacek wrote. "Without that, we do not have accounting principles . . . we do not even have accounting. We have a farce to which we try to give substance by making it mysterious and impossible for the public to understand." May, infuriated at the upstart's tone toward him, told his successor at Price Waterhouse, Jack Inglis, that he was thinking of writing an article about Spacek for the accounting academic journals that he would title, "The Problem and the Charlatan."[12]

May and Bevis also believed that Spacek was hurting the profession by drawing negative attention to accounting. Yet, Spacek's progressive attitude toward systems consulting, recruiting, and marketing undoubtedly moved Andersen ahead of the competition; and other firms took notice. According to Bevis, people would come to him time and time again with more news of what Spacek was doing or saying: "I would immediately say, 'Well, did you want Price Waterhouse to act like that?' They'd say, 'No.' And if Andersen was doing something really constructive, like improving their recruiting procedures so that they could get good people, I'd say, 'Well, why can't we go do that, too?' Let's learn from anybody. Don't be proud. If they've got a good idea, well, let's steal it."[13]

GOVERNMENT CONSULTING

From the debate over audit independence during the period from 2000 to 2002, one could get the idea that auditing inherently provides social benefits to society, whereas consulting, at best, provides a neutral effect on society. This is not the case. The history of consulting includes hundreds of examples of consulting projects performed by accounting firms (and all manner of consulting firms, for that matter) with tremendously positive effects on society. Andersen itself in the late 1990s was the primary consultant hired to investigate Swiss banks in possession of the assets of Holocaust victims.

Many of these public-minded consulting projects were performed for government agencies. Andersen started a large consulting practice serving government agencies out of its Washington, D.C., office in the 1960s, as did the other firms. But while Andersen landed the bulk of the information systems consulting contracts, the other firms competed better on the government consulting playing field. Price Waterhouse, for example, tended to land consulting projects related to high-profile, delicate political situations. According to Bevis's unpublished Price Waterhouse oral history, the firm got the job in the early 1960s when Congress wanted to hire an independent party to monitor Teamsters elections, mainly to ascertain whether Jimmy Hoffa was rigging the elections.[14]

Ted Herz, Price Waterhouse's top partner in Washington at the time, ran the Teamsters project. During the many conferences Herz had with Hoffa, the union leader said little more to Herz's questions than "Yeah" or "Naah." But one day, a number of different vendors in the business of designing and building voting machines came in to make their presentations to Price Waterhouse, which was monitoring the process for the next election. According to Herz, Hoffa's interest was piqued for the first time in months; and he spent the entire time inside the booths, looking at their design, learning all about them. The mechanics of vote getting were obviously important to Hoffa.

Price Waterhouse was so straitlaced that it even had the unique talent of being in the right even when it clearly violated professional ethics. The firm was retained to audit an international organization in Washington, D.C., in the early 1960s. Price Waterhouse's team found certain evidence that made it pretty clear that the vice chairman of the organization (who was appointed by a foreign government; the chairman was appointed by the U.S. government) was embezzling funds. As Bevis put it in the Price Waterhouse oral history: "This was very strong circumstantial evidence. But had we taken it to the board and laid the accusation out, they would have said, 'Where's the proof?' and we didn't have legal proof. And we didn't want to incur a lawsuit for libel or slander. So Ted called me and said, 'I don't know what to do with this thing.'"[15]

Herz and Bevis decided to take the issue to Senator William Fulbright, who had worked with Price Waterhouse on a different case a few years earlier. International affairs was Fulbright's area of expertise. Herz visited the senator and told him about the case, adding that he was now violating professional ethics by speaking about a Price Waterhouse client to a third party without the client's knowledge. Fulbright told Herz, "Just leave it to me. I'm not going to tell you what I'm going to do, or anybody else, or why I'm doing it." According to Bevis, the next thing he knew, the vice chairman in question had resigned and gone back to his home country. Neither Bevis nor Herz ever did find out what Fulbright said or did to make his point. Said Bevis, "And we didn't want to know."[16]

Some of these government consulting projects were not for the U.S. government but for foreign governments. In 1957, for example, Lybrand and its English representatives, Coopers Brothers, were hired by the Iranian government to audit a consortium of oil companies doing business with Iran to ensure that Iran was receiving the oil revenues to which it was entitled.

GROWTH AND EXPANSION

As the accounting firms tried to expand their services in the 1950s and 1960s, they also broadened their geographic coverage to adequately serve the growing number of multistate and multinational companies. There were several ways to do this: purchase an existing firm, build your own practice in a new city by transferring accomplished partners, or serve clients out of hub cities. Different firms were known for different practices. Peat, Marwick & Mitchell acquired so many firms and took in so many people so fast that some of the competition accused them of franchising the firm's name. Peat, Marwick & Mitchell had been furiously merging with and buying up smaller firms in markets where Peat had no presence. Often, the only way for Peat to convince a smaller firm that it wouldn't be lost in the bigger organization was to offer immediate partnership to the smaller firm's more experienced accountants.[17] This led to the impression that the quality of Peat's partner base was declining.

Price Waterhouse, the biggest and most prestigious firm throughout the 1950s, for the most part believed not in growth through merger, but rather in sending trusted partners into an area where the firm had no presence, meeting the local civic leaders, finding some clients, and then perhaps in a few years opening an office. So it tended to become known in the community even before building a major office presence. If the firm did decide to purchase another firm, the target was usually a smallish, high-quality shop with an outstanding reputation. For example, in 1957, Price Waterhouse acquired a small firm by the name of Rankin. The firm had little infrastructure and was easily assimilated, which was the only kind of merger Price Waterhouse liked. Even better, Rankin brought a blue-chip client list to Price Waterhouse that included IBM, Bristol Meyers, and Bankers Trust, star-quality clients virtually unheard of at a small firm.

Despite this Price Waterhouse push for growth in the late 1950s, an article in the July 1959 issue of *Fortune* magazine rocked the firm when it announced that Price Waterhouse had been supplanted by Peat, Marwick & Mitchell as the biggest accounting firm in the United States. It was one thing for Price Waterhouse to pretend not to notice the competition, but quite another to see an article published saying that the white-shoe firm did nothing to stop another firm from knocking it off the top spot. Price Waterhouse vowed to redouble its efforts to compete. To serve more clients, however, Price Waterhouse had to expand faster. So while senior partner Bevis never saw himself as a "growth-at-any-cost" acolyte, he and his firm soon became the key players in the battle for firms to practice anywhere they chose to.

The battleground was Florida, which, along with several other states, had passed laws designed to keep out the national firms and to protect local practitioners. To serve clients in Florida, the national firms would have to operate from a nearby state—for example, Price Waterhouse served clients out of its Atlanta, Georgia, office[18]—and apply for a permit for each engagement.

"Our practice expanded to the point where we had maybe half a dozen Atlanta staff members living out of suitcases 75 to 85 percent of the time," said Bevis in an oral history. "And that's not a good life, so we had difficulty getting staff who would agree to that kind of travel." Price Waterhouse applied to establish an office in Florida and was denied. So Bevis did the next best thing. Price Waterhouse simply installed a partner and his secretary in an office. The Florida Society of CPAs sued Price Waterhouse, and, following a decade of court losses and lobbying, Price Waterhouse finally prevailed when it trotted out some of its big Florida clients, including Walt Disney. "It came to the point where legislators told the Florida CPAs they had to make some kind of a deal with the national firms because pressure was getting too great," Bevis said. "It would be things like our threatening to have our client, Walt Disney, scrap his plans for a Disney World because his auditors couldn't come in . . . that kind of thing." Two future trends that would backfire on the firms in 2001 and 2002 were established through incidents like this Disney episode: (1) strong-armed legislative lobbying and (2) the growth-at-any-cost culture.

International expansion also became critical in the late 1950s and the 1960s. In 1955, for example, London-based Coopers Brothers still had only a few overseas offices when Coopers's New York office set up an affiliation with Lybrand, Ross Bros. & Montgomery. That venture laid the groundwork for when the firms officially merged into Coopers & Lybrand in 1973.

SHOPPING FOR ACCOUNTING PRINCIPLES

One of the things that Leonard Spacek of Andersen got right in the late 1950s was decrying the increasing phenomenon of corporations shopping for an accounting firm that would give a green light to dubious corporate reporting practices. One prominent case in the media illustrated the unequal balance of power between corporate management and outside auditors. In 1958, a company called Alaska Juneau Gold Mining fired Arthur Andersen after Andersen included several qualifications in its audit report.[19] Alaska Juneau then hired Arthur Young, which also found several issues with the company's books. Lastly, Alaska Juneau fired Arthur Young and hired Haskins & Sells for fiscal year 1962, which gave Alaska Juneau a clean bill of health. Today, companies are required to immediately notify the SEC of an auditor change and to provide a detailed explanation, a rule that has thwarted instances of egregious auditor-hopping.

After such episodes as Alaska Juneau Gold Mining, the Accounting Procedures Committee of the American Institute of CPAs (AICPA) was shut down in 1959 in lieu of a new 18-person, part-time, unsalaried panel called the Accounting Principles Board (APB). It was hoped that the new board could sort out—or at least give accountants some guidance on—generally accepted accounting standards. At the time, there were just too many alternative standards.

The chasm only widened in the 1960s between those CPAs who, like Spacek, advocated specific rules-based standards and those who believed broad accounting principles allowed CPAs to best use their professional judgment in specific cases. The infighting spread to the APB, which did little to engender trust at the SEC. The APB was indulged by the SEC as sort of an ill-fated experiment of the profession, and a slightly condescending approach by the commission was the result. The SEC frequently overruled the new board in the early 1960s and did so even more as the APB failed to cut down on what was then a confusing array of accounting methods that companies could employ.

THE FIRMS

Meanwhile, the consolidation of the profession was rapidly occurring. An SEC survey compiled from 3,072 10-K filings for 1955 and 1956 found 558 different accounting firms signing off on financial statements of public companies. Of these, 384 certified to one statement, 77 firms certified to two, and 10 firms certified to more than 25. A similar survey of financial statements in 1946 had found 416 accounting firms represented, of which 279 certified to one statement, 58 certified to two statements, 6 firms each certified to 10 or more, and 4 other firms each certified to more than 25. This shift resulted in larger accounting firms tending to be outspoken about the SEC because there existed a general belief that only firms with many offices did any substantial business before the SEC.[20]

As the ranks of the big firms thinned out going into the 1960s, the firms known as the Big Eight came to dominate corporate audits more than ever. Although the term "Big Eight" had been coined in 1932 by *Fortune,* mergers and bankruptcies had always made the membership of the Big Eight a fluid one. In the mid-1960s, though, eight firms emerged as the ones that would dominate the next 25 years: Arthur Andersen; Lybrand, Ross Bros. & Montgomery; Deloitte, Haskins & Sells; Ernst & Ernst; KMG Main Hurdman; Peat Marwick; Price Waterhouse; and Touche Ross. During this period, the firms carved out distinct identities, related to the kinds of clients they served. Peat Marwick, for example, audited many regulated financial services companies, such as savings and loans. Arthur Andersen audited many old industrials, redolent of their Chicago roots. Price Waterhouse did a lot of work for blue-chip U.S. brands, like auditing the Academy Awards.

Smaller firms still had to be careful in their dealings with the SEC over accounting principles, because practicing public accountants could become subject to SEC rules overnight. For example, a privately held client could decide to go public, thus becoming subject to SEC registration requirements; a company whose securities had been traded in the over-the-counter market might decide to list on the New York Stock Exchange (NYSE) or one of the other exchanges.

In a 1955 speech before a group of practicing public accountants, chief SEC accountant Andy Barr laid down the independence gauntlet. He reiterated that as far as the SEC was concerned, accountants were prohibited from having any financial interest in the registrant or its affiliates. Barr pointed out that the profession's main industry association was dead wrong in requiring only *disclosure* of such an interest. Barr said that the two conflicting independence standards had to come to a head. It was just a matter of time. He continued:

> Some accountants have urged that independence is a state of mind—the accountant's conscience—and that standards of professional work should not be affected by his financial interest in the registrant. However, . . . serious personal embarrassment to the accountant and added expense for the client can be avoided if the accountant is sufficiently foresighted to disengage himself from any entangling relationships with his clients.[21]

Still, the SEC's view of the situation was that accountants were its allies in a pitched battle against corporate managements that did not acknowledge the right of the accounting profession to dictate principles or presentations in financial statements. There were still companies that did not recognize the right of the independent accounting profession—much less the SEC—as legitimate. As much criticism as the SEC took from industry and the accounting profession, it was undeniable that only the enforcement powers of the SEC and the delisting power of exchanges like the NYSE produced the compliance that did exist.[22]

Even though the firms were moving toward the faster, more aggressive world of consulting, the partnership was still an inviolable social institution during the 1950s and early 1960s. Once someone became a partner, he or she was protected as a member of the family and guaranteed a lucrative career until the retirement age of 60 or 62, depending on the firm. There were basically just two reasons a partner would be asked to resign (being fired was unheard of): (1) committing a crime or (2) drinking so much that it affected the work.[23] Most of these professionals realized they were lucky to have such a secure, relatively high-profile, and well-paying job.

But these extended families were growing rapidly. The firms kept opening more domestic offices as their clients expanded their operations. The number of first-year auditors at the firms grew larger and larger, and—with the exception of Price Waterhouse, which insisted its partners be at least 36 or 37 years old—partners were promoted faster. Another reason for the incredible growth of the accounting profession was that the 1964 federal laws expanded the definition of a "publicly traded company." The new laws included companies whose stock traded in over-the-counter markets, in addition to the previously included category of companies trading on a major exchange.

Compared with brokerages or investment banks, accounting firms during the 1950s and 1960s were bastions of stability and consistency—and, for the most part, quality. Soon, though, the auditing profession's technical prowess and commitment to quality—never questioned by Corporate America to this point—was about to come under fire.

A NEW TWIST: BUSINESS FAILURE

The only flaw in Leonard Spacek's—and soon, the rest of the profession's—push for consulting was inattention to auditing, both in practice and appearance. In October 1966, Harold Roth, former president of Continental Vending Machines, a New York City–based maker of vending equipment, was indicted along with three Lybrand, Ross Bros. & Montgomery auditors: two partners and a senior manager. They were indicted on federal charges of mail fraud and conspiring to file false financial statements with the SEC in the Continental Vending 1962 annual report.[24]

From the initial indictment through the unprecedented conviction, the Continental Vending case was a shock to Lybrand, and to the rest of the profession, for that matter. This was the first major case in which criminal charges were brought against auditors for alleged failure to disclose facts they uncovered during the audit of a company. The Continental Vending case—like Enron more than 30 years later—would end up shaking the profession to its core. Also like Enron, the Continental Vending case centered on related-party transactions of the Enron variety.[25]

The government's case against the three auditors centered on the footnote of Continental Vending's 1962 balance sheet, which, according to the indictment, "indicated that an asset item of $3.5 million in the form of receivables due from Valley Commercial Corp., an affiliated company controlled by Mr. Roth, was more than adequately secured. The government contends it wasn't."

In plain English, it sounds worse. For years, Roth had been diverting profits from Continental Vending to himself through Valley Commercial, which turned out to be a shell company. The prosecution's case against the auditors rested on witnesses who said that two of the accountants knew that Roth was siphoning corporate funds for his own use. According to the testimony, two of the auditors knew that the $3.5 million listed as "accounts receivable" in the 1962 balance sheet had actually been transferred to Roth for his personal use.[26] Felix A. Regnie, an accountant at Continental, said that he told one of the auditors each year for several years in a row that he had heard that Roth was transferring money to himself through Valley Commercial. The partner in charge testified that he thought that the 1962 annual report fairly represented the company's position.

Princeton graduate Walter R. Staub had succeeded Alvin Jennings in 1962 as a managing partner at Lybrand, Ross Bros. & Montgomery, and he aggressively exhorted all Lybrand partners and staff to stay close to their clients. Clients had to be reassured directly by the lead partner on their account, and the firms' overall reputation had to be shored up as well. The Lybrand firm stood firmly behind its Continental Vending engagement team. Not only did Lybrand completely support the three auditors, but the entire profession rallied to their defense; and partners from the other Big Eight firms testified for them. After the first trial ended in a hung jury, Staub said, "The great preponderance of testimony from accounting experts was that the audit and auditor's opinion here were in conformity with generally accepted auditing standards and accounting principles. . . . We will do everything we can to support [the partners] in whatever course the litigation takes."[27]

The profession was also in an uproar because the admitted chief architect of the scheme (Roth himself) pleaded guilty to one conspiracy count the day before the trial started and then became the prosecutor's lead witness against the accountants. As David W. Peck, the defense lawyer for the three auditors, put it, "So far as I know, this is the first time an arrangement has been made to treat very kindly the real culprit to go after somebody else."[28]

An interesting aspect of the case with ramifications today was whether the Lybrand auditors had in fact known for years that Roth was siphoning money from the company but didn't report it because they were afraid that their initial inaction would lead to litigation against the firm. Professor Douglas Carmichael of Baruch College in New York City believes that Continental Vending was a landmark case because it convinced auditors that even if they discover fraud, they might get blamed for not finding it even earlier. "That's the thing," said Carmichael. "Even if the firms know something, they are afraid to do anything about it, because the public will say, 'Well, why didn't you do anything about it before?'"

The first trial resulted in a hung jury, and the second resulted in the three Lybrand auditors being convicted, fined, and paroled with no jail time served. Roth was convicted and sentenced to a short jail stay. It was a huge blow for the three men, whose accounting careers ended. Fellow Lybrand partner Bill Campbell said in an unpublished Lybrand oral history, "It was terrible that those three got convicted."

After the verdict, Lybrand issued a statement saying, "If this decision were to stand, the risks assumed by professional auditors would become virtually intolerable. This would necessitate a drastic revision in the auditor's role, which would have grave consequences for the interests of the business community and investors."[29]

It was clear that times had changed. No longer could auditors expect to avoid litigation just by saying that a client's financial reporting adhered to generally accepted accounting principles. The 30-year period since the passage of the Securities laws, in which the big accounting firms denied that auditing had anything to do with fraud detection, had come to an end. Still, the accounting profession would continue to fight the growing sentiment to make it the auditor's responsibility to ferret out fraud in companies. In retrospect, however, the fraud-detection skills required in the Continental Vending case were rudimentary. If auditors were not responsible for ferreting out the manner of fraud perpetrated at Continental Vending (three witnesses testified under oath that they told the auditors that Roth was taking the money), then audited financial statements would lose much of their meaning. Much as Arthur Andersen's inability to ferret out the fraud at Enron made that company's financial statements worthless, so was Continental's financial report virtually devoid of truth.

After the conviction was upheld on appeal, auditors' responsibilities had officially changed. In its decision to uphold the convictions, the court said that once an accountant suspects fraud, he or she can't simply be guided by generally accepted standards, as one would in a normal audit. The auditor must investigate further and report any fraud that is found. The federal court decision pondered at one point "how accountants who were really seeking to tell the truth could have constructed a footnote so well designed to conceal the shocking facts."

Things got worse for Lybrand when, in the middle of the Continental Vending firestorm, another client, Mill Factors, a venerable Park Avenue finance concern, went bankrupt in the blink of an eye. Lybrand allegedly failed to adequately investigate collateral for loans made by Mill Factors. Philip Defliese succeeded Walter Staub as Lybrand's managing partner in 1968 and was given the task of restoring the firm's credibility. He also cleverly indicated his interest in being appointed chairman of the Accounting Principles Board. Although it might have appeared poor timing for such an assignment, it was the perfect move to deflect attention away from "Lybrand the law-breaking firm" to "Lybrand the firm fighting for better accounting principles." Defliese, much like Spacek, opposed the flexibility in accounting that allowed numerous alternatives in corporate financial reporting and used his APB platform to advance his agenda.

Defliese was frequently accused of rigidity by controllers and financial executive groups, but he stuck to his guns and no doubt helped to tighten financial reporting standards significantly, as well as to restore public confidence in the profession. By the end of 1971, stories on Defliese and the APB had completely displaced references to Continental Vending and Mill Factors in the financial pages.

Despite the smart public relations moves by Defliese and Lybrand, Walter Staub was right that no public relations effort could conceal the fact that the Continental Vending case had significantly increased both auditors' responsibilities and, thus, their legal exposure. Everything was about to change.

CHAPTER 5

CRACKS IN THE FACADE

MIKE COOK IS AN ANGRY MAN. HE'S ANGRY BECAUSE HE BELIEVES that the current generation of accountants has done great harm to the reputation of the profession. According to Cook, a longtime CEO of Deloitte & Touche who stepped down in 1999, the global firms in the past made sure that the "attest" function (the stilted term auditors tend to use for their craft, as they are "attesting" to the state of a client's financial statements) was paramount. No matter how much consulting work came in over the transom, the basic audit had to stand up so that the public knew that a financial statement signed by a partner at Deloitte & Touche or Price Waterhouse or Peat, Marwick & Mitchell meant something. And if the profession suffered a serious blow, such as criminal proceedings against an audit engagement team at one of the big firms, the problem would be fixed, both from a substantive point of view and from a public relations point of view—and fixed fast.

"When companies fail, people wonder whether the auditors were asleep at the switch or not," Cook said. "The profession has been through these cycles before. We would make improvements, make changes in the oversight system, and people always would give us good marks for being responsible. But now, the big firms have acted so self-serving that there is very little goodwill left. I'm distressed at the behavior of the profession. We have dropped a long way in public perception the way we have positioned ourselves in the last couple of years."

Cook, even after his 40 years in the business, remains somewhat of a paradox. Cook is one of the last great practitioner/regulators in the tradition of George May, Robert Montgomery, Arthur Andersen, and Leonard Spacek. Not only was he head of a global firm (really, two successive global firms, as he led Deloitte, Haskins & Sells and then, after the 1989 merger of his firm with Touche Ross, the newly formed Deloitte & Touche), but Cook also served as president of the American Institute of Certified Public Accountants (AICPA), chaired the World Congress of Accountants in 1992, served as president of the Financial Accounting Foundation (FAF), and served as the profession's point person on a variety of legislative priorities, including the all-important securities law reform in 1995. In 1999, he was elected into the "Accounting Hall of Fame." (Yes, there is an Accounting Hall of Fame.)

Yet, Cook disagrees with auditors as much as he agrees with them. Some of his stances even seem to contradict a lifetime of hard work building up Deloitte's business. For example, Cook mostly supported Arthur Levitt in 2000 in the SEC chairman's proposal to bar most consulting to audit clients. But it was Cook, as well as fellow global firm CEOs in the mid-1990s—men like Jon Madonna at KPMG and Phil Laskaway at Ernst & Young—who presided over the biggest boom in consulting the profession has ever seen. Cook, though, remembers a time in the accounting profession when such a duality was understood, even welcomed: Work like hell for your firm, but also contribute to the overall advancement of accounting by putting the regulator's hat on, stepping back, and taking a more sober look at the big picture.

Cook and many, but not all, of his contemporaries understood that contributing to public confidence in the quality of accounting standards and the integrity of auditors themselves was the key to becoming a respected professional. "Mike Cook was one of the last guys who came up as an auditor who contributed work in the profession, in terms of setting auditing standards," said Lynn Turner, former SEC chief accountant under Levitt. "Not that we always agreed with him, but he really had a public service mindset when he was leading his firm."

Cook, of course, did have his clashes with the SEC. In the creation of the Independence Standards Board in 1998, Cook had to air his differences with Levitt "because he had his concerns with accounting profession standard setting, and we had concerns with SEC standard setting," Cook said. "We met to try to draft some top-notch people to work on that board. I also worked closely with Arthur at the FAF, which oversees the FASB [Financial Accounting Standards Board]. We knocked heads and we got it done."

In his days at Deloitte & Touche, Cook also had his share of disagreements with the leaders of the other global firms. But again, for him, it was part of the game. "We didn't always agree, but at the end of the day, we worked on problems together," Cook said. "For example, Jon [Madonna] and I worked together on securities litigation reform in 1995. We always had the ability to come together on a common objective."

"Mike has the ability to put his mind to a problem facing the profession, take a stand, and solve the problem," KPMG's Madonna said. "There aren't a lot of people who can do that, in the public sector or the private sector."

There was also a time when the global firms were humble enough to take criticism, address it, and then move on. Today, Cook lamented, that's not the case. For example, until news broke in the summer of 2002 that WorldCom had overstated expenses by $4 billion over a six-quarter period, the profession fought every reform proposal introduced by Congress in the wake of the Enron collapse. As Cook said, "There was no sign that the accounting profession was going to step up and do what's right for the public. There were no reform proposals, while everyone in the profession understands that there are some very important issues."

For Cook, who led Deloitte & Touche for more than 10 years until Jim Copeland unseated him in a bloodless coup (Copeland was unseated in 2001 by Jim Schiro), the evidence points to two general problems. The first is auditor independence, highlighted by Andersen's multiple conflicts of interest that marked its service to

Enron and PricewaterhouseCoopers's 8,000 violations of the rule barring auditors from owning stock in their clients. Pricewater-houseCoopers eventually settled with the SEC, asking five partners to resign and overhauling its independence guidelines. "This was a very serious breakdown in a very respected firm that had always enjoyed a large amount of prestige," Cook said of PricewaterhouseCoopers.

The other problem was the profession's callous disregard for the rule that Cook's generation of old pros lived by: If the public thinks there is a problem, and the SEC thinks there is a problem, and Congress thinks there is a problem, and the media thinks there is a problem . . . well then, there's a problem. Cook saw a myriad of nonresponsive and combative behavior by the accounting profession over 2001 and 2002 that only damaged the profession, from the AICPA's stonewalling of an independent review of the big firms to the global firms' primal hostility toward Levitt's independence proposals. "KPMG, Deloitte, and Arthur Andersen said that commercial interests were more important than the SEC's desire to hold the profession accountable to the public," Cook said. "There's no doubt that even before Enron, Arthur Levitt had won that battle. He exposed those firms for what they were becoming."

OTHER STORMS WEATHERED

Cook is certainly correct that previous generations of auditors responded to their respective crises much more effectively than the current generation does. The savings and loan (S&L) crisis of the 1980s had the potential to be even more dangerous for accountants than the crises of current times. "When bad things happened in the past that tarred the reputation of the profession, such as the savings and loan scandal and its aftermath 10 to 15 years ago, we made constructive changes," Cook said.

The global firms up to their necks in the savings and loan scandal were successful in limiting the fallout so that it didn't impugn their bedrock professionalism. Those firms included KPMG and Cook's own firm of Deloitte & Touche. Cook himself was grilled by Michigan

Congressman John Dingell during Dingell's 1985 series of hearings concerning independent auditors.[1] "You heard the criticism in episodes like the S&L scandal, that as a profession, we were slow in looking at the depth of the problem; but people didn't say you were in cahoots with the client," Cook said. "Until this go-around, I don't think there was a public perception linking independence with audit failures. Now, the question of regaining trust is really different. I think the underlying message from the public today is that 'we don't think you audit very well and we don't think you are trustworthy.'"

Besides the S&L scandal, the 1980s were marked by notorious scandals like the ZZZZ Best case, in which the CEO and entrepreneurial whiz kid Barry Minkow essentially imagined an entire company, took Ernst & Whinney for a ride,[2] and spent more than seven years in prison. Cook said again that auditing got better for it. "Changes needed to be made then, and we made them. Each time, it was hard for many of us to see what the problems were, but we did what we needed to do."

According to Cook, many in the profession today do not possess a similar ability to look at themselves in the mirror: "Now, looking from some distance, it's clear that Andersen just didn't have the distance that is required to achieve objectivity with some of their clients. Yet, they blamed it on somebody else. They said, 'Standards stink,' 'The financial statements contain inappropriate information for investors,' 'The whole system is broken.' They should have just said, 'We did a lousy audit.'"

Cook believes the global firms and the profession in general are in much worse shape than people believe, which was one reason the global firms quixotically clung to the hope of providing consulting services to audit clients. "If you look at the partnership model, almost no organization in business operates like this anymore," Cook said. "Every single partner is financially at risk every day for the action of everyone. The idea that every executive at Merrill Lynch or Bear Stearns is responsible and liable for everyone else's action, you'd just never see that anymore."

Former KPMG corporate finance partner Steve Blum makes a similar point about a major flaw in the accounting firm partnership model. "The Securities laws in the early 1930s were wonderful for transparency of the capital markets," Blum said. "But we [CPAs] made a bad deal in a couple of ways, and the biggest one was that we allowed Congress to bar us from raising capital. That is a huge problem, and certainly one of the reasons all of the big firms have had to develop a number of consulting services. Fifty years ago, it might not have taken a lot of capital to be a big accounting firm. Now, with the technology investment, human resources investments, it takes a lot of capital; and the firms have no way to get it. They can't raise money."

Cook even believes that the limited liability partnership (LLP) status may not be valid. The LLP label became commonly affixed to the names of accounting partnerships in the mid-1990s. The designation was designed to prevent partners in Boston, for example, from being personally responsible for the misdeeds of partners in Boise, and vice versa. The LLP designation has not been tested in any case nearly as big as Enron, however. "We'll find out whether those partners have a meaningful defense," Cook said.

And as far as the future of the profession? "We've got to get our public confidence back to the point where we'll have credibility certifying financial statements. We also have to get this profession restructured," Cook said. "It's incredibly complex right now. You have state licensing boards, the SEC, the court system, the new board created by Congress. I think we need a national licensing system. The profession can't just say, 'What are we going to do the next time we screw up?' We need to do something to strengthen the profession, including the big firms."

A CHANGING PROFESSION

If Cook thinks that in his day the profession was quicker to recover from setbacks, it could be because it got a lot of practice. The late 1960s, a time of tumult in the United States in general, ushered in a period of great change in accounting. Up until the mid-1960s, the accountant had been as good a personification of U.S. diligence and fealty as any professional in United States. CPAs, while certainly not viewed as creative or exciting, were respected as sober and trustworthy.

Accountants, though, didn't have to work that hard to pull off the image. Until that point, third-party users of financial statements simply weren't considered that important. For one thing, there were only a few million U.S. investors in the stock market. And those shareholders were not very vocal. Certainly, CPAs had to be competent enough to do a reasonable check of the company's bookkeeping, but the pressure to certify numbers that would help a company's stock stay afloat was not there.

Since the end of World War II, the country had basically enjoyed unchecked growth, and the profession had enjoyed growth along with it. The 1960s were very good to the accounting industry, in that new publicly held corporations were being formed faster than the profession could certify their securities and approve their books. There was plenty of work for all of the big and midsized firms. But as the 1960s drew to a close, inflation and stagflation meant that Corporate America, accustomed to a thriving economy, had to adjust gears. The market slump that hit Wall Street in 1970 meant that more businesses were failing, and accounting firms—and their hefty insurance coverage—increasingly became targets for lawsuits.

Accountants did not understand how much things had changed until this avalanche of litigation. The late 1960s marked the start of the period when the CPA was threatened by all manner of third parties—litigation by regulators, investors, and creditors. The Continental Vending case, for instance, was having a much greater impact than expected. Lybrand was in real trouble, especially after Mill Factors, a large financial services conglomerate and Lybrand client, went bust right in the middle of the Continental fiasco.[3] Although the profession had rallied around Lybrand, once the firm lost in appeals the united front of the profession broke down, and Lybrand's competitors eagerly scooped up the firm's defecting clients.[4]

There were also serious questions as to how complicit the accounting industry had been in the catastrophic implosion of brokerage firms in the late 1960s. Even today, the role of auditors in the demise of over 200 brokerage firms from 1969 to 1971 has never been thoroughly examined. One infamous collapse was that of McDonnell & Company, which boasted $33 million in revenues in 1968, just two years before its 1970 collapse.[5] At the time, some people questioned the pooling accounting methods that many of the brokerage firms had been using. As Henry Gunders, a Price Waterhouse consulting partner, said in a 1987 unpublished, internal Price Waterhouse oral history:

> In 1967, 1968, and 1969, there were tons of little, unknown companies that would have better remained unknown that went out and sold stock to the public. That, of course, gave the accounting profession a shot in the arm, and it brought with it a lot of unscrupulous practices. The practices skirted at the very outside edge of what might have been acceptable accounting principles. You really started to see these practices during the second half of the 1960s that were in some considerable measure blamed for the crashes of 1970 and 1971.[6]

Both the competence and integrity of the independent accountant were being called into question in the late 1960s and 1970s, really for the first time ever. Lawsuits were just one front on which the accounting profession had to fight; a second front opened with regulators. The SEC in the late 1960s, led by chairman Manny Cohen and chief accountant Andy Barr, took intermittent tough stances on the profession. As early as 1966, Cohen warned the firms to rethink the growing emphasis on consulting, lest the profession neglect its principal job. Cohen was the first SEC commissioner to liberally sprinkle his speeches with references to the "independence" of auditors of financial statements. Cohen and Barr didn't want to simply bar the services, because they obviously didn't want the kind of political headaches that would keep Arthur Levitt up at night many years later. During Cohen's tenure, though, auditing and tax work—the two traditional purviews of accounting firms—still made up over 80 percent of the global firms' revenues; so Cohen and Barr could afford to take a wait-and-see attitude.

The overriding accounting issue during the late 1960s and the 1970s, however, was that the many different—but permissible—accounting treatments made it very difficult to evaluate financial statements coming out of Corporate America, to say nothing about comparing competitors across an industry. For example, the mid-1960s merger-and-acquisition explosion highlighted the fact that companies could use the pooling (or purchase) accounting method in accounting for mergers, and could exploit the method for calculating goodwill. Another embarrassing development for the profession in the late 1960s was the ease with which companies could still "shop" for an accounting firm that would agree with the company's interpretation of the then liberal accounting standards. Peat, Marwick & Mitchell was the big firm most known for its willingness to approve flexible accounting treatments of certain transactions.[7] The malleable standards of the times allowed these kinds of differences in professional judgment.

By the end of the 1960s, criticism of the profession grew to a chorus. To thwart financial reporting abuses, it was clear that enforceable rules needed to be established. The AICPA, however, was still deaf to criticism, clinging to the notion that auditors could only give assurances of the acceptability of the accounting principles used—not whether the balance sheets told the economic truth of the company. This special brand of denial that defined the AICPA marked the emergence of a defensiveness toward any outside proposal, a defensiveness that would fully bloom 30 years later in the battle with Arthur Levitt's SEC.

Auditors' duties, according to the AICPA, were simply to "determine compliance with generally accepted accounting standards (GAAS)." Upcoming court decisions, though, would soon make it more difficult to hide behind the profession's self-made rules, greatly expanding the role of the auditor. On the heels of the Continental Vending case, the question of fraud also hung in the air: When were accountants responsible for sniffing out fraud that was affecting the financial statements? The parameters of this extended role are still debated today.

A PRICE WATERHOUSE MAN

John Biegler was the head of Price Waterhouse during the 1970s. Like most middle-class kids from Chicago who wanted to go to college in the 1940s, he went to the University of Illinois, which for years and years sent scores of accounting graduates every year to Arthur Andersen. Even though he had a good offer from Price Waterhouse, Biegler had his heart set on joining his friends from Northwestern at Andersen. Alas, when he showed up for his interview at Andersen, they told him it was a mistake and there was no job for him.[8]

After 10 years working for Price Waterhouse in Chicago, Biegler, who had recently made partner, was asked in 1956 to relocate to the New York office to start up the firm's new SEC department. Price Waterhouse decided to start the department because it felt it was being singled out for criticism by SEC chief accountant Barr. It is interesting that today Barr isn't even known as one of the tougher chief accountants of the SEC. "Andy Barr was actually pretty cozy with the accounting profession," said Lynn Turner, the SEC chief accountant under Arthur Levitt from 1997 through 2000.

The criticism of Price Waterhouse's methods could be traced to the legacy of George May, its legendary senior partner from 1911 to 1936. May believed that any company ought to be free to use any allowable accounting standard that made sense for that particular company. Therefore, U.S. Steel, a Price Waterhouse client, might be audited in a fashion different from that used for another steel company that also used Price Waterhouse. This was all well and good, but Price Waterhouse had no quality control process to categorize for the SEC which accounting standards were being used by which clients. Barr complained that the firm was being inconsistent and, practically speaking, was impossible to monitor, as it would take a watchdog agency many times the size of the SEC to compare Price Waterhouse's work across its roster of clients.

The SEC department Biegler led was created for the purpose of centralizing and reviewing client documents to be filed with the SEC. Whether it was registration statements or annual reports, the idea

133

was to improve the consistency and the quality of what was being put into the SEC. Biegler also had major client responsibilities in New York, particularly with Royal Dutch Shell, headquartered in London but with extensive U.S. operations that had to be audited. Biegler soon became partner in charge of this major worldwide engagement. In 1965, Biegler was elected to the firm's executive committee. With only eight members, the committee afforded Biegler the opportunity to set policy and really to understand the administrative underpinnings of the firm. Biegler was chosen as senior partner of the firm in 1969, succeeding Herman Bevis. Biegler would lead the firm for the next nine years, the first five of which were some of the toughest times that Price Waterhouse—or the industry in general—had seen since the early 1930s. The recession hit in late 1969 and would last through 1974.

"No one saw it coming," Biegler said of the economic downturn in a 1987 unpublished Price Waterhouse (PW) oral history. "The economy was pretty good when I took over, and then . . . not so good."[9]

Henry Gunders headed Price Waterhouse's consulting practice throughout the late 1960s and the 1970s. According to Gunders, the work just flowed into the big firms during the stock market boom of the 1960s, making the recession that started in 1969 all the more difficult to navigate. As he said in the PW oral history: "In 1967, '68, '69, the stock market was just going nuts, and as a result of that we were getting a tremendous amount of work. We were so spoiled in the sixties and so used to being very successful. People were coming to us, the phone was ringing off the hook; and we became so spoiled that we didn't really have the muscles that we needed to deal with or cope with the 1970s."[10]

Bill Miller was an audit partner in Price Waterhouse's Los Angeles office and appeared for nearly 20 straight years on television as the Price Waterhouse partner monitoring the Academy Awards (incidentally, Miller would later come to chafe at his affiliation with the Academy, as his renowned technical skills at Price Waterhouse were largely overlooked by his colleagues). In the PW oral history, Miller described how events just took over Price Waterhouse and other Big Eight firms during this period: "It was just one damn thing after another. I never really thought we were reaching any desperate situation; I thought we had things under control and could handle these things. I'm sure in retrospect, from a business competitor's point of view, everybody, from Inglis on down, wasn't rapid enough on the MCS [management consulting services] end of things. Other firms built up their MCS departments, usually by hiring people from the outside. We tried to do with homegrown talent for a long time."[11]

The stock market implosion and no-growth economy had dire implications for the profession. For one thing, when companies failed, it was now clear that shareholder suits against accounting firms followed. What was even worse was that the big firms were making more tangible auditing mistakes, which meant that plaintiffs' attorneys had the ammunition they needed to pin the business failure on the accounting firms, even if the business failure ultimately had nothing to do with accounting gaffes. One reason so many mistakes were being made was a shortage of good partners to monitor all the new clients signed up during the go-go 1960s.

For example, entering the 1970s, Price Waterhouse had fewer partners per staff member (and thus higher per partner salaries) than any of the other firms, and the partners were too thinly stretched. When the economy went south, the firm slowed down its hiring of junior accountants, meaning that Price Waterhouse's manpower shortage would exist for many years to come. Price couldn't serve its far-flung client base as well as it should have because it just didn't have enough partners in the right place. It couldn't even open new offices in some instances because it didn't have the manpower. When senior partner Biegler did try to open a new office with a senior manager, who was supervised by partners from a nearby office, it typically didn't work out well because leaders of the local community didn't want to play golf or go to dinner with a perceived flunky. They wanted to deal with their equal, a Price Waterhouse partner.[12]

The shortage of good partners at the big firms also meant a shortage of good partners to take the top management jobs. The dearth of leadership talent raised the stakes; the firms had to be absolutely sure that those tapped to lead were up for the job. During Biegler's day, for example, Price Waterhouse had a medical program under which partners would submit to physicals and the reports would go to the firm's medical consultant. The medical consultant would advise Biegler if a partner up for a top management job had a serious medical problem. "That was very confidential," Biegler said. "I was the only person who would have the information."[13]

COMPETITION AND CONSULTING

Entering the 1970s, Biegler had every reason to worry about the relatively small number of Price Waterhouse partners and domestic offices because an era of unprecedented competition was about to descend on the industry. One reason for the intensifying competition was the fact that the government was insisting that the profession obey antitrust laws. Until the 1970s, the global firms were basically splitting up a lucrative pie eight ways and—consistent with AICPA prohibitions on competitive bidding and solicitation—pledging not to steal each other's clients. In 1973, under threat of litigation from the Federal Trade Commission (FTC) and the Department of Justice for violating antitrust laws, the AICPA lifted the ban against competitive bidding. For a few more years, the accountants clung to the bans against advertising and approaching other firm's clients and employees; but again, the government threatened litigation. A Supreme Court ruling in 1976 striking down such bans in the medical and architectural arenas signaled the end of the accountant's fight to retain their restrictions as well; and by the end of 1977, all such bans were lifted.

Roger Hermanson, an accounting professor at Georgia Tech who writes frequently about competition in oligarchies, thinks that the 1970s cutthroat competition for audits and the subsequent embrace of consulting services can be directly tied to the government's forcing the profession to compete. It is ironic that in 1973 the government told accountants that they had to act more like businesspeople, and today admonishes them that they are acting too much like businesspeople. "The whole thing evolved from the government's changing the rules and trying to force competition," said Hermanson.

"It immediately changed everything. About this time, I once met a partner of one of the big firms in Atlanta, and he'd just lost a client because someone cut his price. He told me that he was going to steal one of this guy's clients, even if he had to do it for nothing. As time went on, I'd go to these state CPA society meetings, and the partners at the big firms wouldn't come at all. No one wanted to see the guy whose clients you were stealing."

Although most observers agree that action by the U.S. government to enforce competition among the global firms negatively affected the profession, some say that the auditing profession could easily have avoided the lowballing bidding frenzy that resulted. "I totally disagree with the presumption that auditors moving away from professionalism is the fault of the government," said Lynn Turner, the SEC's former chief accountant under Arthur Levitt from 1998 to 2001. "There is no doubt that the FTC made a disastrous decision back in 1973. But the accounting firms could still have acted like professionals. They still had the responsibility to act in the public trust under the mandate given them by the SEC."

But Hermanson said that the result was predictable. "In a business, it's important to get the lowest price. In a profession, when you start underbidding, you start losing some of the other stuff. The government created the climate where it was a dog-eat-dog situation. I suppose the firms could have concentrated just on the audit and refused to cut the prices. I don't know how you do that without collusion."

The pressure to compete introduced a new dynamic into accounting, one in which sales skills and intelligent marketing were rewarded. Once the gloves had come off, the pure technical auditing types tended to be uncomfortable, whereas the consultants were happy to finally get unleashed. "At Price Waterhouse, most of us were distressed by it," said Shaun O'Malley, former CEO of the firm. "We knew that before we got our lunch eaten, we had to act to survive, do marketing, develop new services. All the firms reacted the same way; I don't think anybody was crazy about it. It was sort of deprofessionalization. I know it upset a lot of people because they thought the FTC was actively deprofessionalizing accounting."

O'Malley, though, said that consultants saw their opportunity coming to the fore with the relaxation of selling restrictions: "To some degree I think the consultants thought it was great stuff. Consultants don't have the same boundaries; the idea of unrestrained competition is fine."

Eminent accounting historians, too, trace the devaluing of the audit—which partly led to the expansion of consulting services—to the government's insistence on forcing competition among the global firms. As Gary Previts of Carnegie Mellon University, one of the deans of accounting historians, wrote in his paper *Accounting History and Public Policy*: "Price competition for a professional service, which is fundamentally judgmental and qualitative and not tied to a physical commodity, strengthens the posture of the lowest bidder and encourages diminished investment in the human skills to serve such a low-value line of endeavor."[14]

The 1970s lurch toward price competition started to chip away the ethical norms in the profession and also ushered in an era of litigation. "As the firms became more like big businesses, they took their eye off the ball," Hermanson said. "Once you start doing that, you start getting more brazen. It happens incrementally. It's not like one day you are honest and the next you are a crook. The idea is not to do that first thing if you know it's wrong."

The accounting firms proved to be naturals at landing consulting contracts, not out of any innate sales skills, but because they were already firmly entrenched at their clients doing audits. The presence of the audit team also meant that the firm knew the key decision makers at the client, individuals they could run all their great ideas by. "The accounting firms had the in, because they knew all the players," Hermanson said. "And there is always plenty of consulting work to go around."

Partners started cold-calling clients and announcing they were dropping by, like vacuum salespeople or Bible salespeople shopping their wares. Felix Amenkhienan, a native of Nigeria and a British chartered accountant trained in London, arrived in the United States at the infancy of enforced competition. He was surprised at what he saw and said that the profession suffered great harm to its reputation as partners started hustling for business. "I think a lot of the mess we're in today can be attributed to the deregulation wave that the professions have seen," Amenkhienan said. "It used to be a CPA could not advertise or solicit each other's clients. It was like overnight the CPA suddenly became a business. Certain types of lawyers are called ambulance chasers, and some of that did infect the CPA profession. It's possible that a good deal of ethics went out the window."

That's certainly the case for one man who worked as an investigator for the U.S. Treasury for over 20 years after a short stint in the early 1970s as an auditor at Ernst & Ernst (E&E) in St. Louis. He left E&E to work for the Treasury largely because he felt the people with whom he worked were totally bereft of ethical standards. He found public accounting "distasteful. I'm not driven by the acquisition of money. Integrity means nothing at these big firms."

The former Treasury investigator, who didn't want to be identified for this book, said that in his time at E&E, the entire energy of the firm was focused on getting and keeping clients. "When I worked for E&E, we had to go out and eat lunch in a restaurant in the hopes that you'd meet someone that would turn into a client. They'd fire someone for eating lunch at their desk."

The crunch for new clients also led to chronic underbidding for audit work. "Let's say you are bidding on ABC widget company. You do a quick estimation of how much work it will take you to do the job, but you really don't know because you've just been for one or two meetings with the potential client," this source said. "So you bid $60,000 for doing the SEC filings and issuing an opinion on the financial statements. You get the work, but then you get in there and do tests on internal controls—which tell you how well the client can maintain an accounting system—and you find that it's the same guy balancing the books and signing the checkbook or [that] they don't always send a bill after a business sale. Now, as an auditor, your sampling has to go way up, because you don't know what you're dealing with."

At one major client, the former auditor said that he was told not to find any accounting errors because that would mean much more rigorous testing and E&E couldn't afford a time-consuming client.

"My manager told me, 'You will not find any errors. If we find an error, we have to increase the sampling and we'll go bankrupt.'"

His team couldn't go and tell the client that the audit would cost much more than estimated because the next year the client would simply hire a different auditor. This led to a common practice in public accounting, which is billing the client for just a portion of the hours worked. "The staff is there working sixteen hours and the firm is billing the client for eight," said the former auditor. "It's like that movie *The Firm*."

At one small client, his team discovered that the president of the company was siphoning money from the company to support a mistress. When the fraud was discovered, a partner meeting was called. At the meeting, according to the E&E source, the discussion centered not on disclosing the information, but on how to keep E&E out of trouble. "If the company found out about this, they're going to wonder why we didn't find it last year. The board of directors could say, 'Hey, we're going to sue you; you should have found it last year.' The second conversation at the meeting was, 'How can we cover this up so we didn't find out about it? How can we justify trashing what we just learned?'"

Loss-leader audits like the ones described by the E&E source made consulting projects look very attractive to the accounting firms. Another factor leading to the profession's embrace of consulting was that the big firms rewarded audit and tax partners who helped consultants land projects at their clients. Arthur Andersen, for example, aggressively went after all the business it could get. The reaction in the profession was not to censure or ostracize Andersen, but to lionize and emulate its ability to sell consulting services. "I think all of us admired the way that Andersen went in and saturated a market," Shaun O'Malley said in the PW oral history.

Indeed, all of the big firms held a grudging respect for Andersen and how clearly it set itself apart from the pack through its aggressiveness, single-mindedness, and unbeatable organization. From a philosophical point of view, Price Waterhouse, Haskins & Sells, and Arthur Young were genteel competitors, in the words of Biegler, "our kind of people." Peat Marwick was thought of as the most commercial of the

CRACKS IN THE FACADE

big firms, even more so than Andersen. One reason Peat was thought of as so overtly commercial was that Peat basically franchised its brand, allowing firms all over the country to hang up Peat signs where the firm needed a presence. According to Biegler: "The firms like Peat, particularly, were just going really commercial, and so there was shopping for accounting principles and all sorts of things, which was new; and, of course, it's everyday today. But in those days, it was a new atmosphere; the profession was starting to look like a business and not a profession."[15]

Andersen's iconoclastic senior partner, Leonard Spacek, personified its competitive instincts in the 1960s and 1970s. The intense dislike between Spacek and, well, just about everyone else in the profession was palpable throughout the 1950s and 1960s. Spacek was intensely critical of the established accounting industry and the Accounting Principles Board (APB) for allowing flexible accounting principles to proliferate. Flexible accounting principles, of course, were exactly what George May had championed for half a century, so Spacek's criticism of the industry did not sit well with Price Waterhouse. The feud spilled over from philosophy to the real world of serving clients. Price Waterhouse's blue-chip clients were used to using their judgment when it came to accounting, and Price Waterhouse naturally wanted to ensure that that was in tune with the philosophy of its client base. Spacek started out as a bookkeeper in a small utility in Chicago. Public utilities are very unusual in that they are subject to very rigid rules. Those rules formed Spacek's perspective, and he couldn't see why that didn't apply to all accounting areas. During this time, Spacek infuriated the accounting establishment by saying that accounting without strict rules was meaningless and misleading and that accountants had been failing at their primary duty for years and years by not establishing strict accounting rules. While Bevis had frequently clashed with Spacek, Biegler, when he took over leadership of the firm in 1969, didn't want any part of the feud between Bevis and Spacek.

One of the many unrecognized ways that accounting firms attempted forays into consulting was through industry specialization. On the face of it, the layperson might think that a qualified, professional accountant could judge financial statements across industries. But if a firm really could talk the industry talk with a client's CEO or CFO, the firm would be in an excellent position to win lucrative consulting projects, not to mention a shoo-in to retain the audit. Industry specialization, however, has proved elusive to all of the big firms since the efforts began. In the PW oral history, Biegler said:

> The matrix got too complicated when you try to put an overlay of industry specialization over everything else, and I considered it one of my great frustrations and great failures that I just couldn't get that thing going the way it should have been. A typical situation would be where an office X would get an inquiry from company Y in industry Z. And there wouldn't be anyone in that office that would know anything about that industry; and we would find those guys making a proposal on that work without ever contacting Joe Dokes over here who is an industry specialist and has lots of experience and should have gone out there and presented himself so that they would get the feeling that somebody understood their industry. It wouldn't happen.[16]

The competition among the firms was also heating up internationally. Again, Andersen and Peat Marwick were the aggressors. Whereas Peat established the most international offices, Andersen said to any potential client that listened that Andersen operated on a worldwide basis and that it was the only unified international firm. That wasn't really accurate, but that's the way Andersen presented it.

Price Waterhouse, it could be said, grew obsessed with Andersen in the 1960s and 1970s to an unhealthy extent. People like Biegler and fellow Price Waterhouse executive Russell Zimmerman—individuals who had spent a considerable amount of time in Chicago, Andersen's headquarters—kept one eye on their business and one eye on whatever innovation Andersen was coming up with. Zimmerman, in particular, was known to scream at other partners about what newfangled idea Andersen was implementing and why Price Waterhouse wasn't keeping up.[17]

When Price Waterhouse did come up with an innovation, it was along the lines of ethics and propriety. Price Waterhouse started the practice of partner rotation, in which a partner could stay with a client for a certain number of years before transferring to a new client. Price Waterhouse wanted to avoid situations where a partner became too closely identified with a client. The conservativeness that marked Price Waterhouse and the aggressiveness associated with firms like Arthur Andersen and Peat, Marwick & Mitchell were manifested in the companies' internal operations. Peat senior partner Walter Hanson handpicked his successor in 1978, only to have the partners reject the choice and throw the firm into turmoil. Andersen let senior partner Harvey Kapnick go when his plan to separate Andersen's audit and consulting practices caused an uproar. Price Waterhouse, by contrast, had smooth handoffs from John Inglis to John Biegler to Joe Connor to Shaun O'Malley.

Andersen, in fact, raised competing to a whole new level in the 1970s. The economic slowdown had caused many companies to eliminate nonessential expenditures, which made the quest to sell extra services all the more heated. "The FTC investigation had all the normal charges—collusion, fee fixing, etc. This was all directed at the anticompetition clauses that were in the canons of ethics in the professional code," said Price Waterhouse partner Henry Gunders in the PW oral history. ". . . That [investigation] turned up nothing because there was plenty of competition already, God knows, because we were all starting to scramble at the beginning of 1971."[18]

Healthy competition is in the eye of the beholder. Before the government forced the profession to relax the bans on solicitation, Gunders himself would never have attempted to perform a consulting project for another firm's client. While Gunders was working in St. Louis in the 1960s, a Price Waterhouse vendor phoned him to tell him that the vice president of finance of a major manufacturing concern would soon be calling him about doing a systems project. This executive had heard about Price Waterhouse's great new systems product that could solve a problem at the company. The problem was that Ernst & Ernst was the company's auditor. According to Gunders: "I had already been around long enough to know that you just don't do that kind of thing. . . . In the meantime this [executive] calls me three times, and I won't answer the phone because I know that it's dangerous. So [PW chairman John] Inglis calls the senior partner at Ernst & Ernst, and that very night a consultant from Ernst & Ernst is on a plane to St. Louis and ultimately does a piece of consulting work. Today, I'd walk into [the client]; I probably wouldn't wait for him to call."

Contrary to the widely held notion that the big accounting firms charged into consulting with little regard for the effect the new services would have on their auditing operations, in several of the firms, there was enormous resistance to consultants, particularly from the audit partners at big clients. The partners weren't afraid that they would be compromised; they were afraid that the consultants would screw up the consulting project and hurt the audit team's relationship with the client. According to Bill Miller, the Price Waterhouse partner on the Academy Awards: "The MCS people were trying, but they were having a harder time because there was more resistance. . . . The reason I saw for their failure, at least in Los Angeles, was that they didn't always do a real good job, and so there was resistance to them. People were reluctant to have them around, and I've heard people say, 'I wouldn't let an MCS partner on my job,' and part of it was deserved. . . . I think Henry Gunders came to New York, and I think he was the first really modern type of MAS [management advisory services] partner."[19]

Steve Blum, the former KPMG corporate finance partner, also saw internal resistance to this type of investment banking consulting when he switched into that practice from auditing in the mid-1970s. "There was a set of partners that wouldn't want us anywhere near their clients, because with our kind of deals, we're not just talking to the controller, we're talking to the CFO and the CEO," Blum said. "We also found that we got more resistance, oddly enough, in situations where the audit partner had a good client relationship. When they were trying to get new clients, on the other hand, they loved bringing us in because they could show what range of services we had."

Most telling of the firms' ambivalence toward consulting was that none of the firms used the words *management consulting* to describe these services. Throughout the 1970s, Price Waterhouse, taking its cue from the AICPA, used the term *management advisory services* to refer to consulting. The idea was that the word *advice* was a little weaker than the word *consulting*, because advice can be accepted or rejected, whereas consulting implied a clear endorsement of a certain course of action by the accounting firm. None of the big firms used the term *consulting*. For example, Arthur Andersen called consulting "administrative services," and Ernst & Ernst called it "specialized services."

Management consulting is by its very nature a risky product because consultants, by definition, go into a company and try to change things. But consulting isn't risky in the same way as auditing. There are rarely lawsuits related to consulting projects because an unsuccessful project is usually heavily discounted and shareholders never find out the specifics of most consulting projects anyway. The big accounting firms knew that shareholder lawsuits stemming from consulting projects would not be an issue with these new services. Rather, maintaining independence from client management, "in fact and appearance," as the saying went, was their real concern. So, the firms started saying, early on, that there was "no evidence" to suggest that consulting contracts with audit clients could impair the objectivity of auditors. This was to remain the profession's defense of consulting to audit clients for the next 25 years. As early as 1978, an AICPA-sponsored report found that "There is no evidence that provision of services other than auditing has actually impaired the independence of auditors. However, the belief of a significant minority of users that independence is impaired creates a major problem for the profession. Decisions on the other services offered and used should be made by individual public accounting firms and boards of directors of the client."[20] The AICPA's stance would remain essentially the same for the next 20 years.

THE AGE OF LITIGATION

Continental Vending opened the litigation floodgates. Before John Biegler became senior partner in 1969, Price Waterhouse had seen only three cases of litigation related to auditing in its history.[21] Before Biegler knew it, he was inundated in the early 1970s with 40 to 50 lawsuits. This was fewer than the other firms had, but still unheard of at the industry's most blue-chip and self-satisfied firm. "During my tenure, litigation became an industry," Biegler said. "I mean, my God, we had to create an office of the General Counsel, we had reports to the executive committee. That was the age of litigation."

According to Henry Gunders, there was a sense of disbelief at the litigation throughout the organization: "For us to have even one lawsuit, much less dozens, was unthinkable. . . . [W]e were trying very hard to hold up that Holy Grail of Price Waterhouse being free from professional errors, and you have to remember that the people in charge of the firm those days were not far removed from McKesson. . . . I would say the mood of the partnership in the early 1970s was affected by all of these lawsuits. . . . [A]lmost without exception, serious lawsuits involved partners in the partnership for a year or two—relatively inexperienced people."[22]

Price Waterhouse, however, generally stayed out of the news as they adroitly managed the litigation. Peat, Marwick & Mitchell was on the defensive all throughout this period. Before 1965, for example, Peat, Marwick & Mitchell had zero lawsuits filed against it by major companies whose books Peat audited. By mid-1966, the firm had 28 lawsuits filed against it, with total requested damages of over $20 million. By the mid-1970s, the firm had over a hundred lawsuits.[23]

The lawsuits did not materialize because, overnight, auditors forgot how to read a financial statement. To some extent, class-action shareholder suits were new devices being somewhat abused by plaintiffs' attorneys. But the litigation did not occur in a vacuum. "You had a whole number of things going on," said Lynn Turner, SEC chief accountant under Arthur Levitt. "For one thing the sixties bull market blew up. Then you had a very aggressive group at the SEC coming in who really ferreted out fraud, commissioners like Ray Garrett and Harold Williams."

The AICPA didn't choose to defend the profession in all, or even most, of the hundreds of lawsuits that were filed against the global firms in the late 1960s and early 1970s. They did fight alongside Lybrand in the Continental Vending case, however, not necessarily because of the merits of the case, but because of the high stakes for the profession. In addition to Continental Vending, the late 1960s and early 1970s litigation produced landmark cases that created an entire body of precedent that often superseded the standards the profession had carved out for itself. One case that went a long way toward enforcing the impression that independent auditors were not satisfactorily performing their roles was the Equity Funding case. The culmination of a series of alarming audit failures came when Equity Funding collapsed in March 1973. Equity Funding fabricated thousands of fake insurance policy sales, while Peat, Marwick & Mitchell, though openly questioning among themselves in 1971 whether there was a problem at their client (there was even a Peat memo concerning Equity Funding titled "Regarding Possible Fraud" at Equity Funding), never issued a qualified opinion. The scheme was revealed only when a former employee notified regulators.[24]

The accounting profession knew that it would be under greater scrutiny than before when Equity collapsed. Officials from the AICPA met with SEC chairman Bradford Cook on April 30, 1973, to discuss what needed to be done. Wallace Olson, representing the AICPA, wanted to lend the trade group's support to fixing the profession, if it needed fixing. In his memoir, *The Accounting Profession*, Olson said: "I concluded that we could not afford to leave the meeting without giving some assurance that the profession would take appropriate action. We agreed, therefore, that the AICPA would immediately conduct a study of the Equity Funding case to determine what, if any, corrective action the profession could take."[25]

The AICPA study, however, only confirmed the profession's reflexive stand that no new standards were needed by the profession relating to finding fraud. The AICPA said that the existing standard governing fraud—that the audit of financial statements was not designed to detect fraud, although fraud might be uncovered in the application of auditing procedures—was sufficient.

The interesting aspect of the AICPA's investigation of the Equity Funding fraud was that one myth had to be demolished, because if the standards were fine, the auditors must not have followed the standards. If the auditors did their job, there was a much more fundamental problem: The standards were bad. The AICPA chose the profession's interest—and their own interest, since they made the standards.

THE AGE OF REGULATION

By the late 1960s, it was clear that the APB was hamstrung. Critics of corporate governance had had enough of standards established by the profession that were too broad to establish consistent reporting. George May–style principles-based reporting fell out of vogue, and with it the APB. Practical problems also doomed the APB: It was strictly part-time, under the thumb of the AICPA, and clearly not interested in reform. Because the SEC and many critics of the profession blamed many of these alleged audit deficiencies on the loose auditing standards championed by the APB, it was clear that the insular standard-setting body sponsored by the AICPA had to disband. While the SEC blamed the APB for failing to establish rigorous and clear standards, accountants countered with their own charges. By law, the SEC oversaw the accounting profession. Failures in standards could just as easily be blamed on the SEC, according to this argument by the accounting profession.

The most vociferous proponent of this point of view was Harvey Kapnick, who had succeeded Spacek as the leader of Arthur Andersen. Kapnick's view was that the SEC wanted to expand the accountant's responsibilities in the areas of management fraud, interim financial statements, and forecasting future performance. Kapnick cited the Four Seasons Nursing Home case as an example of the SEC abusing its power. The Four Seasons case was in many ways similar to the Continental Vending case. Three auditors were charged with colluding with management to approve financial statements with fabricated information in them. The Four Seasons case, to Kapnick, epitomized the new culture of investors and regulators blaming accountants for business failure. Kapnick said in a speech in Dallas on April 24, 1974:

> In large measure, these attempts are an overreaction by such regulators to investors' cries of anguish when they took a risk and lost, even though those same investors were willing to accept huge profits when they occurred. Now these attempts to soothe the investor who is looking for someone to blame by accusing the accounting profession of failures to fulfill its public-interest role are largely defensive by regulators who may not have fulfilled their responsibilities in the past and, at best, are cosmetic cover-ups that impede rather than enhance our ability to serve the public.[26]

The other firms, while initially reluctant to take Kapnick's tack, eventually fought back against the SEC. For example, Arthur Young was accused of fraud by the SEC in May 1973 in connection with its audit of Geotek Resources Fund, Inc. Arthur Young said in a statement at the time: "This action was not commenced in good faith by the plaintiff Commission. . . . The Commission instituted this action against these defendants not out of any convictions that they had violated the federal securities laws, but as part of a policy to obtain injunctions against such firms in order to impose controls over said firms which the Commission cannot impose by regulation."[27]

These were serious charges, and they equaled the level of discourse between the profession and the SEC in the final days of Arthur Levitt's tenure as SEC chairman. Peat, Marwick & Mitchell also had harsh words for the government when two Peat employees were charged with violating federal securities laws in the audit of National Student Marketing Corp.

Certainly, the SEC had some bedside-manner problems with the accounting profession. For one thing, the SEC has always had a policy that it would not comment on the status of an investigation. Typically, after notifying an accounting firm of an investigation, the SEC tended to lock the accounting firm out of any negotiations, and the firm would not get a chance to respond before the case was referred to the Department of Justice.

The standard-setting body that succeeded the APB was the Financial Accounting Standards Board (FASB). The study that gave rise to the FASB was the Wheat Report, commissioned by former SEC commissioner Francis Wheat, with the grudging cooperation of the AICPA. "The Wheat Committee wasn't formed for fun," said Henry Gunders in the PW oral history. "It was formed . . . to say that we don't want the SEC or another government institution to legislate accounting principles; we want to keep that in the private sector. We're going to say our mea culpas as necessary, but we're going to look at this on a broad scale and we'll come back with recommendations to give the government."[28]

John Biegler of Price Waterhouse was the only big-firm senior partner on the Wheat Committee. Biegler received an earful at public hearings about how poorly the accounting profession was performing. He was shocked at what he heard. Until then, Biegler hadn't really understood how the twin forces of shareholder litigation and infighting between leaders of the profession had coalesced and hardened into a deep distrust of the big firms: "It gave me a perspective about what the public and clients and other people were thinking about—what their views were of the accounting profession. It wasn't a very pretty picture. . . . It was a change from the past; I think that all that built up during the late 1960s. I think they felt [that] they see these companies going belly up, so to speak, and they figure, well, 'Geez, these accountants must have been in cahoots with them.'"[29]

The Wheat Report established the Financial Accounting Foundation, comprised of nine trustees: the president of the AICPA, four CPAs in public practice, two financial executives, and one accounting professor. The FAF's main duty was to choose the members of the new FASB, which would consist of seven full-time members: four CPAs with backgrounds in public practice and three individuals with significant experience in financial reporting.

Don Kirk was a Price Waterhouse partner when the APB was in

the middle of its death throes. It was clear to Kirk that the APB needed to be supplanted by something very different. "The standard-setting process had to come out from the umbrella of the AICPA," Kirk said. "The late 1960s were referred to as the go-go years. There were incredibly high multiples; and as the downturn occurred in the marketplace, there was a long, lingering criticism that accounting standards and principles were too flexible. It was definitely a crisis, and one thing that people kept coming back to in those times was that it was the auditors that were setting the accounting standards."

Kirk also believed that the members of the FASB had to be sufficiently removed from the everyday hustle and bustle of the big accounting firms. So, when a spot on the new board was offered to him, Kirk jumped at the chance to join the FASB. He was the youngest member of the original board. "I was pleased to be asked," Kirk said. "I was an audit partner in the field and very interested in accounting standards. In my experience, you could see that there were just different philosophies among the firms; every firm thought about financial reporting in a different way. I thought that it was essential that the people deciding these issues should not be dealing with clients."

According to Kirk, the new FASB, while encountering some resistance, was given a stamp of legitimacy almost right away by a prominent member of the business community. At the dinner marking the official creation of the FASB, the keynote speaker was General Electric's Reginald Jones, whose endorsement of the new board gave it some much-needed clout. Jones said, according to Kirk, that it was inevitable that with the new board, "Someone's ox is going to be gored, and the real test will be getting behind the FASB after that."

"The FASB was very consistent with what the Wheat Commission recommended," Kirk said. "It was independent and it was fully staffed and funded. This was really the first time that the setting of the principles was taken away from the profession itself to any extent. Once the FASB started to make the standards, the profession got behind it, and so the SEC acknowledged that this new entity would be the source of authoritative standards."

Although the accounting profession, as Kirk said, lost some of its standard-setting mandate to the FASB, Mike Cook said that the AICPA understood that getting behind the FASB was really the only way to regain the trust of the public. "Those moves were a big part of why we were allowed to remain a self-regulated profession," Cook said.

THE METCALF REPORT AND THE
COHEN COMMISSION REPORT

The growing dissatisfaction with, in particular, the global firms resulted in two major studies of the profession in the late 1970s: the Metcalf Report in 1977 and the Cohen Commission Report in 1978. The Metcalf Report was the result of the first real government inquiry into the accounting profession since the 1930s, an investigation conducted between 1975 and 1977 by Senator Lee Metcalf and, on the House side, by Representative John Moss.

"Pretty soon the politicians started to get hold of [accounting debates]," said Henry Gunders in the PW oral history. "The notion went something like this: You guys in the major accounting firms have the privilege of having a semimonopolistic business handed to you. There it is, and you'd better be prepared to be accountable to government inquiry because you've got a fiduciary responsibility and we aren't sold on the fact that you're discharging a product. That ultimately led to the Metcalf Report."

The Metcalf Report issued four main recommendations:[30]

1. Establish a self-regulatory organization of firms that audit publicly owned companies.
2. Limit types of management services to those relating directly to accounting.
3. Relax artificial bans on advertising and promotion.
4. Encourage the formation of corporate audit committees.

The Metcalf Report recommendations were less than earth shattering. The Justice Department and the FTC had already pushed the profession toward rescinding the ban on advertising and promotion, and the AICPA soon established a new self-regulatory organization of firms known as the SEC Practice Section of the AICPA. Corporate America had also already come around on the idea of audit committee formation, so the only really controversial cause the Metcalf Report backed was the limit on consulting to accounting-related projects.

Biegler, senior partner of Price Waterhouse, was called to testify before the committee. The day Biegler testified was remembered by Gunders, who sat with Biegler during Biegler's testimony: "Well, there was a lot of the usual thing going on, people walking around and whispering, and there was a lot of commotion. . . . Biegler's sitting in the Senate hearing room, and I'm sitting there and Lee Metcalf says, 'Next witness.' And John doesn't say anything for what seems like a full minute, and finally he says, 'I'm John Biegler, the senior partner of Price Waterhouse,' and you could hear a pin drop because he commanded that kind of respect."[31]

Biegler had an ace up his sleeve in his testimony that would establish Price Waterhouse as the firm most committed to the public trust. Biegler felt that the AICPA was adrift and going every which way, with no real plan to extricate the firms from the multitude of lawsuits and negative publicity about accountants. To the shock of everyone, including many partners in his own firm, Biegler dropped a bombshell at the hearings, suggesting that the SEC form an oversight body for the profession, one that would supersede the AICPA and state accounting boards. According to Biegler:

That was the point at which I felt that the profession, the organized profession, was just going every which way and there was no way. . . . It was very difficult to get their attention. We put forward some proposals . . . on the theory that it would force the Institute, the organized profession, to do something to get the house in order, because while we weren't completely blame free, we were getting hurt by association from some of the practices of a number of the other firms. We had very clearly understood that even though ours was an informal legislative proposal, the odds of it ever becoming legislation were virtually nil, and therefore it was a safe thing to propose because it would force the profession to react.[32]

The Metcalf Report did not result in any new legislation, but the spotlight shining on perceived failure of the profession prompted the SEC to propose a rule mandating that companies include in their financial statements the total fees they pay their accountants, broken down into audit and nonaudit fees. The resulting howls of outrage from the AICPA occurred because the rule, in effect, required accounting firms to give to the competition sensitive internal information. But the accountants were also upset at the implication that the profession's burgeoning cash cow, management consulting, somehow tainted the audit. According to Gunders in the PW oral history:

[T]hey also didn't particularly want a disclosure of the payments because the Metcalf Report has in it the implicit suggestion that if you're doing consulting work for an audit client, you can't be as independent an auditor. I met privately at the Republican Club with Jack Chesham, who was chief of staff for Metcalf in Washington. I said, "Jack, all you guys are trying to do is to make us say that we're taking unfair advantage." . . . I said I thought it was insulting, that everything that I know about a professional is that what you hold dear is what's good for the client and what's right for the client, not what's good for you; and I think any suggestion that's not the drum beat we march to I'm going to resent very much personally and so will anybody else in the profession. We're not a bunch of prostitutes.[33]

It is interesting that even in Gunders's impassioned defense of his profession to Chesham, his point is that being a good professional means that what "you hold dear is what's good for the client and what's right for the client, not what's good for you." There is no mention of the public or a client's shareholders in Gunders's reasoning.

This inability to transcend the client service relationship between accounting firm and client is what defined the accounting profession for the past 30 years. Gunders and so many smart, accomplished professionals like him believed that it was the job of the auditor to help and defend company management, not to act as an aggressive watchdog on company management.

The compromise rule worked out with the SEC was that companies had to report in their annual reports the aggregate fees they paid to their accountants for nonaudit services. The rule would stay on the books for only a few years, until Ronald Reagan's SEC chief, John Shad, rolled it back. Even with the rule on the books, consulting opportunities flourished for accounting firms in the years following the Metcalf Report. Though the consulting growth was most likely attached to a growing economy, the irony wasn't lost on Gunders, the head of Price Waterhouse's consulting services: "I said laughingly a couple of years after Metcalf, 'I hope we have another Metcalf very soon. This is a great shot in the arm.' The market was there, and I have become convinced that no matter what they do in Washington, when you have a staff, and you have a capability, and you have a market, and you have clients, you don't fold your tent because of anything that goes on in Washington, D.C. Never have and never will."

The Cohen Commission, commissioned by the AICPA and headed by former SEC commissioner Manny Cohen, was important for two reasons. First, its final report included at least one example of an audit that had been compromised because of a consulting project, that of Westec Corporation. Professor Douglas Carmichael of Baruch College in New York City, who served on the Cohen Commission, said, "It was quite clear that the jury believed that the Westec case had impaired the independence of the auditor. It's irked me over the years that you get this constant refrain from people speaking on behalf of the large firms that says there's no report that has ever cited one case of consulting affecting audit independence. It's not true, and yet they continue to go on making the point."

Second, the Cohen Commission Report contained an item that the accounting firms have been trying to fight until this very day: the fact that there is no product differentiation in the audit, which by definition must adhere to formal auditing standards. The Cohen Commission even predicted a decline in audit quality if the profession insisted on competing by lowballing audit fees. Ever since the Cohen Commission Report, firms have been "reengineering" their audits every few years to "capture more information" and to "add value" to the client.

WATCHING THE WATCHDOGS

The 1970s also saw many attempts to reform the profession from within. One crusader who emerged in the late 1960s and the 1970s was Eli Mason, who put forth several proposals to reform the profession. Mason, senior partner at Eli Mason & Company, submitted his plan to Congress as part of the "Accounting Establishment" report issued by Senator Lee Metcalf. Mason, a former president of the New York State Society of Certified Public Accountants, wrote in his plan that Congress should create, by law, an oversight body that would unite all the different standard setters, rule makers, and regulators that ran the profession at the time. It was actually quite similar to the plan proposed by Price Waterhouse's Biegler. Under Mason's plan, licensing of CPAs, adoption of accounting standards, and regulation of practitioners would all be performed by this oversight body, which Mason dubbed the Institute of Certified Public Accountants of the United States. Mason was an unusual critic because he was actually a practicing accountant and not an academic or a regulator.

Other reformers from within the industry emerged in an attempt to ward off regulation from outside. For example, J. S. Seidman, a partner at the New York City firm Seidman & Seidman, suggested that mandatory rotation be instituted—that companies be forced, at a fixed interval, to switch auditors. Seidman was a former president of the AICPA, but that didn't help his proposal garner much support.

Another reformer at the time was Itzhak Sharav, then at Herbert H. Lehman College of the City University of New York (CUNY). Sharav believed that the best way to ensure true independence was to strip the power of management to hire, yes, but most important to fire the auditors. The prospect of losing the engagement over an audit dispute, Sharav rightly pointed out, was a more basic issue than, say, separating auditing and consulting. Sharav also believed that mandatory auditor rotation would ensure two things: (1) Auditors would know that another firm would soon enough need to look over their work; and (2) auditors, knowing that they would be handing the client to another firm in several years, would have little allegiance to management.

PEER REVIEW

The peer review process developed as one way of watching the watchdogs. The idea of accounting firms reviewing each other was floated in the late 1960s by the AICPA in response to some firms who thought voluntary reviews of their processes would stave off potential lawsuits. The idea was rejected then, but emerged again when the SEC and the AICPA struck a deal to, in some cases, allow firms accused of negligent auditing to undergo quality reviews in lieu of facing SEC civil charges. The first firm to ever undergo such a review was Laventhol, Krekstein, Horwath and Horwath in 1972 (Laventhol Horwath would implode in 1990 due to third-party litigation), followed by Touche Ross in 1974 and Peat, Marwick & Mitchell in 1975. A team of partners from the other big firms conducted the reviews. That system stalled, however, and in 1976 Price Waterhouse voluntarily invited Deloitte, Haskins & Sells to perform a one-on-one review. That "one firm" review model became the model for the rest of the big firms, and soon it was established that the global firms would review each other's audit quality control systems every three years.

CHAPTER 6

THE END OF THE AUDIT

B OB N<small>ICOLLS</small> <small>GRADUATED FROM THE</small> U<small>NIVERSITY OF</small> I<small>OWA IN</small> 1980 and went to work that summer in the Chicago office of Ernst & Whinney with a hundred other newly minted accounting graduates. At the first orientation session for these new graduates, an Ernst & Whinney partner announced to the group, "Look around. Five years from now, there are only going to be ten of you left at the firm." Determined to be one of those ten, Nicolls rushed around to his clients—mainly small banks—for the next four years, working 12-hour days and lugging around his heavy, ungainly computer that could hardly be called a "laptop." Like many accounting graduates fresh out of school, Nicolls rarely saw a partner in the course of his work. Partners were mostly hobnobbing out in the community trying to land clients; and, besides, the partners leading Nicolls's engagements invariably had bigger clients to visit. If something important came up or if Nicolls had a technical question, he could always go to a senior manager, who in turn would bring the partner in.

The biggest bank client being served out of Ernst & Whinney's Chicago office was Continental Illinois National Bank and Trust Company. Continental was a client that partners could sink their teeth into, a major lender to some of the nation's leading gas and energy companies. Ernst & Whinney had 30 staffers full-time over at the bank. Continental had been wise enough to team up with another bank that really knew the energy industry, Penn Square Bank of Oklahoma City. In 1979 and 1980, Penn Square lent more than $2 billion to companies serving the industry, positive that oil prices were bound to go up. Continental decided to buy more than $1 billion of these loans, effectively making it the lender to Penn Square's customers. This was done in the belief that, with energy prices poised to soar, these companies would not only pay back the loans at a healthy rate, but might even come back to Continental to finance other projects.

While Nicolls was in the trenches at his small bank, doing the necessary sampling and testing that is the core of an auditor's work, his colleagues on the Continental Bank audit were, shockingly to him, simply taking a cursory glance at Continental's internal audit work papers and signing off on them. "Here was Continental making these participating investments in Penn Square. Friends of mine were on the job. They never created their own work papers; they were vouching for the bank's internal audit work papers," Nicolls said. "But Continental hadn't even gone down to check the oil situation and these companies that were getting the loans. And we didn't send people to see which wells were where; it would have been impractical. But to do the job right, we should have done it."

As is so often the case with such failures of due diligence, all would have been forgotten—or never even come to light—had a booming economy borne out everyone's optimism. As it turned out, the 1981–1982 recession put many of Penn Square's and Continental's less-than-stellar borrowers out of business. Penn Square could not collect, and the bank failed. Continental was not broke but eventually had to be rescued with a $4.5 billion federal bailout plan.[1]

Just as in many business failures, attention shifted to the auditors next. There was plenty of blame to spread around for both Ernst & Whinney and Peat Marwick, the firm auditing Penn Square. Eventually, Continental fired Ernst & Whinney, and several Continental and Penn Square bankers were charged with fraud.[2]

THE TROUBLE WITH AUDITS

The competition that had been unleashed at government insistence in the 1970s had ushered in a new era of fee pressure in the early 1980s. On those Chicago-area audits where Ernst & Whinney did do quality work, the firm didn't get paid for it. Nicolls was shocked to find out in his first few jobs that those 12-hour days were being billed as 8-hour days to the client. According to Nicolls, when Ernst & Whinney would submit a proposal to a company, the proposal included an estimated number of hours for the job, broken down into partner, manager, and staff hours. This is how they arrived at the price of the job. Unless they are the incumbent firm, however, their bid would be made with a minimum amount of information because the potential client would often be too busy or similarly unavailable to give the team much information. The price included in the bid was typically a best-case scenario.

Often, perhaps even a majority of the time, the audit didn't go exactly as the work plan so neatly laid out. More hours were needed just so Ernst & Whinney could get the job done. But the firm couldn't charge all those hours to the client; they had already told the client exactly what the hours and the fee would be in the written proposal process and the contract that was signed afterward. So Ernst & Whinney had to eat the extra hours, driving the profit margins of an audit further down. "You'd have a budget to go out in 100 hours or 1,000 hours or whatever; and if you didn't come in under that, you'd be fired," Nicolls said. "Fee competition did exist, and it led to breakdowns at the client." Nicolls's comments suggest that the rise of consulting per se is not to blame for bad auditing as much as is fee pressure in any form.

THE ACCIDENTAL CPA

It wasn't only at Ernst & Whinney that price competition was driving down audit quality in the 1980s. A lack of professional skepticism was endemic throughout the Big Eight. Todd Walker was anything but an eager young accounting graduate like Bob Nicolls. Walker, who today runs a small CPA firm in the town of Munford, Tennessee, never really saw himself as a CPA and didn't major in accounting as an undergraduate. Rather, he majored in chemical science and worked for the 3M Company while working toward an MBA at night. After receiving his MBA degree, for which he had taken several accounting courses, Walker sat for the CPA exam and passed the whole thing the first time.

When he joined Peat Marwick's Milwaukee office in 1983, Walker could already see the troubles plaguing the firm. "You couldn't help but notice," Walker said. "Peat was pretty heavy into the S&Ls, and you'd get these periodic purges of partners." The increasing tendency of fairly large partner layoffs of 50 to 100 at once, in fact, was a previously unheard-of development at accounting firms. At Price Waterhouse in the late 1960s, for example, John Biegler had nearly caused a partner revolution when he tried to fire a rogue partner in one of the firm's outlying offices.[3]

"I think in 1983, there was still a lot of good auditing being done," Walker said. "There weren't a lot of jobs where they'd all been shaved to nothing. A good audit is where the client has everything ready for you when you get there. They pay you a good enough fee where you can have a couple of managers running the day-to-day stuff and also have a partner who can do some real thinking about the audit. If a company pays enough money for a team of high-quality people to lend a high-quality service, the job will get done right."

What happened in the 1980s, according to Walker, was that when the firms started cutting prices, huge clients were getting less experienced people for less time. "It was stupid to cut these fees on these huge clients," Walker said. "Because if things got fouled up because you didn't have enough good people on the job, you'd have to throw more bodies at the problem. Pretty soon the audit had no value for the firms because they weren't making any money on it."

Fees spiraling downward and legions of inexperienced auditors attending to important clients also meant that it would be difficult for auditors to marshal the resources and the expertise to deter or to find management fraud. The litigation that had exploded in the 1970s, and the body of judicial opinion that accompanied it, made it clear that auditors could not hide behind generally accepted accounting principles (GAAP). In 1984, for example, U.S. Supreme Court Chief Justice Warren Burger wrote that auditing was a "public watchdog" function that demanded complete independence on the part of the auditor. But auditors in the 1980s, like Nicholls and Walker, witnessed a continuing slide—not an improvement—in auditing. Public opinion, a flood of litigation, and judicial pronouncements had not done the job. Auditors still refused to believe that an important part of their job was opening their eyes to what was going on around them at a company.

According to Walker, clients could tell when rigorous auditing meant nothing to an audit partner, when it was simply a "loss leader" on the way to lucrative tax and consulting jobs. A savvy CFO or controller also knew that this lack of resources devoted to auditing, combined with the pressure not to lose the client, would make for a very favorable balance of power when it came to discussing the financial statements with the auditing team. So not only were auditors both unwilling and unable to ferret out management fraud, but also they were frequently outwitted in the boardroom during debates on what qualified as income, what kind of income could be deferred, and so on. Indeed, the widening gap between the top-flight financial minds at U.S. blue-chip companies and the increasingly mediocre outside audit teams stands out as one of the biggest reasons for debacles like Enron and WorldCom. Now that accounting as an occupation is even less attractive than it was before, that gap is bound to grow.

"As the pressure on auditors to make money became acute, they had to do whatever clients wanted," Walker said. "The audit side has, over 25 years, really lost its backbone; and it really started to accelerate in the 1990s."

Walker said that a young auditor is not faced with tough decisions about an audit every day, or even every year. But they do come along, and the decision is ultimately based on the professionalism of the partners running the engagement. "Toward the end of my career at Peat, a client was doing some things with estimating a product's liability that were clearly wrong," Walker said. "Our partners didn't do much about it. The partners basically caved. If you stay at a big firm 10 years, are you likely to run into one of these? Yeah. Is there a good chance the outcome will be disagreeable to you? Yeah. At the same time, I never had a partner where I'd say, 'Whoa, get me away from this guy.'"

As of the end of 2002, Walker was planning on joining a fellow practitioner in Munford—a merger, if you will. "The big firms might have destroyed the audit forever, I don't know," Walker said. "But I'm in a small rural environment. Here, someone with a CPA is respected. It's almost like being a doctor; you have this skill that's needed and appreciated."

THE CONSULTANTS ARRIVE

Peter Cohan is a business consultant who joined Price Waterhouse's consulting division in the mid-1980s. Here's how he describes the decline of auditing standards that marked the 1980s and 1990s: "It's not something that happened at one time. It's like the old story about the frog in the pot of water. The water kept getting turned up 10 degrees at a time. Before you know it, it was boiling." And the frog—like the books—gets cooked.

Cohan grew up in Worcester, Massachusetts, where his grandfather, father, and uncle all worked together in their family-owned accounting firm. As respected members of the community, they audited several local, privately owned companies and worked on the tax and estate work for the community's leading citizens. Cohan worked for the firm when he was in high school and decided that the career path of his father and grandfather wasn't for him. "I just found it kind of boring," said Cohan, who became a consultant instead. "But you could really see what a skill it was. It's sort of a whole mindset. It's the ability to sniff out problems, to have the patience to follow a bunch of procedures to find the right answer."

Cohan joined Price Waterhouse's strategic management consulting practice in 1985 after he received his MBA from Wharton. At Price Waterhouse, Cohen found that the audit had been devalued.

"Basically what I discovered, at about the time accountants were about to set up consulting practices, was that auditing was a commodity, that the idea was cross-selling."

Not that the strategy was working very well. Price Waterhouse's consulting and auditing divisions, according to Cohan, were not working with the cross-selling synergy that had been advertised. "I was led to believe there would be this culture of working together and cross-selling," Cohan said. "But it was incredibly balkanized. It was like every single responsibility center had its own profit-and-loss statement." According to Cohan, the problem was that the incentive structure at Price Waterhouse was not set up to produce the kind of behavior the firm wanted. The consultants represented a huge risk for the auditors because the consultant's project could easily go awry and leave an angry client with only the audit team to take frustrations out on.

Greg Neu joined Touche Ross's consulting practice in 1980 from the brokerage firm Shearson Hayden Stone. Neu chose Touche Ross because the firm's consulting practice had a growing reputation as modeling itself after deep-thinking McKinsey Consulting. "Touche Ross, from a consulting standpoint, was a class act," Neu said. "They were more of a real management consulting practice. I was under the impression we were doing strategic consulting as opposed to accounting-related consulting, which the other Big Eight firms were doing."

Because the consultants of Touche Ross saw their skills as not meshing much with the firms' auditors, Neu seldom went on client pitches with auditors. "Actually, consulting represents as much a risk for auditors as it does an opportunity," Neu said. "The audit partner gets some brownie points for helping the consultants get work at an audit client, but he'll really get nailed for losing the audit client."

After five years, Neu took a vice president's job at Bankers Trust, but he found he still had the consulting bug. A year later, he went to Coopers & Lybrand, where one of his first assignments was assisting a client in the United Arab Emirates (UAE) who wanted to start a business importing specially bred white-skinned chickens to the UAE from the United States. Neu's job was to figure out how feasible such a business would be. "This was not that long after the Iranian hostage crisis," Neu said. "Your basic southern chicken farmer would tell me, 'I don't want the Ayatollah coming here. You got it?'" While Neu was at Coopers, he saw the financial-planning-and-analysis group grow to almost 300 people. In 1989, Neu went to Andersen to help the firm rebuild its consulting capability after the reorganization that made Andersen Consulting a separate division of Andersen Worldwide.

"In 1989, Arthur Andersen had a plan in mind," Neu said. "They had just finished their battle with Andersen Consulting. I was coming in to develop a consulting practice at an accounting firm. What was important was salesmanship ability and how well you embraced the culture."

Auditors and consultants like Nicolls, Walker, Cohan, and Neu were all witnesses to—and participants in—a tangible shift in focus among the leadership of the big firms from auditing to consulting, primarily due to the brutal competition that had taken hold of the industry.

A tangential issue in the new era of intense competition for clients was that the global firms' international affiliates were dumbfounded by their U.S. colleagues' clumsy forays into marketing. An internal memo to Price Waterhouse employees in 1980 said, "All partners and staff members should be aware that many Price Waterhouse member firms do not practice in the same ethical environment that exists in the United States. In this era of advertising, brochures, and other efforts to enhance the firm's image, we may inadvertently cause other firms to suffer embarrassment or worse treatment from the organization that regulates the practice of accounting in their countries."

SEC ROLLBACKS IN THE EARLY 1980s

The SEC has done many good things in its oversight of the accounting profession, but its relationship to the profession is not designed to be consistent. The worldviews and political stances of the past two chairmen—Arthur Levitt followed by Harvey Pitt—illustrate that the oversight role of the SEC over the accounting profession is necessarily related to the person sitting in the White House. The result, occasionally, is a complete about-face, within just a few months, in how the SEC's mandate over the accounting profession is applied. After the defeat of Jimmy Carter by Ronald Reagan in 1980, for example, Reagan appointed John Shad as chairman of the SEC. Just as Pitt's chairmanship seemed out of place following Levitt's, so did Shad's following Harold Williams. "The difference between Harold Williams and Rod Hills under Carter and then John Shad under Reagan is just night and day," said Lynn Turner, the SEC's chief accountant under Arthur Levitt.

It did not take long for the Reagan administration's deregulatory philosophy to be implemented by Shad at the SEC. In January 1982, Shad repealed ASR 250, "Disclosure of Relationship with Independent Public Accountants," the rule that the SEC itself had proposed several years earlier, which required public companies to list the percentage of their accounting firm payments that was for consulting services.

According to Lynn Turner, an opportunity to squelch the gathering momentum toward a massive shift in emphasis to consulting was lost with the revocation of the requirement. "For the couple years when the public saw those percentages published, audit committees cut down on consulting," Turner said. "Then Reagan came in, the firms regained their influence, and, boom, Shad took the steps to eliminate the disclosures."

In 1981, the American Institute of Certified Public Accountants (AICPA) committee that deals with the SEC reaffirmed that accounting firms auditing public companies could not provide services that were "inconsistent with the firm's responsibilities to the public," such as psychological testing, public opinion polling, merger-and-acquisition assistance for a contingency fee, executive recruitment, and actuarial services to insurance companies.[4]

Steve Blum was a partner at Peat Marwick in the early 1980s; at age 29, he had been named the youngest partner in the firm's history. His experience is instructive of what consultants were encountering during this time as restrictions like the ones mentioned earlier proliferated. Blum said that one of the challenges in those days for Peat Marwick's investment banking consultants was complying with essentially two layers of restrictions: (1) the AICPA's fee restrictions (no contingency fees) and (2) the SEC's scope-of-service restrictions (no investment banking to audit clients). Investment bankers from Wall Street always expressed amazement to Blum that he and his colleagues could operate within the structure of an accounting firm. But they did, and sometimes they even beat the Wall Street firms at their own game, snatching middle-market deals away from the Goldman Sachses and the Merrill Lynches of the world.

"Wall Street folks know finance, where to raise the money, there's no question about that," Blum said. "But we were accountants who knew the language of business. We knew what to pay for a company, how to structure the deal. In a lot of ways, we could run rings around the Wall Street people."

S&L AUDITS IN THE 1980s

The Penn Square Bank and Continental Bank debacle that Bob Nicolls saw up close was one of the first big S&L failures that garnered a lot of attention. In March 1982, Peat Marwick finished the annual audit of Penn Square and issued a clean opinion. Four months later, the bank was liquidated by the Federal Deposit Insurance Corporation (FDIC). For Ernst & Whinney, Continental wasn't the only bank it had a difficult time auditing. The firm's clean audit opinion of United American Bank in Knoxville, Tennessee, had an even shorter shelf life than Peat Marwick's last audit of Penn Square. Ernst & Whinney gave United American a clean bill of health in January 1983, and just 20 days later the bank was shut down by federal regulators, who convinced another bank to merge with United American.[5]

Ernst & Whinney responded to criticism of its bank auditing by designing an "early warning system" that was supposed to closely monitor its bank clients for potential problems. But like most programs such as this one, it languished unheeded as partners and managers rushed about, trying to meet client demands and make filing deadlines. Preemptive processes within firms have proved very ineffective at stopping bad audits, but review processes centered on firms' resident accounting experts have been effective (indeed, if Andersen's Enron engagement team had listened to the firm's Chicago-based professional standards group, which ruled against certain Enron transactions, the firm might be around today).

In 1984, Nicolls himself went to work for one of his S&L clients as a loan workout specialist. "There was a lot of pressure to put up more and more loans," Nicolls said. "And the auditors that we had out there were virtually clueless." As Nicolls observed, both as an auditor at Ernst & Whinney and later as someone who dealt with auditors in his job at the S&L, auditors had great difficulty trying to account for the risk that bank loans inherently contained. Indeed, all kinds of banks, not just S&Ls, were getting much more difficult to audit in the 1980s. Banks are difficult to audit to begin with because there is very little physical inventory. Short of traveling all over the country checking those companies out for themselves, for example, it was impossible for Nicolls's friends auditing Continental Bank to properly gauge the risk of the bank's loan portfolio.

Auditing banks only got more complicated in the early 1980s. Well-known bankers like Citibank's John Reed had been pushing for deregulation. As banks ventured into new frontiers like discount brokerages and venture capital services, auditors had to broaden their skills, too. Then, banks started to make huge loans to Latin American countries, real estate companies, and other risky creditors. Accountants like those at Ernst & Whinney had to gauge the creditworthiness of loans like Continental's, and they didn't do a very good job of it. It shouldn't be a surprise, however, that auditors were not any better than the banks themselves at deciding whom to loan money to. Citibank, for example, was nearly bankrupt with bad loans in the early 1990s when the Federal Reserve bailed them out. In the 1980s, though, it wasn't the global banks like Citibank that caused the most problems, but S&Ls big enough to make huge loans but not big enough to cover them.

By 1990, the government had filed more than a dozen lawsuits—seeking more than $2 billion—against accounting firms related to audits of failed thrifts. The biggest suit was against Ernst & Young, the firm resulting from the 1989 merger between Ernst & Whinney and Arthur Young. Even though Ernst & Whinney had its share of troubles in the early 1980s, Arthur Young had run into even deeper troubles in its work with S&Ls. Arthur Young certified financial statements of Western Savings Association in 1984 and 1985 that were overstated by almost $400 million.[6] According to one source, the prospect of major S&L litigation was so great that if it had not merged with Ernst, Arthur Young probably would have gone out of business altogether. The FDIC sued Ernst & Young for $560 million in connection with Arthur Young's previous problems. Ernst & Young was also the target of another suit by the government, for $250 million over its audit of a group of Tennessee banks.[7] Mike Cook's Deloitte & Touche was being sued for $300 million over its audit of Beverly Hills Savings & Loan and for $250 million over its audit of a Florida S&L, Sunrise Savings.[8]

The accountants' defense was that they were not the ones making the loans. Holding an accounting firm responsible for loan losses, they insisted, represented an absurd perversion of an accountant's duty. For the accounting industry, the only good thing about the S&L crisis was the timing. While many of the audits in question stemmed from the early 1980s, many of the lawsuits and much of the publicity did not come until several years later. The profession had just spent much of 1985 and 1986 bobbing and weaving through Congressman John Dingell's House hearings on independent auditing, just before the lawsuits really came down in full force. If the S&L lawsuits had materialized a little sooner, Dingell's proposed Fraud Detection and Disclosure Act, which would have dramatically increased auditors' responsibility to look for fraud, might have had a better chance at passage. Of course, the big firms thought the legislation was wrongheaded and based on fundamental misunderstandings of the auditors' role and were influential in the legislation being stymied.[9]

Besides bank failures, other business failures occurred in the 1980s. Andersen's audit of mutual fund company Fund of Funds in the early 1980s went so awry that a federal jury ordered the firm to pay $80 million to the fund's shareholders, at that time more than twice the previous biggest judgment ever levied against an accounting firm. The big question was whether Andersen had enough insurance to cover the award. Rumors swirled that the firm was underinsured for such a huge verdict, and the possibility of Andersen being litigated into oblivion was not unthinkable. It didn't happen, but not every firm would be so lucky in the years ahead.

PRICE WATERHOUSE AGAIN TAKES THE LEAD

Just as Price Waterhouse senior partner John Biegler had surprised people with his reform suggestions during the Metcalf Committee hearings, another Price Waterhouse partner stepped up with more ideas in the mid-1980s. Biegler's successor, Joe Connor, suggested that the firms open up more and give more information to the SEC. He came out for proposals to reform reporting and registration to the SEC; he suggested that each accounting firm register with the SEC, supply a list of all its clients, list all partners on the clients, and really let the SEC know how the firm was serving clients.

"He really wanted to be open about all of this and come clean. Connor made his proposal, and practically no one in the profession would even speak to him," said Shaun O'Malley, Connor's successor. The profession, in fact, took the opposite tack. They began to line up lobbyists and to contribute to political action committees. "Lobbying became more and more commonplace; it seemed like it worked," O'Malley said. "During Joe's time, they started having regular meetings to discuss pending legislation." O'Malley continued the meetings, but he says that they included other subjects, like training.

In 1990 the firms learned a hard lesson. The 350 partners of

Philadelphia-based Laventhol & Horwath filed for bankruptcy that November. The seventh-biggest firm in the country, Laventhol had at least a hundred lawsuits pending against it, claiming more than $2 billion in damages.[10] The original firm that became Laventhol was founded in 1915 and for many years had been known as *the* accounting firm to the hotel and entertainment industry, including Hyatt. One of the biggest claims against the firm was the $184 million lawsuit against Laventhol and other professional services firms by the donors to Jim Bakker's PTL ministries. "Whenever we go through one of these cycles, we lose a firm or two," said former KPMG head Jon Madonna. "It was not unthinkable at that time that we'd lose another one of the really big firms." The likelihood of getting sued from an S&L failure or other case was so high in the early 1990s, in fact, that the firms took to having regular meetings on the subject, as the rash of cases threatened their very survival.

Madonna was the head of KPMG's San Francisco office when he took over as CEO from Larry Horner in 1990. He often spent time in meetings trying to figure out KPMG's response to litigation. "When I got to New York in 1990, we had a lot of litigation," Madonna said. "I'd say about a certain case, 'Okay, who's the partner on the case, and what are they doing today?' The reply would be that the person was still around because he had to testify. But meanwhile, the other work he would be doing was bad, too." One of the reasons firms typically didn't just fire auditors who had proved themselves poor performers was fear of the Andersen–David Duncan scenario in 2002. Andersen fired Duncan, the firm's lead partner on the Andersen account, and he became the prosecution's star witness, albeit one who did not ultimately make as big an impact as expected.

Indeed, the firms often recycled partners who had been accused in a lawsuit of being a bad auditor. The lead partner of Andersen's audit of Charles Keating's Lincoln Savings and Loan, the 1989 failure that came to embody the S&L scandals, later served as Andersen's lead partner on the audit of the Baptist Foundation of Arizona, which collapsed over a decade later.

"It's not a coincidence that it was the same guy who audited Keating and the Baptists," Madonna said, "which leads you to the skills and talent of the person doing the auditing. Look at what happens with the IRS. They get gamed. People say whatever they have to say to get through an audit; and with a weak adversary, it's an easy game, whether you're talking to an IRS auditor or a Big Six auditor."

Sometimes, though, a firm can be vindicated when it keeps an audit team around that is involved in heavily publicized litigation. For example, in 1985, the SEC charged Price Waterhouse and three of its partners with fraud in connection with its 1980 audit of Chicago-based AM International, which went bankrupt in 1982.[11] Price Waterhouse defended itself by saying that it had, in fact, been documenting problems at AM International when it was fired. On November 25, 1981, according to an internal Price Waterhouse partner newsletter, the Price Waterhouse team delivered to the AM International audit committee a 10-page draft of the report that the accounting firm planned to issue on the company's 1981 financial statements. The report was discussed by AM International's full board of directors on December 2, 1981, and Price Waterhouse was fired soon after.[12]

Price Waterhouse stood behind its team of partners, including one who was a partner in charge of the firm's Tucson office, a position he was allowed to retain. In 1992, a federal judge dismissed the SEC lawsuit, saying the SEC had not provided proof that the three had not acted unprofessionally in any way in their approval of AM's 1980 financial statements.[13]

Another Price Waterhouse client in the early 1980s also caused a furor. Advertising agency J. Walter Thompson shocked the advertising world when it announced a $24.5 million restatement in 1981 when it was found out that an executive was falsifying client billings to prop up a failing division. The firm said it was the victim of an elaborate cover-up, involving schemes carried out by trusted J. Walter Thompson employees (including a department head) to sabotage the system of internal accounting controls.

Shareholders started to ask, "Can a J. Walter Thompson happen at a company I invest in?" Much to their discomfort, the global accounting firms starting hearing these questions at client visits, client shareholder meetings, and board of directors meetings. People asked them all the time: "How are you going to stop fraud at my company?" Price Waterhouse responded by issuing an Executive Letter every year that went over the firm's, as well as the entire industry's, most embarrassing cases and what to say about them when asked at a shareholder meeting.[14] The annual memo included this tip, applicable when caught by surprise: "Ask the questioner what specific part of the case they are asking about, as that will ensure that everyone is talking about the same thing. Also, it will give you more time to formulate an answer."

Marc Cheffers is a former Price Waterhouse manager who surely must be doing one of the most useful services for the profession: He runs a web site, accountingmalpractice.com, for CPAs on how to conduct themselves to avoid getting sued. "The gun has always been pointed at accountants," Cheffers said. "You can look at it two ways. You can say it's unfair, or you can be extra careful."

Joshua Ronen, accounting professor at NYU's Stern School of Business, said that 1980s litigation led to a reluctance on the part of auditors in the 1990s to offer investors a full look at financial statements. "Unfortunately, auditors cannot provide full disclosure because they are afraid of legal liability," said Ronen. "They are really in a bind. They've been hiding behind the rules, saying, 'We're conforming to GAAP.' Accountants lobbied for more rules because it gave the 'bright line' defense in court. But the rules are such that you adhere to measurements that you can defend."

Unfortunately for auditors, conforming to GAAP wasn't enough to keep them out of the firing line during the other S&L crises. "Conforming with GAAP doesn't exonerate you from responsibility," said Ronen. "It is possible to mislead with the financial statements even if you conform to GAAP. On the other hand, you would certainly be liable if you didn't conform to GAAP." One way the firms said they were being careful was through their peer review process. Peer reviews, however, were conducted just once every three years and were not broad enough in scope to point out flaws in the big firms' processes.

MERGER MADNESS

The eight global firms that had emerged in the 1970s and kept their market share in the 1980s were competing so hard in the 1980s that everyone was looking for an edge. With their rosters of Fortune 500 clients getting more and more global, several firms decided to act to build their worldwide breadth and, hopefully, gain market share. In early 1987, Peat Marwick and KMG Main Hurdman merged to form the largest firm in the world, KPMG Peat Marwick. In 1989, Ernst & Whinney merged with Arthur Young to form Ernst & Young, and Touche Ross merged with Deloitte, Haskins & Sells to form Deloitte & Touche.

Arthur Andersen took a different tack toward global expansion when it set up a *société coopérative*, Andersen Worldwide SC, in 1989. A société coopérative is a uniquely Swiss corporate structure, sort of an international holding company to unite member organizations. Andersen Worldwide SC became the umbrella organization that linked Andersen's global network of firms. In its marketing pitches to win new business during the 1980s and 1990s, Andersen touted itself as the only truly global firm. In 1989, when Arthur Andersen structured its consulting group as Andersen Consulting, it became a separate entity within the société coopérative. One of the attorneys who negotiated the split between Arthur Andersen and Andersen Consulting was none other than Harvey Pitt. While the legal split wouldn't come for more than 10 years, with Andersen Consulting recast as Accenture, the problems began to accelerate for the auditing firm with that 1989 split.

With the mergers that brought the eight global firms to six global firms and the enmity between the consultants and the auditors at Arthur Andersen, 1989 marked one of the most publicly tumultuous years the accounting profession had ever seen. A publication titled *Big Eight Valuation by Fortune 1000 Executives 1990* said, the "Depression-wracked 1930s was the most traumatic decade, but the 1980s were not far behind." According to the publication, their research showed that clients didn't like the mergers, hated seeing stories about the failed S&Ls and the accountants' involvement in them, and were angry at the advent of marketing.[15] In short, Fortune 1000 CFOs were disgruntled with accountants.

MEANWHILE, BACK AT THE AUDIT

A curious transformation took place in audit services in the early 1990s. Consulting, as can be seen from the statistics and the firm's business plans, was firmly in place as the business model. The audit was certainly reduced to a commodity, but it still had some uses, one of which was to ingratiate accounting firms with the management team. In an ingenious move on the part of the accounting profession, the audit was resurrected as an informational tool for the client, thus enabling audit teams to burnish their standing as "trusted advisers" to company management.

In April 1993, Price Waterhouse was unveiling its "audit of the future" at client AlliedSignal. The firm presented AlliedSignal with findings and recommendations developed during pilot testing of the "Audit of the Future" project at its Safety Restraint Systems Division. Here is the text from Price Waterhouse's New York office newsletter (the managers referred to in the first sentence are Price Waterhouse auditors):

> [Our] managers took on the challenging assignment with tremendous enthusiasm. Their observations and recommendations went far beyond management's expectations. The results of their work resulted in immediate direct savings for AlliedSignal and will enhance the company's competitive position going forward. Their work led directly to an additional consulting project in another automotive sector division and has enhanced and deepened our relationship throughout the organization. In addition, we have been asked to expand this approach within AlliedSignal as well as to assist in training the internal audit department in the process.[16]

UNACCOUNTABLE

While the closeness with the management team that this language implies appears to stretch the imagination that Price Waterhouse could provide an "independent" audit of AlliedSignal, one audit partner at a global firm believes that firms should not be criticized for building a strong relationship with management. "Those are the people we have daily contact with, and if you don't communicate well with them and work well together, we'd have more Enrons," this partner said. "A good auditor knows what the job is, and you have to be pretty dishonest to violate those concepts. I have never had a situation when a client said, 'Report it this way, or we'll go to another firm.' Anyway, it can't be worth the risk to make money for the firm by signing a bad audit. I don't think firms are rewarding partners equivalent to the risk of doing that."

Still, Price Waterhouse's AlliedSignal audit suggests that auditors in the 1990s altered the audit to be sufficiently agreeable to corporate management. In Price Waterhouse's "traditional" audit, according to the example, the auditors:

Understand and analyze the business through financial statement analysis, utilize staff accountants to perform a majority of the detailed audit work, and develop management recommendations centered on administrative efficiency and internal accounting controls. In the audit of the future, auditors obtain a better understanding of overall business processes, operations, and strategies of the company, which will in turn increase our level of audit satisfaction, increase the efficiency and speed of the audit process through the use of industry and functional specialists, and develop recommendations which will provide payback to the company as well as comments on internal accounting control.[17]

This language about the audit of the future was typical of global-firm propaganda in the 1990s intended to at once aggrandize the role of auditing and eliminate the rationale for auditors to spend long hours immersed in the nitty-gritty of a company's accounting systems. After all, what company wouldn't want business "recommendations" in lieu of nettlesome questions about off-balance-sheet debt?

This repackaging of the audit in the 1990s to make it an information-gathering tool to benefit the client resulted from the price wars in the 1970s and 1980s. By focusing on a company's business processes and not detailed sampling, an audit could be done in fewer hours for the same fee. Most companies don't look that hard at the hours the auditors put in; they look at the fee. "Eventually prices got so low that the firms couldn't compete on price anymore; so firms had to compete in being more flexible in accounting treatments and compete by building into the audit approach things the client would see as a service," said Douglas Carmichael, accounting professor at Baruch College in New York City. Other features of 1990s auditing included the value-added "scorecard," where an accounting firm would provide a list of all the value the audit brings to the business besides the financial statement examination. "The audit team never had contact with investors," Carmichael said. "There was nothing in their training and experience that would make them think that part of their role was to help the investor. The risk-based audit just made them focus more on what the client wanted."

Some of the things about the new risk-based audits, according to Carmichael, were good for auditing. "Going out and talking to the client's operational people to understand their business, that could be very helpful in doing a good audit. The question, though, was how was the information being used—to do a good audit or to help the management team."

A STUDY OF FRAUD

In 1997, 10 years after a landmark study by the Treadway Commission on corporate-reporting fraud, the group that sponsored the Treadway Commission decided to launch another study that would break down the corporate fraud cases brought by the SEC between 1987 and 1997. In some cases, the results were surprising. For example, the companies committing fraud generally were very small, with approximately $15 million in assets. Perhaps the most striking statistic was that in just 45 percent of the cases, the auditor qualified the company's audit report in some respect in the year before the alleged fraud came to light. Reasons cited by the auditors for the qualifications included such concerns as whether the company would remain in business, litigation the company was facing, and dubious accounting principles (although just 3 percent of the audit reports were qualified because of a departure from GAAP).

In 72 percent of the cases, the CEO was implicated; and in 29 percent of the cases, the outside auditors were implicated. Most of the auditors named in the cases (46 out of 56) were non–Big Eight/ Six auditors.[18] Although this report has occasionally been used to support the industry's contentions that the global firms were not doing bad audit work in the late 1980s and early 1990s, one of the authors of the report believes the report impugns the big firms. "For one thing, there is no question that the SEC has limited resources," Dana Hermanson said. "There are many cases that never make it to the enforcement stage. Also, when there is massive fraud at a big company, it's catastrophic. It doesn't take many disasters to shake investor confidence."

Much of the fraud during the period came, as Hermanson said, in an effort to "preserve upward trends. The greatest incentive for fraud may be when the economy has been outstanding and times are starting to turn. When the stock price is growing, people seem to want it to keep growing and not let the party end."

NOT YOUR FATHER'S ACCOUNTING FIRM

By 1992, nonauditing work brought in the majority of revenues for the Big Six for the first time—$6.2 billion out of $11.5 billion.[19] In many small ways, from slowing recruiting of auditors to reorganizing their firms along industry, not functional, lines, the firms were slowly distancing themselves from audit work. Now, the consultants were fighting for control of the firms.

At KPMG, that meant recasting the staff. The accountants weren't going to be classified as auditors, tax professionals, or consultants anymore; they were going to be identified by their industry focus. A partner would be a manufacturing services partner if he served Pepsi or a financial services partner if she served Citibank. "I remember at one point at Peat, there were all these battles about whether we were going to be defined as functional professionals—audit and tax professionals—or by lines of business," said Todd Walker, the former KPMG senior manager. "Eventually, we had this dual reporting structure, with line-of-business heads and heads of each office. I remember thinking, 'Who's the boss around here?' And I think that was a function of the audit losing its status and auditors starting to lose their power at the firm."

Lynn Turner had left Coopers in 1989 for a two-year stint as an SEC fellow under Commissioner Richard Breeden. In 1991 he went back to Coopers, and after just those two short years, he was stunned at what he saw. "The firm had totally changed," Turner said. "We had an Atlanta consulting firm, a marketing firm, and an HR consulting practice in Chicago. I was walking around saying, 'I think we ought to have mandatory rotation.' Saying things like that got me in trouble."

Turner found himself on the outside looking in on some dubious practices. "We had partners at Coopers that just could not say no. There was one manager who never said no. I remember voting against him for partner, but of course he still became a partner."

The consulting culture—urging its practitioners to sell, sell, sell—had become legitimized due to its importance to the firms' growth. Subsequently, the consulting partners started to wield power in the organizations. "The people who became the head of these firms were the ones who were really pro-growth, pro-consulting," Turner said. "You could see it happening; the whole culture of the firms [was] changing."

One thing that should not be overlooked is that the consulting practices that Turner refers to were filling a market need. Increasingly, companies were faced with technology challenges, global competition, and the pressure to hit quarterly expectations. And nobody knew them better than their auditors did.

Former Price Waterhouse CEO Shaun O'Malley, who led Price Waterhouse through 1991, agreed that in the 1990s salesmanship became one of the core attributes for getting a leadership position. "More and more, you had people coming into the profession, aspiring to get to the top of the firm, and knowing that growing the practice was a good demonstration of your capabilities," O'Malley said. "It used to be that far and away, technical expertise was the most important facet. Over time, practice development (selling) came to have greater importance.

"The CFOs were telling us in the late 1970s and 1980s, 'You guys are sort of a luxury. You just give us this opinion, and we need more. You're not telling us anything about our business,'" O'Malley said. "They needed help, and a lot of times they didn't know where to turn. And lots of auditors found the opportunities interesting, the chance to be more of a problem solver, to bring in some people who could solve the problem, and not just be a 'techer and checker.'"

Several years after he retired, O'Malley led a commission called the Panel on Audit Effectiveness. Among other things, O'Malley's team examined the correspondence from the leaders of the big firms in the mid-1990s to their employees. What they saw was too little emphasis on the audit. Another manifestation of the firms' swerve away from audit services was their aggressive revenue-building tax products. The goal of these products was to help a company get its effective tax rate down and then take a percentage of the savings. There is no law against advocating for a client's aggressive tax position. But as firms made more nonaudit revenue from audit clients, including millions on a single tax project, they opened themselves up to further curbs on their activities. In a way, any business that seeks to add new products runs the risk of losing sight of its core activities. So, in a sense, the accounting profession made an understandable mistake in abandoning the audit. But bad audits have a bigger downside than a lot of products do—business failures and lawsuits.

THE ABANDONED AUDIT

To Joshua Ronen, auditors also abandoned the audit during this period because financial statements during the late 1980s and 1990s became much less auditable. "The FASB [Financial Accounting Standards Board] has been one of the main culprits because it allowed so many intangibles to creep into the statements," Ronen said. "Cash, accounts receivables are verifiable. Cash flow from future projects is nonverifiable and nonauditable. A major portion of financial statements became unauditable."

Will Shafer, an accounting professor at Pepperdine University who worked at small firms in Houston in the 1980s and 1990s, believed "the big firms became known for very bad quality work" in Houston during this time. Shafer said that the big firms during the 1980s and 1990s played off their brands, even while reducing the quality of work. "It's the big firms that have destroyed the reputation of their own firms. They got too big and started behaving like a commercial corporation. The constant push for new lines of business, diversifying products, more and more consulting, you can draw a parallel between the big accounting firms and a commercial corporation."

KPMG CREATES AN INVESTMENT BANK

Given the emerging dominance of consulting, it seemed in the spirit of the times when KPMG decided to create an investment-banking affiliate, Baymark Capital, in 1995. After all, KPMG and the other global firms already were advising on hundreds of mergers-and-acquisitions (M&A) deals every year. KPMG, in fact, often claimed to be the leader in providing M&A services in the United States when measured by numbers of deals, which is a little like someone claiming to be the greatest artist in the world by the number of paintings completed. The total value of KPMG's deals was far less than what big investment banks like Goldman Sachs and Merrill Lynch earned every year brokering their megadeals.

Still, KPMG and the other big accounting firms had made real headway in providing M&A consulting. The problem for KPMG and other accounting firms was that as accounting firms, their investment banking fees had to be on a flat or hourly fee basis, not on a contingency fee basis. All they needed was the right structure, and they could underwrite deals and make the big killings.

The plan was that Baymark Capital would be a separate but affiliated investment bank, a place where KPMG could send clients who wanted underwriting help on a deal. According to a consultant who was involved in the dissolution of Baymark and who did not want to be identified, when the investment bank was first started and the SEC did not immediately halt the deal, KPMG thought they "had built a better mousetrap."

"Basically, the idea was that Baymark was going to charge big investment-banking fees and contract KPMG people out at lower rates," the consultant said. "Lawyers and bankers and people from Wall Street in 1998 and 1999 were making multiples of what the accounting partners were making; and when you met with these people, it was clear that they were looking for Wall Street salaries."

But the SEC, which had been tentatively eyeing the deal ever since KPMG announced it, charged KPMG in 1997 with independence violations relating to Baymark and a KPMG audit client that was also a client of Baymark. KPMG loaned $100,000 to a Baymark executive who later was hired by the KPMG audit client to turn the company around.

The charges brought KPMG to the negotiating table with the SEC to try to figure out a way to save Baymark. "KPMG tried to find a way to make it allowable," the consultant said. "Charge people at a fixed hourly rate, whatever. They had access to all these audit clients, a vast middle market that would potentially need help in M&A deals. I think they wanted to be on the map with the first real investment bank at an accounting firm."

One problem that may have caused the Baymark incident, according to this anonymous consultant, was that some of the Baymark executives involved "were not exactly the best guys. They had some former Drexel guys doing it. They could have hired a very high class group of people; you would have thought they wanted to go that way."

Another odd aspect about KPMG's relationship with Baymark was that even had KPMG never run into the problems, no one was ever clear how KPMG actually planned to make money from Baymark. KPMG, when it announced the deal, said it did not own any of Baymark, would not collect fees for referrals to it or share in Baymark's revenue.[20] "One of the issues that KPMG had that fall of 1995, when they started Baymark, was they were trying to figure out how they would collect the fees," said the consultant. "When the fee went into Baymark, how were they going to get it out?" As it turned out, KPMG never really had to figure that out.

The consultant was hired to try to wring some value out of the firm by trying to sell it to some medium-sized investment banks. There were no takers; and Baymark, dissolved in 1996, exists only in the continuing SEC case against KPMG. In May 2002, the U.S. Court of Appeals for the District of Columbia supported the SEC's contention that KPMG had violated independence rules.[21]

Cautionary reports about the state of the industry began to surface in the early 1990s. One of these was the 1993 Kirk Report, which came out of a commission led by former FASB chairman Don Kirk. The report emphasized that a company's audit committee should grill the auditors about the quality of the accounting standards, not just their acceptability. "It's now embedded in the professional standards, but very little was expected from the audit committee back then," Kirk said.

SECURITIES REFORM BILL STOPS THE LEAKING

The last real deterrent to rubber stamping the audit fell in late 1995 with the passage of the Private Securities Litigation Act. The bill, designed to thwart frivolous class action lawsuits against public companies, law firms, and accounting firms, would place a time limit for bringing securities suits and would force plaintiffs to prove that company executives *intended* to mislead investors when making their forecasts for future earnings. Best of all for the accounting industry, the law would exempt accounting firms and other "aiders" and "abetters" from being sued in a private, class action suit. Litigation against an accounting firm would now have to be brought by the SEC.

The six global firms heavily supported the bill, with Mike Cook and Jon Madonna, among others, helping to frame the debate. Opponents of the bill, including many longtime critics of the accounting industry, said that there was no great proliferation of class action lawsuits and that the bill would make it much more difficult for investors to sue for stock fraud and shoddy auditing. As in so many of the debates that involve public companies and audits, the statistical evidence was used by both sides to back up their respective arguments. Opponents of the bill showed that the number of suits amounted to less than 1 percent of SEC-registered companies, meaning that there existed no flood of frivolous suits. Proponents pointed out that class action legal claims averaged 295 from 1990 to 1993, up from an average of 110 in the four years before that. The Senate passed the bill by a 69-to-30 vote and then overrode President Clinton's veto.

Now, with private litigation seemingly taken care of, it seemed that nothing could stop the firms in their push for annual double-digit growth. But, even as 1995 was ending, Arthur Levitt, head of the SEC, was looking more closely at the consulting services that had been the salvation of the global firms.

CHAPTER 7

THE FIGHT OF HIS LIFE

TOWARD THE END OF HIS TENURE AS HEAD OF THE SEC, ARTHUR Levitt dreaded airports. It wasn't the actual travel that was getting to him, although Levitt certainly logged plenty of miles spreading the word about the need for protecting individual investors. Rather, it was the trip through the terminal that Levitt loathed, the treacherous few hundred yards where Levitt would see the slick, hyperbolic advertisements from the global accounting firms with such slogans as, "There isn't a business we can't improve" and "It's time for clarity." The text of the ads, of course, never said anything about auditing.

"It would bug me walking through the airport to see the accounting firms advertising all these nonaudit services," Levitt said in an interview. "You don't see those signs anymore, not today. Now I know at least one thing: If anything in this fight was worth it, at least we got the damn airports cleaned up."

Making airports safe from Big Five advertising campaigns was not exactly Levitt's goal, however, during his last two years as SEC commissioner. Levitt spent 1999 and 2000 doing "armed battle" with the accounting establishment over auditor independence, an epic struggle that has now passed into U.S. regulatory lore, like Reagan versus the air traffic controllers or Kennedy versus the big steel companies.

The difference, of course, is that Levitt was not the president but the head of a smallish government agency that depended on an often unimpressed Congress for its funding. As Levitt now says: "We basically had a hostile, deregulatory Congress the whole time we were there, and we had the most proactive agenda of any commission in history."

THE MAKING OF AN ACTIVIST

Appointed by President Bill Clinton in July 1993, Levitt spent nearly eight years as head of the SEC, the longest tenure of a commissioner in the history of the agency. His style contained elements of Clinton's, in that Levitt was not averse to pursuing incremental advances and small victories: He improved broker sales and pay practices; introduced the concept of using plain English in prospectuses and other investment literature; enticed major foreign companies to list on U.S. exchanges; established an office of investor education and assistance; and made available to the public, at no cost, all SEC press releases, corporate filings, and hearings via the commission's web site.

But Levitt also pursued bigger fish, like the accounting industry. Levitt's battle with the firms centered specifically on his proposal to ban accounting firms from providing most consulting services to their audit clients. By the time he retired from the SEC on February 9, 2001, Levitt was much praised for his efforts in that arena, but his track record was mixed. Levitt didn't get all the concessions he wanted from the accounting industry. In fact, he didn't get most of them. But Levitt's legacy changed forever just nine months after he left the SEC, when Enron imploded. The energy trading company's 2001 annual report showed that in 2000 Enron paid Andersen $27 million in consulting fees and $25 million in audit fees.[1] The astounding degree to which Andersen's financial interests were intertwined with Enron's became clear only because Levitt's SEC passed a rule in November 2000 mandating disclosure of both nonaudit and audit fees in the annual report. The consulting fees that Andersen earned—printed in Enron's annual report for all to see—and possibly galvanized the Congressional hearings that first put Andersen CEO Joseph Berardino and his firm on the hot seat.

The Enron/Andersen debacle prompted some of Levitt's biggest critics from the previous year's battle to cry out: "Where were the auditors?" In fact, many of those same people, well-known members of Congress included, tried to intimidate and bully Levitt into dropping his proposed independence rules. Jon Madonna, a former chairman of KPMG, never agreed with Levitt's characterization of consulting and its potential to adversely affect the audit. But Madonna, who serves with Levitt on the board of directors of the mutual fund company Neuberger Berman, said, "It's hard to see Arthur these days. Whenever we talk about this, I have to say, 'Yes, Arthur, you were right and we were wrong. Can we change the subject now?'"

Levitt didn't oppose accounting firms with all of his actions as commissioner, however. Occasionally, his stances and the accounting profession's interests coincided. For example, Levitt supported passage of both the 1995 Private Securities Litigation Reform Act and the 1998 Securities Litigation Uniform Standards Act, bills designed to reduce the number of frivolous class action lawsuits brought against Corporate America. The accounting lobby strongly supported these bills, which it correctly anticipated would lessen accounting firms' liability for poor audit work. In fact, opponents of Levitt during his battles with the accounting profession might be surprised by some of the stances Levitt took earlier in his career, particularly during his first stint as a regulator, as head of the American Stock Exchange (AMEX).

Levitt was born and raised in Brooklyn, New York, where his mother was a public schoolteacher. His father was the New York State comptroller for more than 20 years. After graduating Phi Beta Kappa from Williams College in 1952 (without ever taking a single economics course, incidentally) and serving in the air force for two years, Levitt worked as a small-town newspaper reporter in Massachusetts. Then, he spent five years in the ranching and cattle business before joining a tiny Wall Street brokerage called Carter Berlind & Weill. Soon, the firm was called Carter, Berlind, Weill & Levitt (or "corned beef with lettuce," as some detractors referred to the upstarts),[2] and Levitt proceeded to spend the next 16 years working side-by-side with future Citigroup chairman Sandy Weill.

"I think the experience I had working with retail customers, the method of doing business on Wall Street, highlighted the awareness of conflicts for me," Levitt said in an interview. "Also, I saw my mother's concern with her pension as a retired city school teacher. It just gave me a sense for individuals and the fact that people weren't really looking out for them."

Levitt's innate activism manifested itself in early attempts to fight for the "little guy." In his speeches and public statements as president of the brokerage firm (Weill was chairman), Levitt fretted over unscrupulous brokers and started advocating a rigorous certification process for professional brokers. In a speech he titled "Profits and Professionalism" before MBA students at Columbia Business School (a speech that Weill ridiculed, incidentally[3]), Levitt criticized the brokerage profession for its lax training, saying, "It makes for an interesting comparison that doctor, lawyers, and accountants are granted licenses to practice only after years of formal education, training, and apprenticeship, while registered representatives in the securities industry become full-fledged brokers after six months of training that is often perfunctory."[4]

Along with Weill, Levitt built a firm that made its fortune providing retail investment services to individual investors. Early members of the firm, including Arthur Carter and Marshall Cogan, wanted to turn Carter Berlind & Weill into an investment bank, but Weill and Levitt wanted to keep the firm a retail shop. Their unlikely alliance—Weill was, and still is, as narrowly focused as Levitt is interested in the wider world—at the brokerage firm lasted until 1978, when Levitt was recruited to lead the AMEX.

Levitt's empathy for the small investor only increased at the AMEX. The small and midsized companies that dominated the AMEX needed all the promotion they could get, as did the exchange itself, which was dwarfed in resources and prestige by its downtown New York neighbor, the New York Stock Exchange (NYSE). After taking the helm at the AMEX, Levitt's first priority was giving voice to the concerns of the 1,000-plus small and midsized companies that populated it. In a speech to a group of personal financial planners on May 22, 1978, Levitt presented a point of view that became his defining worldview two decades later as head of the SEC: "I am passionate about the subject of the individual investor. Unfortunately, the individual investor has been taken too much for granted in recent years. But now the small investor is surfacing again as the most important—if not the most essential—customer for brokers, bankers, advisers, and exchanges."[5]

Oddly enough, the future defender of the individual investor was no fan of government regulation at this point. In fact, Levitt's zeal for the small company led him to take a few positions that seemed at odds with his later persona as a reformer. For example, in a January 17, 1979, speech to the Securities Regulation Institute, Levitt expressed concerns about the SEC requiring the formation of audit committees for companies that wanted to be listed on stock exchanges.

> Take the question of audit committees. The SEC has been insisting for some time that the exchanges make the existence of an audit committee, consisting entirely of outside directors, be a requirement for a company's listing. The other exchange has incorporated such a requirement. While I agree in principle that audit committees are useful—I formed such a committee for the AMEX itself last year—such a requirement can work a distinct hardship on the smaller companies listed with us.[6]

Levitt, however, said that he always understood the important gatekeeper role that an audit committee played. "In my early years at the AMEX, we were conducting a life-and-death struggle with the New York Stock Exchange. I was looking for every advantage I could find. A lot of these companies were beset with regulatory challenges, and I wanted to help them to respond to some of these."

It is interesting that one of Levitt's allies in those days was the accounting profession, which in its quest for more profit centers had found a market for consulting services at small and midsized companies. In a speech to an organization called the Citizen's Union on April 17, 1979, Levitt praised Peat Marwick (later his biggest critic of all the global accounting firms) as an "incubator for small business":

> [Peat Marwick] has also worked long and vigorously to set up a Small Business Advisory Service to concentrate on smaller firms. Within a year it had more than 800 professionals help 1,100 new clients to grow and develop. It continues to expand this effort, bringing these fledgling corporations the same resources and skills enjoyed by giants. Like Peat Marwick, the AMEX sees itself not merely as an accommodation for small business, but as an incubator for growing ones.[7]

Levitt took these positions because he viewed himself primarily as an advocate for the small companies that would be hard-pressed to comply with burdensome regulation. Indeed, these examples suggest a core modus operandi for Levitt: His activism is nearly always channeled toward fighting for the underdog. Viewed in this context, it's easy to reconcile Levitt, the fighter for small companies, with Levitt, the regulator. At the AMEX, the underdog was the small company trying to thrive under an avalanche of regulation. At the SEC, the underdog was the individual investor trying to get a fair shake on Wall Street.

ACCOUNTING 101 FOR LEVITT

Only one group of individuals has the right—and, indeed, the legal obligation—to delve deep into a company and to extract raw, unvarnished information: CPAs. It wasn't long after he was sworn in as SEC chief in 1993 that Levitt began to suspect that auditors weren't so much critically examining this raw data as much as parlaying it into lucrative consulting contracts. Although he had never necessarily viewed the accounting profession as one he would eventually have to take on, Levitt wasn't going to let any one group stand in the way of what he wanted to accomplish at the SEC. "Every SEC chairman establishes their own agenda," Levitt said. "My goal was to create the most investor-friendly commission in history, to provide the transparency and fairness in the markets. I did not think accounting would be my legacy."

Knowing he had to confront the global firms that audited almost every Fortune 500 corporation, Levitt, famous for his affability even with avowed enemies, tried Plan A: to engage, charm, and evaluate. Plan A, however, did not fare well, as Levitt's efforts to create a dialogue with the leaders of the firms and Barry Melancon, head of the American Institute of Certified Public Accountants (AICPA), fell flat. "During my first years at the commission, I tried to develop a rational agenda with the firms, but their leadership was so inept," Levitt said. "Their inability to agree among themselves to just about anything—and if you could sit in a room with them, you'd see that—made accomplishing anything just impossible. They'd say they want to help, and then when I called on them, they were not there. The trade association, so poorly led, so archaic in its cheerleader approach to the profession, had no concern about, or notion of, the profession's public interest responsibility."

Lynn Turner, in addition to being Levitt's chief accountant at the SEC, was his point man for the confrontation with the accounting industry. Turner, a former partner at Coopers & Lybrand, is today a business professor at Colorado State University. He believes that partners at the global accounting firms—including most of the individuals with whom he and Levitt negotiated—misplaced their priorities in the 1990s. "These guys want the government franchise that requires everyone to go to them for audits, but they don't want the responsibility that goes with it," Turner said. "They want to treat it like a business. They have to decide whether they want to be businesspeople or people with a responsibility to the public."

While still early in his first term, Levitt started to hear about what he called "corporate numbers" games. For example, companies would place ordinary expenses into the category of one-time or nonrecurring costs (WorldCom would play a similar game when it treated expenses as capital expenditures under Andersen's watch).[8] As time went on, Levitt and Turner started to see more and more companies restate their earnings. From 1997 through 2000, 700 companies were forced to restate earnings due to misrepresentations in their financial statements. In 1981, by contrast, only three companies needed to restate earnings.[9] It had also become apparent that many companies, with the blessing of their auditors, were just managing to meet their quarterly projections, time and time again. In fact, between 1992 and 1999, the number of companies that beat quarterly earnings projections by one penny quadrupled. And while companies did not have to disclose audit or consulting fees, it was becoming obvious that the global firms, in particular, were focused throughout the 1990s not on balance sheets but on growing their high-flying consulting practices. The profession's inattention to auditing during this period is startling when looked at from a statistical perspective: Audit fees made up 70 percent of accounting firm revenues in 1976 but only 31 percent in 1998. To Levitt, the bottom line was that the global accounting firms, and the AICPA along with them, had for all intents and purposes absolved themselves from acting as independent watchdogs of their clients and were also overlooking evidence of fraud in Corporate America.

"Accounting fraud has always been of interest to regulators," Levitt said. "And it really escalated in my days at the SEC. Very often, there are many subjective judgment calls in the course of the audit. [Whereas] in the past, those calls have generally been made with an interest to the well-being of the shareholder, now, these things started to go to the interests of management."

Though it went largely unnoticed due to the rampaging bull market, Levitt and chief accountant Turner were essentially seeing the fruits of 20 years of audit neglect by the accounting profession. Each of the global firms had experienced the same evolution from professional accounting firm to multiservice conglomerate. "The true sign of a professional accountant is someone who can put the public first, regardless of the economic consequences," Turner said. "Certain members of the accounting profession lost that ability."

Dana Hermanson, an accounting professor at Atlanta's Kennesaw State University and director of research at their corporate governance center, said that client service, not public service, was the theme of his years at Ernst & Ernst. "We were taught from day one that we weren't really auditors," said Hermanson, who started with Ernst & Ernst in 1986 and left three years later to enter academia. "You were a business adviser to the client. Certainly, you were supposed to get the financials right. But it was clear that your job was to add value to management." Hermanson's generation of entry-level auditors in the mid-1980s are today's young, up-and-coming partners at the global firms. These auditors have grown up lowballing the audit, emphasizing sales or marketing skills, and, generally, identifying themselves as anything but auditors.

Recognizing these developments, Levitt became more confrontational toward the profession in the mid-1990s. If leaders of the accounting profession had been paying attention, they would have known long ago that Levitt was eventually going to offer tough new independence rules. Often, these clues were given to the accountants themselves. In a speech to the AICPA on December 10, 1996, Levitt said:

> The accounting agenda for the millennium is no different from the accounting agenda of 1934, or 1996, or any other year: to act as an independent check on the natural inclination of companies and governments to show themselves in the best possible light. I'm not just talking about auditors. All accountants are professionally bound to splash a bucket of cold water on overly exuberant ideas about performance. Your work provides a reality check—in many cases, the only reality check—before important economic and investment decisions are made.[10]

That speech was important because it struck a blow at the profession's argument that, because certifying financial statements is a service that only a minority of CPAs perform, the independence rules that apply to auditing public companies are not relevant for most accountants. Levitt destroyed this line of reasoning by saying that accountants—all accountants—are supposed to act as a check on the greedy, self-serving impulses that strike human beings now and then. You are not supposed to be enjoying the party, Levitt was essentially telling the group of accountants; you are supposed to be monitoring the party.

Whereas early in his first term he would couch his criticisms with niceties such as "this most noble of professions" or "the profession has done 60 years of great work," Levitt instead aggressively developed his theme that auditors at accounting firms were almost as responsible for faulty corporate reporting as the companies themselves were. In his well-known "Numbers Game" speech at the NYU Center for Law and Business in 1998, he said: "As I look at some of the failures today, I can't help but wonder if the staff in the trenches of the profession have the training and supervision they need to ensure that audits are being done right. We cannot permit thorough audits to be sacrificed for reengineered approaches that are efficient, but less effective."[11]

PRICEWATERHOUSECOOPERS VIOLATIONS CHANGE THE CLIMATE

In the winter of 1997, a fired staffer from Price Waterhouse called the SEC and said that the Tampa office was in egregious violation of independence rules prohibiting ownership of a client's stock. Ultimately, the newly formed firm PricewaterhouseCoopers (from the merger of Price Waterhouse and Coopers & Lybrand) admitted committing more than 8,000 independence violations. The SEC could have refused to recognize certification of audit papers handled by PricewaterhouseCoopers, something it hadn't done with a firm since Peat Marwick was sanctioned in the early 1970s. The PricewaterhouseCoopers (PwC) revelation was a signpost to the SEC that pervasive independence violations persisted even after Levitt had repeatedly raised the issue. In addition, Levitt finally had some leverage over the profession—especially over PwC, the world's largest firm.

Despite the PricewaterhouseCoopers violations and other damning information coming in to the SEC, it was difficult for Levitt to pursue sanctions against the firms on an individual basis because it was difficult to link lack of independence with audit failure. "During my years at the commission, we saw a great many auditor fraud cases," Levitt said. "It was such a slow, gradual thing, and I'm not sure when it became the case that I really thought we'd have a war with the accounting profession. They were difficult cases to bring, because the law was really not broad enough."

Part of the difficulty in bringing cases against the firms through-out Levitt's tenure was that some of the SEC's weapons had recently been stripped away. Levitt points to a Supreme Court decision in 1994 that took away one of the SEC's and the plaintiff's lawyers' prime weapons against the accounting profession: the law against "aiding and abetting" securities fraud. The court decided in *Central Bank of Denver N.A. v. First Interstate Bank of Denver* (1994) to effectively elimi-nate the "aiding and abetting a securities law violation" liability. This theory of liability had been a primary weapon that plaintiff's lawyers used in litigation against accountants. "When the Supreme Court ef-fectively took away the aiding and abetting statute, that really handi-capped our ability to bring those cases," Levitt said.

The global accounting firms' peer review system also provided some defense to the firms. Each of the global firms could point to 30 years' worth of assurances that their auditing standards were high. Also, because the AICPA had no effective mechanism to punish neg-ligent auditors, even those who committed egregious independence violations were seldom sanctioned. "The SEC has constantly urged the AICPA to sanction those auditors guilty of wrongdoing, and the AICPA constantly failed to do it," Levitt said. "Then, laws were passed to mandate they punish them, and they failed to do it again."

NOT JUST INDEPENDENCE

Levitt is most associated with the issue of separating auditing and consulting. But even as auditor independence became the paramount issue in his mind, he and his staff saw other accounting problems distorting the reality of corporate performance. Levitt had to decide which problems to address immediately, which ones would best be tackled when he had roused all of his allies, and which ones would have to wait for another time and another commissioner. He had to choose wisely; one misstep and his credibility would be destroyed and any chance of reform would be lost.

"This was the least progressive, least enlightened, most hidebound industry that I'd ever dealt with," said Levitt. "As each year went on and each new effort to deal with them failed, I came to the conclusion that in my later years, rather than have an open fight, I would leave the field without addressing certain issues. I knew these fraud cases would come out, and I knew that people would look back and say, 'Why didn't we do something about it?'"

Accounting issues came to the attention of Levitt and his relatively undermanned SEC staff of attorneys and accountants from many different sources, including anonymous tips, raw data contained in corporate 10-Ks and annual reports, and the media. Levitt, though, also had another weapon at his disposal: a network of experts all over the country who, in support of his ideas for reform, would constantly bombard him with articles, speeches, research papers, and informed opinions based on their own business experience.

One of these correspondents was professor Michael Porter of Harvard Business School. In late 1998, for example, Porter wrote a letter to Levitt saying that "accounting and reporting practices are contributing to mergers being consummated that do not earn an acceptable return on investment, but which distorted scorekeeping seems to justify." Porter asserted that "deals are being done based on misleading accounting numbers rather than real economic benefits." In addition, Porter pointed out that studies routinely show that most mergers do not "recover their premiums."[12] Soon after getting this letter, the SEC started to mention pooling treatment of mergers as an issue that needed to be addressed. About this time, another accounting issue came to light via Levitt's informal network of advisers. Levitt received a letter from James E. Wheeler, a professor of accounting at the University of Michigan Business School. Wheeler pointed out a problem to Levitt that had been getting very little press: the abuses of "last in, first out" (LIFO) inventory systems.[13]

Another major issue for Levitt and Turner was mined straight out of the available data in audit reports filed with the SEC by foreign-owned companies. The mid- and late 1990s saw an increase in the number of foreign companies registering securities for sale in the United States; and Levitt and Turner felt that foreign affiliates of U.S. accounting firms were not even aware of existing AICPA auditor independence rules, much less enforcing them. In fact, as early as August 1993, Levitt warned that he would not buckle to New York Stock Exchange lobbying for a relaxation of accounting standards for foreign companies wanting to list on the exchange.

The evolving structure of accounting firms was another important issue that Levitt wanted to address. One alternative structure became evident in the 1990s: A public company acquired an accounting firm, integrated the firm's staff into the parent entity, and then conducted audits through leasing of those employees back to the shell organization that still remained. The New York City firm Goldstein Golub Kessler entered into an "alternative practice structure," as they called it, with American Express Tax and Business Services in 1997. The arrangement meant that the employees of the accounting firm had become employees of American Express as well. Another example is McGladrey & Pullen, the eighth-largest firm in the country when it entered into an alternative practice structure with H&R Block in 1999. Accounting firms find these arrangements attractive because, among other things, the parent company has plenty of capital available for the firm, and the firm can offer corporate-style benefits packages. The companies find it attractive because they can add accounting services to the laundry list of financial services they already perform for clients. Levitt's SEC felt that an accounting firm owned by a public company ceased to be independent.

Levitt also wanted to pursue the issue of audit committees' independence. In 1998, Levitt created the Blue Ribbon Committee on Improving Corporate Audit Committees, chaired by former Goldman Sachs senior partner John C. Whitehead and Ira Millstein, a senior partner in the law firm Weil Gotshal & Manges. This was an enormously effective move on Levitt's part because this committee provided him with a ready-made group of allies for his upcoming battle with the profession. Many of the panel members came out strong for Levitt's position two years later.

The Blue Ribbon Committee also provided the SEC with recommendations on which to act, and gave Levitt at least some political cover: The new rules were based on recommendations from another independent body. The committee determined that "common sense dictates that a director without any financial, family, or other material personal ties to management is more likely to be able to evaluate objectively the propriety of management's accounting, internal control, and reporting practices."[14]

The Blue Ribbon Committee also recommended that the SEC require all reporting companies to include a letter in their annual report stating that the audit committee, relying on its review and discussion conducted with management and the outside auditors, believes that the company's financial statements are fairly presented in conformity with generally accepted accounting principles (GAAP). Through the Blue Ribbon Committee, Levitt became so strongly associated with the subject of audit committees that after a May 1999 speech Levitt made on the subject, James Taranto, the then-deputy editorial features editor at the *Wall Street Journal*, jotted down this humorous poem and sent it to Levitt:

I have a great passion
for audit committees
They're far more romantic
than bustling cities

When I sit upon them
I can't help but start
to feel something stirring
Deep down in my heart

The ecstasy builds
As I serve this board function
This ardor inspires
Not the slightest compunction

I shout from the rooftops:
"I feel such elation!"
And though some have warned me
I risk litigation

These naysayers don't
Cause me any distress
For on the committee
I found my wild cress.[15]

In December 1999, the audit committee issue came to resolution, as the SEC adopted amendments to its rules that further established the audit committee as a wedge between the auditor and management. The SEC required that audit committees disclose whether they have discussed auditor independence issues and the quality of the companies' financial statements with management and outside auditors. In a parallel move, the New York Stock Exchange and the American Stock Exchange altered their listing company requirements to make clear that audit committees must be independent from management and that the audit committee, as opposed to management, maintains the ultimate authority to hire and fire the outside auditors. Now, Levitt was ready to tackle the Holy Grail of auditor independence.

AUDITOR INDEPENDENCE

On January 14, 1999, the SEC censured PricewaterhouseCoopers for the pervasive ownership in clients that had come to light. PwC agreed to complete an internal review supervised by an independent consultant appointed by the SEC. Still, Levitt was not ready to announce any sweeping independence proposals yet. He needed more time to convince the AICPA and the global firms of the singularity of his purpose and the strength of his evidence, putting him in a better position when the inevitable negotiations began.

As was his wont, Levitt left the arm twisting to Turner, his chief accountant. Turner was by far the most aggressive member of the SEC staff when it came to confronting the global accounting firms, the pit bull behind Levitt. Levitt was not a CPA and rarely ventured into granular discussions of accounting issues. Turner was the one who wrote long memos for members of Congress and other SEC constituencies explaining the accounting issues about which the SEC was most concerned. "I would say that our efforts to educate the public and Congress about financial fraud and 'managed' numbers could never have succeeded without Lynn Turner," Levitt said. "He saw this problem, he alerted me to it, he supported me any time I wavered. He constantly pointed toward the right direction. I think the rest of the staff viewed him somewhat as a radical and that I had to keep chains on him, but that was just more a question of style than substance."

Accounting irregularities, from either the corporate management side or the accounting firm side, were constantly being pushed to the forefront of the SEC agenda by Turner. One member of Levitt's staff said, "We were all wondering why we were spending so much time on the accounting stuff." At one point, SEC lawyer Harvey Goldschmid jokingly said to Turner, "You know, Lynn, it would be nice if we had one week of calm around here. Just one week."

Turner, however, said that once the evidence started to come in like a torrent, Levitt and the SEC staff didn't need any convincing to go after the accounting profession. "Every SEC administration comes in and is pretty chummy with the accounting firms," Turner said. "And then you start seeing the cases. When we kept seeing these cases coming in—Microsoft, Sunbeam, Waste Management, Xerox—nobody needed any convincing."

In a letter to Michael Conway of the AICPA, Turner sent a message to the profession saying that the SEC was gearing up for the independence battle and that the AICPA must "reassess whether the quality controls and training programs of firms and their affiliates that practice before the SEC are adequate to ensure compliance with the independence requirements set forth in Securities Acts and the Commission's rules and regulations."

Levitt also enlisted the Independence Standards Board (ISB) in his campaign. The ISB, chaired by William Allen, had been created in 1997 as sort of a neutral zone for the AICPA and the SEC to discuss accounting issues. The ISB was made up of four individuals from the accounting profession and four from outside the profession. While Levitt thought of the ISB as glacially slow in its deliberations, the board seemed to enjoy tweaking Levitt. They would tell him how they got along famously, often saying that they had never experienced a four-to-four split of those inside the profession versus outside the profession, implying that Levitt's perspective was simplistic. Some members of the ISB strenuously objected to the manner in which Levitt later proposed his independence rules, saying that the ISB had been bypassed even though it was making great progress on this front.

"The ISB had been working on the auditor independence issue," Turner said, but the leadership wasn't strong enough. "So, just before Christmas 1999, Manley Johnson and Bob Denham, two members of the ISB, came to us and said the SEC has to take the auditor independence issue back. They said that this issue had to be decided with a broader public debate and that the ISB wasn't the forum for that. So, in January of 2000, we basically decided that we were going to go ahead, take back the issue, and propose new independence rules."

Levitt was happy to have the auditor independence issue thrown back to him because he believed that the ISB had been dragging its feet on the issue. As early as the previous January, in fact, Levitt had gotten impatient with the ISB. It was Turner who wrote a letter to ISB president Bill Allen on January 7, 1999, requesting that the ISB "place certain issues on its agenda: the form and structure of practice of independent auditors; valuation services provided by auditors; mutual fund audits and investments; legal advisory services; and executive compensation and actuarial consulting services." In addition, Turner chided Allen and the ISB for being too solicitous toward the accounting profession when he wrote, "The staff has noted that some . . . papers prepared by the ISB appear to provide an auditor's perspective on independence topics, and certainly this should be considered. However, it is ultimately the investor who relies on the report of the independent auditor and who must consider the auditor to be independent."[16]

CONGRESS AND AUDITOR INDEPENDENCE: MONEY TALKS, NOBODY WALKS

In an interview in the autumn of 2002 promoting his book, *Take on the Street,* Levitt said that many of the nation's economic problems are caused by "legislators who don't care at all about individual investors. The public has all the power to influence Congress but acts as if it's impotent."

Levitt's dim view of the average member of Congress was forged largely by two issues: (1) expensing stock options and (2) auditor independence. In 1994, when he was still feeling his way around Washington, Levitt, under enormous pressure from Senator Joseph Lieberman of Connecticut and other lawmakers, made the self-acknowledged "mistake" of advising the Financial Accounting Standards Board (FASB) to forget the idea of expensing stock options, which the standard-making body had proposed. Lieberman, Senator Barbara Boxer of California, and others believed that the ability of infant companies to grant stock options was a crucial fuel for the New Economy. Expensing them would make this fuel too costly. After seeing options and executive pay spiral out of control in the mid-1990s, Levitt vowed to himself that he wouldn't be intimidated by Congress again.

So, during the auditor independence battle, Levitt gave as good as he got. For example, on May 25, 2000, Senators Charles Schumer, Robert Bennett, and Evan Bayh of the Senate Banking Committee sent Levitt a letter with a list of 15 questions that sounded like they were dictated by the Big Five to stump Levitt (e.g., "Compromising audit quality because a firm provided nonaudit services to audit clients risks lawsuits and firm reputation. Please identify all studies or analyses undertaken by the Commission to evaluate the effectiveness of these disincentives to compromised audit quality"). Levitt assigned Turner and his staff to answer the questions. But Levitt allies like Eli Mason, a New York CPA and longtime industry reformer, heard about the congressional strong-arming. Mason, in turn, wrote a blistering letter to Schumer expressing concern that "a legislator with your reputation for fairness would participate in such an obvious effort to discourage a great public servant."[17]

Levitt also had to fight Congress over SEC funding. In 1999, when Levitt was gathering his forces for the assault on the accounting industry, House Republicans decided to hit Levitt where it hurt. The House Subcommittee on Commerce, Justice, State, and the Judiciary appropriated $324 million to fund the SEC, nearly $10 million less than the previous year and $26.8 million less than what the SEC said it needed to keep the same level of staffing. Levitt wrote in a letter to subcommittee chairman Harold Rogers, "At a time when the SEC must be more aggressive and expand its activities, a funding level of $324 million will have serious consequences for the markets and investors."

Congress didn't just stop there, however. The threats to cut off the SEC's funding hung over Levitt during his last two years in office. "There was a threat to cut off funding at the end of my stay at the Commission and also to delay this rule until my successor came in," Levitt said. "It was clear to me that what was galvanizing these public officials to act this way was political contributions from the accounting firms."

"As far as the budgetary issues, you've got to remember that for about a dozen or so years, we had virtually no increases, while the number of investors in the market has increased by 60 percent," Turner said.

Levitt's most persistent congressional opponents included Representative Billy Tauzin of Louisiana; Representative Michael Oxley of Ohio; Representative Tom Bliley, chairman of the House Commerce Committee; Senator Michael Enzi of Wyoming, the Senate's only CPA; Senator Robert Torricelli of New Jersey; Senator Wayne Allard of Colorado; and Senator Robert Bennett of Utah. These individuals could not be faulted for their enthusiasm, as they often wrote or called Levitt with their "suggestions." "They were all over me many times a day, urging me to compromise and talk with the accounting firms," Levitt said. "I'd already been talking to them for six years."

Turner believes that the SEC never had a chance of winning over many members of Congress. "Our problem was that the accountants just had very thick bank accounts," Turner said. "Those bank accounts went a long way toward establishing their stance on this issue."

Levitt, of course, understood Congress and its motivations. Not only had he been through the stock option expensing debacle in 1994, but he'd been testifying before Congress in some role or another for over 40 years. As SEC commissioner, Levitt always wrote his opponents back, often in a handwritten note with a personal joke or two. He'd always suggest they stop by and visit him (especially the Democrats). As he said in an interview: "There are three things you need to be successful as a regulator. You need to be incredibly lucky. I had a great market. Second, you have to know how the media works. Since I had been a reporter and owned a newspaper, I actually liked journalists and newspapers. Third, you have to deal with Congress. My first testimony to Congress was in the 1950s. I knew the way the system works; and the way it works is that you can't be at war with everyone at the same time. You have to have a dialogue with people."

Levitt had his friends in Congress, but that list was much shorter than his lineup of adversaries. Congressman John Dingell of Michigan, one of the deans of House Democrats and the ranking Democratic member of the Commerce Committee, was often Levitt's staunchest ally in the House. Dingell had been a thorn in the side of the accounting profession for years. If anything, in fact, Dingell wanted Levitt to be more aggressive confronting the profession. In early 2000, he urged a much more offensive tack, thinking that the battle was being lost. In a letter to Levitt, he said that the ISB "has done little more than hold inconclusive 'standard-setting meetings' since that time, while the conflicts of interest have multiplied and the problem has aggressively worsened." Dingell added: "Moreover, common sense tells us that the problems revealed in the PwC report are not confined to that firm. The accounting profession is now the management services industry: The profession and the companies that it is charged with auditing . . . are quickly becoming wholly-owned subsidiaries of one another. Self-interest has replaced much of the profession's fidelity to the public trust."

What Dingell didn't know was that Levitt basically agreed with his points about the ISB and the profession; he just couldn't say it. Not at that point anyway.

LEVITT MAKES HIS MOVE

On June 20, 2000, KPMG, Deloitte & Touche, and Arthur Andersen—the three firms most determined to fight Levitt's proposals—met him at Deloitte & Touche's Manhattan offices. The meeting did not go well, as Levitt, Turner, and SEC lawyer Harvey Goldschmid got nowhere with the three CEOs. Bob Grafton, CEO of Arthur Andersen, which was aggressively building its consulting unit in the wake of its final divorce with Andersen Consulting, told Levitt that if he went ahead with aggressive independence reforms, "It will be war."[18]

Within the next week, Levitt proposed rules barring CPA firms from providing most consulting services to their audit clients, including information technology services. This was by far the most lucrative nonaudit service Levitt wanted to ban, and the one he knew the global firms would go to war over. Levitt's proposal also addressed the increasing tendency of companies to outsource their internal audit functions to their external auditors, basically in the name of efficiency and convenience. The rules also strengthened the Public Oversight Board, particularly from a funding point of view. Levitt cleverly grouped the proposal for liberalizing the rules in investments by personnel of CPA firms and their families with the explosive issue of limiting consulting services to audit clients. This coupling had the disconcerting effect of forcing the accounting industry to voice full endorsement of one of Levitt's proposals.

When confronted with the threat of losing a significant portion of their business through the separation of auditing and consulting, the global firms did not exactly close ranks. Although the firms all had the overriding mutual interests of retaining the right to provide consulting services to audit clients, each had its own concerns that ultimately drove its actions.

"If I were running such a firm, and I saw regulators doing what we were doing, that might inspire a fortress mentality," Levitt said. "If I saw the competitive pressures bearing down on me, and suddenly a pot of gold appeared before me in the form of new kinds of services, and everyone was moving closer and closer to that pot of gold, well, you see what happens."

KPMG, with its laconic midwestern CEO Steve Butler, was the most conservative firm and the most averse to change. After Levitt's proposal came out, Levitt called Butler three times and never got a response.[19] Finally, Levitt called Representative Billy Tauzin, a close friend of the accounting industry, and told Tauzin that he should get on the phone to Butler with the message that if Butler wanted to have any input at all in the final rules, he had to engage. Butler, however, was not having problems communicating with just Levitt. The relationship between Butler and Phil Laskaway of Ernst & Young (E&Y) was marked with intense animosity, bitterness that lingered from their failed 1998 attempt to merge their two firms into what would have been at that point the biggest professional services firm in the world.

Indeed, E&Y and KPMG had shared an intense rivalry all throughout the 1990s, and it intensified after their merger fell apart. E&Y and KPMG were the most alike of the five global firms, with a similar number of employees and partners and similar size, industry expertise, geographic coverage, and partner pay. This similarity bred a competition for clients and, subsequently, intense rivalry. For example, in 1997, when bidding on the Columbia Presbyterian Health Care Center, Laskaway entered a bid of zero for the first year for the audit, simply to keep KPMG from winning the client,[20] which it did.

There was also another issue with Butler. In the fall of 1998, he approached the SEC to get its approval to spin off the firm's consulting practice. The SEC countered with an offer that Butler could spin the practice off, but he had to sell 80 percent of it and get rid of the remaining 20 percent over five years. Butler initially turned down the deal, only to accept the exact same conditions in February 2000. The bruising negotiations over the consulting-firm spin-off may have had something to do with Butler's reluctance to negotiate on the auditor independence issue.

Laskaway was viewed by Levitt and Turner as the one leader of the firms with whom they could really work. "I think out of the five leaders of the accounting firms, Laskaway was the only one I'd say was on a par with effective chief executives," Turner said. "The rest of them were not even close; they don't match up well with other executives. It's the structure of the firms. A powerful group rises to the top, and their leader gets the top job and takes out the competition pretty quickly."

There was another reason Laskaway, who supported Levitt's proposals for the most part, was easy to work with: He was about to sell his entire consulting practice to Cap Gemini, the French conglomerate. PricewaterhouseCoopers and CEO Jim Schiro were already running scared because of its highly publicized independence violations and was the firm most amenable to cutting a deal with Levitt. Laskaway and Schiro decided that they would meet Levitt halfway on his auditor independence rules.

"I think PricewaterhouseCoopers and E&Y probably played it out and decided that was their best move," Levitt said of the two firms. "They each had their own issues that made them more susceptible than the other firms. PricewaterhouseCoopers had severe regulatory problems. Laskaway was about to sell the consulting firm to Cap Gemini. It wasn't totally nobility, and it wasn't totally self-interest; it was somewhere in between. They were certainly more intelligent than the guys leading the other firms."

Arthur Andersen, led by Bob Grafton, was slightly less hostile toward Levitt than KPMG was. Deloitte & Touche, the smallest global firm of the five, was led by new CEO Jim Copeland, who had a much worse relationship with the SEC than did Mike Cook, who had led the firm the previous 10 years and to a large extent supported many of Levitt's reforms in 2000, though for his own reasons. "I said to

Arthur at one point, 'You have contributed greatly to the concerns about consulting, and maybe this is more a perception problem than a real problem, and maybe you helped create the perception,'" Cook said. "But the fact is, the perception is the deciding factor." Cook's old firm, though, stood fast against Levitt and his independence proposals.

Levitt probably would not have been able to muster the political capital to take on the accounting industry had he not gathered a head of steam during his second term. Levitt was clearly emboldened in late 1998 by a deal that the SEC struck with banking regulators on accounting for loan-loss reserves. In an internal memo to three SEC staffers who participated in the negotiations—Turner, Harvey Goldschmid, and Gregg Corso—Levitt called it a "huge win." Shortly after this victory, Levitt turned his attention more fully to the accounting profession.

Another victory was Regulation FD, which mandated that public companies must provide nonpublic information simultaneously to all investors. For example, highly restricted quarterly conference calls with analysts used to be a popular way for management to announce whether a company had hit its quarterly earnings targets. After the passage of Regulation FD, web casting of company conference calls emerged as one of the most efficient and effective ways for the average investor to get full access to newly released information.

Turner said that Levitt picked just the right time to rev up his campaign against the accounting profession. "Arthur was the most phenomenal CEO I have ever worked with. He was very strategic in his thinking, and the tactical implementation of his ideas was superb. His ability to communicate meant he could reach out to everyone."

Levitt certainly reached out to many allies in his fight to increase independence in the accounting profession. One was Bevis Longstreth, a former SEC commissioner and a retired partner at the New York City law firm of Debevoise & Plimpton. Levitt would later tell Longstreth that during his battle against the firms, he often asked himself, "What would Bevis do?"[21] Longstreth saw the independence issue in even more black-and-white terms than Levitt did. He felt that

Levitt had courageously challenged the monopoly and that the monopoly was fighting back with full force.

Another important ally was Levitt's occasional golfing partner in Santa Fe (where Levitt owns a house) and then-CEO of TIAA-CREF, John Biggs. Biggs was a longtime critic of the accounting industry who made sure that the corporate practices at TIAA-CREF reflected his convictions. Biggs and Levitt saw eye to eye not only on audit independence but also on such issues as the responsibilities of the audit committee, the importance of high-quality international accounting standards, and the need for corporate government practices to replicate U.S. practices (Biggs was very critical of German corporate governance, for example) in other countries.

John C. Coffee Jr., professor of law at Columbia University, was a key sounding board for Levitt, as well as an important adviser when it came to the evolving legal situation of the accounting profession. For example, Coffee put to Levitt a very convincing argument that despite the fact that litigation against accounting firms was increasing, developments in the 1990s resulted in a decrease of liability for them. This lack of legal liability, according to Coffee, could be traced to four developments:

1. The Private Securities Litigation Reform Act of 1995 (PSLRA) made it much more difficult to convict an auditor of fraud (legislation that Levitt supported, incidentally).
2. The PSLRA substituted proportionate liability for joint and several liability as the normal standard of damages under the Securities Exchange Act of 1934, and this change meant that in the future, auditors would be held liable only for the portion of the influence they had, which typically would be much less than management's role.
3. The 1994 Supreme Court decision in *Central Bank of Denver N.A. v. First Interstate Bank of Denver* effectively eliminated the "aiding and abetting a securities law violation" liability.
4. The passage of the Uniform Standards Act in 1998 meant that accounting firms would not be facing fraud litigation in state court (if only the tobacco companies could be so lucky).

Many important business publications backed Levitt in his proposals to separate auditing and consulting. As the *Economist* said: "Of course, if accountants are barred from selling other services to their audit clients, then the cost of audits may well go up. But companies should be happy that they are not having their arms twisted into buying other sorts of advice from auditors' colleagues. Auditors, too, would be freed from the insidious pressure of selling or reviewing colleagues' work. And for shareholders, surely the price of truly independent audits is one worth paying."[22] The *New York Times* said in an editorial, "The SEC has proposed nothing draconian, only commonsense rules to make sure that outside auditors perform and appear to perform independent audits."[23]

Levitt sometimes cast his net a little too wide in his search for allies. On June 13, 2000, he wrote a letter to Ken Lay of Enron, thanking him for joining a panel on New Economy valuation. Levitt said in part: "Your experience and judgment will be invaluable as we confront the major issues born out of advances in technology and business and consider how they affect the future of financial disclosure in the capital markets."[24] The SEC came under heavy criticism from the Senate in October 2002 for not aggressively reviewing Enron's annual reports in the late 1990s. Because Congress was cutting Levitt's budget and threatening to close the spigot on SEC funding altogether, that reprimand was highly hypocritical.

FORMIDABLE ADVERSARIES

In the 75-day "comment period" (the actual time period was about a week longer because the clock starts ticking only when it's sure that all relevant parties have access to the proposals) between when Levitt's tough new rules governing auditor independence were announced and when the SEC held public hearings, Levitt tried to live by the maxim "Keep your friends close, but your enemies closer." He spoke and met with congressional opponents, in particular, nearly every day.

The five global accounting firms, however, were a different story.

Part of the accounting profession's objections to the new independence proposals and its tangible hostility to Levitt had to do with the fact that it was the SEC pushing the issue. Although the SEC had every right to address a problem it felt was harming the nation's investors, the accounting profession had for years been chafing under the rule of the SEC. Since the mid-1970s, relations between the SEC and the global accounting firms—whether it was the Big Eight, Big Six, or Big Five—had been deteriorating. As the global firms turned more and more to consulting, the commission grew more and more determined to keep them focused on the audit. Prior to this debate, the SEC tended to rule with a light touch when it came to enforcing accounting standards. In fact, from its very inception, the SEC could have exercised its right to mandate accounting standards. Instead, it followed the advice of experts in 1934 to let the industry continue to create its own standards.

Another reason the profession fought so hard against Levitt's independence proposals was that it knew this fact: A high percentage of consulting services to Fortune 500 companies valued at $1 million or more are provided by the auditor. Getting stand-alone consulting contracts is not something big accounting firms are good at, particularly because most accountants are not polished salespeople. They procure these contracts because they are so deep in the numbers that they can tell management things about the company that management doesn't even know. "If you understand the numbers, you start to wield power," said accounting professor G. A. Swanson. "That's how these firms get the business in the first place, because they're digging down deep in the company. If they're not doing the audit, they don't have that inside track." As one global firm audit partner put it, "The audit client is such an easy target."

Levitt's congressional opponents sent a signal to Levitt that they were galvanizing support. One strategy was to hit Levitt on several fronts. Senator Lieberman, one of the key legislators in the successful gambit to face down the FASB in 1994 in the stock options battle, brought up the issue again in early 2000. Even while the independence debate was ramping up, Lieberman grew concerned about the FASB wanting to address another aspect of the stock option issue. In a letter to Levitt on March 21, 2000, Lieberman said that "not allowing companies to 'reprice' underwater options without forcing them to recognize a compensation expense will have the practical effect of eliminating stock options for many lower and midlevel workers at growth companies."[25] Levitt responded by saying that the FASB had indeed compromised with the tech community. Senators Spencer Abraham and Robert Bennett sent a letter to Levitt on December 16, 1999, bringing up yet another accounting issue, saying, "We are troubled by FASB's proposal to require that all mergers and acquisitions be accounted for as purchases. . . . We are also very concerned about FASB's stock compensation exposure draft."[26] The senators were concerned that the proposed changes would hurt the tech community's ability to competitively recruit people.

Levitt knew he had to do something to get his opponents in Congress to at least take the independence issue seriously. He was able to set up a closed-door meeting with the Senate subcommittee holding the hearings. His SEC predecessor also attended the meeting. During that meeting, Levitt gave many skeptics reason to reconsider their opposition. "Ideally, we could have gotten total separation of auditing and consulting," Levitt said. "But we couldn't have gotten anything if we hadn't gotten a confidential briefing with the Senate subcommittee. We at least gave them pause to consider their position."

In addition to Congress and the global accounting firms, there were institutions that opposed Levitt. One was the Financial Executives Institute (FEI), a professional group of corporate officers. In his speeches as SEC commissioner, Levitt relished assigning the FEI the role of bad guy for its lobbying to sharply curtail the strength and viability of the FASB in 1994. At one point in the mid-1990s, the FEI called the FASB "antibusiness," and Levitt repeatedly said in his speeches that "calling FASB antibusiness is like calling the College of Cardinals anti-Catholic."

The FEI came out vocally against some of the findings of the SEC's Blue Ribbon Committee, including one that recommended that the outside auditor discuss with the audit committee the auditor's judgments about the quality, not just the acceptability, of the company's accounting principles. The FEI also repudiated a recommendation that the auditor provide judgments about the clarity of the company's disclosures and aggressiveness or conservatism of its accounting policies. In a letter to Levitt, the FEI said: "External auditors should have free and private access to the audit committee at any time the auditor has a concern about the appropriateness of a company's reporting or the actions of management, as provided for in auditor and audit committee practices today; but on matters having to do with business factors, management judgments, and selection of the most appropriate accounting policies, a three-way discussion should take place."[27]

An organization called the American Business Council (ABC) also was determined to stop Levitt. In the summer of 2000, even as the auditor independence battle raged, the ABC and its president, Barry Rogstad, tried to change the subject in the same manner as Congress, sending a letter to Levitt that aggressively attacked the FASB over its refusal to change its proposed new rules on accounting for mergers. Rogstad accused the FASB of wanting to prove something after the 1993 retreat on expensing stock options: "The FASB's failure to mandate the valuation and expensing of stock options a few years ago apparently left deeper scars than I ever realized. My sense is that the Board would view any extensive revision of its business combinations project as yet another defeat for accounting purity at the hands of business. And, having framed the issue in warlike terms—as a choice between advancing and retreating—the FASB will charge ahead."[28]

The five global accounting firms became only more upset midway through the 75-day comment period, on August 31. The Panel on Audit Effectiveness—nicknamed the O'Malley Panel after its chairman, former Price Waterhouse chairman Shaun O'Malley—released its final report on August 31, 2000. The O'Malley Panel came out strongly in favor of an exclusionary ban on nonaudit services to audit clients, recommending that the SEC bar:

Everything other than the work involved in performing an audit and other work that is integral to the function of an audit. In general, the touchstone for deciding whether a service other than the straightforward audit itself should be excluded from nonaudit services is whether the service is rendered principally to the client's audit committee, acting on behalf of investors, to facilitate or improve the quality of the audit and the financial reporting process rather than being rendered principally to provide assistance to management in the performance of duties.[29]

"The O'Malley Panel Report reads almost like a blueprint for what was about to go wrong in the following year," said Mark Cheffers, a former Price Waterhouse senior manager who now runs accountingmalpractice.com, which educates accountants on how to avoid actions that could result in shareholder litigation. "Today, when I run seminars for accountants, I write the 10 main recommendations on a board, and say, 'Hey, this one looks pretty good right now, doesn't it?'"

Levitt's opponents, however, seized on the fact that the O'Malley Panel found that occasionally a consulting project can help an accounting firm understand a client's business better, thus helping the firm do a better audit. Soon, the AICPA and the global firms were integrating this point into the presentations they would give at the upcoming public hearings. "Our report was like the Bible," O'Malley said. "People on both sides of the argument were using it to support their version of events."

Perhaps it is fitting that the O'Malley Report was cited by both sides in the debate, because O'Malley himself is of two minds regarding the barring of consulting services to clients. "The press became interested in corporate governance and independence issues because of Arthur, and that's good," O'Malley said. "But it wasn't all consulting. It was weak auditing, and I think that got lost."

Several weeks before the public hearings, PwC and Ernst & Young met with Levitt to discuss the proposed rule. One thing that impressed each of them was how hard their opponents worked. To Laskaway, who had been with E&Y for many years, the meeting with the SEC harkened back to the old days, to the "positive and productive relationship that has traditionally existed between members of the accounting profession and the Commission."[30] After meeting with the

Commission, E&Y and PwC took matters into their own hands and together drafted their own independence rule. They handed it in to the SEC staff, who were to evaluate it before the first public meeting, on September 20, 2000. Just days before that meeting, rumors spread that the other three global accounting firms were preparing to challenge the SEC on the grounds that it was misinterpreting the word *independent,* used in the Securities Act of 1933. That approach, however, would have likely led to ignominious defeat for the firms.[31]

The stage was set. Going into the all-important public hearings, civility between the SEC and the profession was at an all-time low. Three of the firms were going to play hardball, two were trying to advance with their own independence agenda, and the AICPA was prepared to go on the offensive.

THE HEARINGS

One of the problems from which the accounting profession suffered in the late 1990s—which was evident at the hearings—was that it had bought into New Economy jargon. The leaders of the global accounting firms testified time and time again throughout the hearings that the "information age" required a "real-time reporting" so that "intangible value could be captured."

Indeed, representatives from the AICPA and every global firm testified that audited financial statements have ceased to correctly measure the value of a company. As James Schiro, CEO of PricewaterhouseCoopers, said in his testimony at the first public hearing on September 20, 2000: "A decade ago, even a couple of years ago, most investors formed economic judgments based on historical financial information. Today, a more complex set of factors has an effect on value. To make decisions in this environment, reliable, contemporaneous information, supplied by a trusted and objective third party, is increasingly necessary."

The antiquated accounting model is an especially handy culprit because of its inability to defend itself. The firms were blaming an idea—a condition—rather than anyone setting the standards or performing the audits. The accounting model argument has also been discredited because the key aspect of its formulation—that New Economy companies contain intangible value that financial statements cannot capture—has been discredited. More often than not, New Economy companies whose value proved hard to capture turned out to have no value at all. Hence, the difficulty capturing it.

"The notion that all of these problems were being caused by an antiquated accounting model is just a load of nonsense," said Don Kirk, a former chairman of the FASB. "There was a great tendency to blame these audit failures on anything else other than the people responsible for it."

KPMG in particular, through the testimony of Terry Strange, global managing partner of audit, came out with both barrels blazing at the first public hearing. The firm had apparently decided that to effectively negotiate its position, it had to start off as far from Arthur Levitt's solution as possible. Strange said in his prepared statement:

The proposal states that "common sense" tells us that the proposed rule is the correct outcome. We believe that common sense, in fact, cuts exactly the other way. Let's consider first the real incentives an auditor with common sense would face. Accounting firms have survived for decades on the basis of their reputation for quality and integrity. If that reputation is lost, inside or outside one's firm, the auditor's career is over. If the auditor looks the other way on an audit engagement, he or she, and his or her firm, face tremendous liability exposure. Audit relationships with a client often last many years; consulting engagements are frequently short-term and sporadic.[32]

The fault with that reasoning, however, is that during boom times—like the 1990s—it's very rare for audit negligence or fraud to ever come out, because shoddy audit work often comes to light only after businesses fail. If Enron never declared bankruptcy, Andersen's winking at Enron's unusual partnerships might never have come to light. Auditors are very unlikely to get called on pushing the envelope when the economy is humming, and they know this. Therefore, there is actually very little disincentive in a growth environment to maintain strict independence.

Another tack that the accounting profession took was to repeat this mantra: There is not a single shred of evidence that any audit had ever been compromised due to consulting services that were performed at the client. There is, however, ample evidence. For example, the 1978 Cohen Commission concluded that Arthur Andersen's audit of Westec was compromised by its merger-and-acquisition services to Westec.

"I thought the argument that there is no link was specious," Levitt said. "I didn't really care if they thought there was no evidence. Perception is the ultimate reality. Perception creates confidence, or lack thereof. If there is a very dark cloud hanging over a profession, you have to deal with it."

Levitt got his chance at the hearings. Fed up at one point with criticism toward the SEC by AICPA head Barry Melancon and AICPA chair Robert Elliott, Levitt commented: "It was the Commission, not the profession, that pushed for the creation of the ISB and the O'Malley Panel, the Garten Panel, and the Blue Ribbon Committee on audit committees, the whole use of EDGAR, our Internet fraud unit, our use of exemptive authority that was given to us in recent congressional action. Where are we lacking?"[33]

Only one firm came out tentatively supporting the barring of consulting to audit clients. It was no coincidence that it was the firm that had recently sold its entire consulting capability: Ernst & Young. Laskaway said in his testimony, "I might note that now that we have sold this practice, we have not discovered that we are somehow enfeebled, unable to perform effective audits or to maintain a topnotch audit and tax practice. In fact, we have found the opposite to be true: Without a large consulting practice to manage, we are now more targeted and more focused on our core audit and tax business."[34]

What really upset Levitt at the hearings was what he called the "scare tactics" that Barry Melancon, head of the AICPA, used to get smaller firms to support his opposition to Levitt's proposals. Several leaders of small and midsized accounting firms testified at the hearings that Levitt's proposals would hurt them. This tactic infuriated Levitt, because he was trying to position his argument as pro small firm and anti big firm.

"I thought the AICPA was soulless and gutless, suggesting a bulk of their membership were auditors at small public companies and would be affected by these rules," Levitt said. "That was the most cowardly, deceptive thing I'd seen in Washington. Melancon knew perfectly well that those firms had no horse in that race. He tried to convince them otherwise."

Overall, though, the public hearings were a huge victory for Levitt and his staff. Going in, they didn't know if they would survive the onslaught by the profession. Coming out, it was obvious that the SEC's credibility was intact and that there was support for a good many of its proposals.

"The public hearings were absolutely essential to us getting our message out," Levitt said. "The firms would stand up and say that this was not a problem, and then there would be all these witnesses standing up and saying these guys are like a bunch of criminals. A few days after one of the hearings, I went to my dentist in Washington, and he said to me, 'Boy, those accountants are really a bunch of crooks.' When you people on the street are saying, 'You're a bunch of crooks,' you definitely have a perception problem."

But this "bunch of crooks" was not finished yet. They still had plenty of clout in Congress that would swing the momentum back to them.

THE FINAL NEGOTIATIONS

Shortly after the end of the public hearings, Republican Senator Phil Gramm of Texas notified Levitt that fellow Republican Senator Richard Shelby of Alabama was preparing an "appropriations rider" that would effectively defang the SEC if Levitt went ahead with his independence proposals. In his book, *Take on the Street,* Levitt recounted his critical phone call with then–Senate Majority Leader Trent Lott:

> I pleaded with the Mississippi Republican not to let this important issue be resolved by dead-of-night appropriations riders. "No matter what you think about the issue," I said, "the process should be aboveboard." I told him that such publications as the *New York Times,* [the] *Washington Post,* and *Business Week* had all endorsed the rule. "Well, Arthur," Lott said, "I'm not familiar with what you're proposing to do, but if those liberal publications are in favor of it, then I'm against it."[35]

Levitt sent Jim Morhard, clerk of the Senate Committee on Appropriations, a warning missive on October 19, 2000, in a handwritten note on his personal stationery. It read, in part: "Dear Jim: Thank you for your valuable help in connection with the SEC's effort to ensure the independence of auditors. I view the auditor independence proposal as one of the most important initiatives pursued during my tenure. I hope that it does not also become the first time in the Commission's 65-year history in which Congress chooses to override the agency's independent rule-making authority."[36] That same day, one of Levitt's supporters in the House, Mark Udall of Colorado, gave a speech on the House floor, saying that he "strongly opposed any attempt to delay the final rule-making process through legislative means." Levitt later thanked him with a warm personal note for his support.

At one point, Senator Robert Bennett, one of the most partisan of the Republicans fighting Levitt, offered to broker a compromise solution between Levitt and the firms, which Levitt politely brushed aside with a note saying, "We are working hard to craft an agreement."

There was someone else who offered his services as a diplomat that Levitt would not turn down. Arthur Andersen audit practice head Joseph Berardino—representing the firm that basically invented management consulting—offered to help broker a deal. In the accounting world, when Arthur Andersen offers to act as a selfless mediator, most Big Five partners from the other firms would have been highly skeptical. But the group had little choice. Berardino shuttled back and forth between Levitt and the firms. This diplomacy, in fact, later played a large part in Berardino being elevated to the chairmanship of Arthur Andersen. According to Mike Cook, the former CEO of Deloitte & Touche, "Berardino came through with Arthur [Levitt] respecting him a lot."

During the final month, when Levitt and his team were putting together the final proposal, the Clinton administration signaled its support. "They didn't get involved until the last month," Levitt said. President Clinton assured Levitt that he would veto any legislation that would disable the SEC.

The rules passed on November 15 by a 4-to-0 vote of the SEC commissioners. In the end, Levitt was forced to abandon the ban on firms providing information technology consulting to audit clients. Instead, he had to settle for the requirement that made companies disclose the dollar amount of the audit and the consulting fees they pay. In addition, audit committees would now be required to state in the proxy statement if they considered any nonaudit services being provided to be compatible with the auditor's independence. On November 27, Levitt sent out a batch of letters to various players in the battle over accounting rules. On his letter to Arthur Andersen CEO Joseph Berardino, he scribbled this additional note: "Joe, your leadership, at the critical moment, helped make this possible. Thank you for your patience and thoughtfulness." Levitt's note to Steve Butler said: "Steve, I appreciate the passion and directness that you brought to the discussion. I hope the outcome is something to which you can lend your support."

Levitt didn't get his separation of auditing and consulting, and less than two years later, Arthur Andersen had ceased to exist. Levitt seemed a bit saddened by the whole affair. "I don't think the developments at Enron totally surprised me," he said. "Over time, I've come to believe that fraud is fraud and deception is deception, and it happens in big companies as well as small companies."

And Andersen? "The Justice Department need not have brought that case against Andersen," Levitt said. "I knew the other firms had just as many problems as Andersen. They could have brought the case against the individuals in the firm who did it."

Both Levitt and Turner lay much of the blame for the latest string of debacles at the feet of Congress. "The culture of gamesmanship in Corporate America, with the end result being bad numbers, together with a complete meltdown of the public confidence is exactly what we were worried about at the SEC," Turner said. "Unfortunately, though, that concern wasn't shared at all by Congress. I think everyone could have done a better job: The boards of directors, the auditors, the regulators, all of us could have done a better job. But I put a lot of the blame on Congress. Going back several SEC administrations, regulators did try to make reforms and each time ran into a congressional buzz saw."

Asked about his take on the state of the accounting profession, Levitt recalled some of the past well-respected leaders of the accounting profession and expressed concern that today no one seems to be stepping forward to set an example for the profession. "I think it generally takes time to produce a leader," Levitt said. "And it's not just the accounting profession. You couldn't name five people in business right now you'd call a real leader. I don't know how far you get past Paul Volcker." Even Volcker, a former Federal Reserve Board chairman, would have his hands full with the challenge he faced in 2002—saving Arthur Andersen.

CHAPTER 8

ENRON AND THE FALL OF ANDERSEN

HEN SHE WAS A MEMBER OF ARTHUR ANDERSEN'S PROFESSIONAL standards group in Chicago from 1998 to 2000, Melinda Lawrence couldn't have been prouder. Being invited to join the professional standards group meant that Lawrence was one of the firm's top technicians, or at least showed the potential to become one. Andersen's best pure-audit and tax specialists from all over the country vied to be invited to Chicago for the two-year stints in the professional standards group. As a member, Lawrence had no direct client responsibilities and could lose herself analyzing a Financial Accounting Standards Board (FASB) bulletin or an SEC pronouncement all day—not long ago the highest calling of the best and the brightest in the Big Five.

The lack of contact with Andersen's clients did not mean that the 30 or so partners and managers in the professional standards group were caught in a professional backwater. On the contrary, Lawrence and her colleagues were in-house technical gurus for Arthur Andersen partners and managers. The professional standards group reviewed, debated, and then ruled on the most complex technical transactions that Andersen's clients were engaged in. When an Andersen audit team was presented with an unusual or problematic financial reporting issue at a client, they were to contact the professional standards group for a ruling on the matter. As it turns out, the technical ability of many accounting firm partners has suffered as a result of the deemphasis of auditing and the proliferation of consulting, and all of the global firms had developed comparable groups of partners devoted to thinking deep thoughts about tricky problems encountered in the field. "You have a lot of partners who are not real good technicians," said one Big Four partner. "They really need to rely on the guidance of a national office."

Quite literally, Lawrence and her colleagues were the accountants' accountants and tended to be—in the best sense of the word—nerds. "You'd walk around the office, and most of the conversations around the halls went like this: 'Okay, so they entered into this lease agreement, and then guess what happened?'" Lawrence said. "The real technical stuff had to be your forte. You had to enjoy it, or you wouldn't have been there. I was known as sort of a nerd myself."

Lawrence was a manager (two rungs below partner in accounting firm hierarchy) when she came to the professional standards group from Arthur Andersen's Dallas office, where she had developed a knack for helping clients deal with rules and proposals coming out of the SEC and other rule-making bodies. Like the other 30 or so partners and managers on her team, once she settled in, Lawrence polished the skills that got her there in the first place. Lawrence became an expert on what foreign-based companies had to do to comply with U.S. generally accepted accounting principles (GAAP), usually in an effort to be listed on the New York Stock Exchange (NYSE) or another U.S. exchange. When Andersen partners in other parts of the world called Lawrence's group about a client that needed advice on complying with GAAP, Lawrence would often be assigned the call.

ENRON AND THE QUEST FOR INNOVATION

While Lawrence was an expert on the SEC and GAAP, some partners in her group specialized in issues relating to complex industries, such as the energy industry. Knowledge of the energy and utilities industry was a point of professional pride with Andersen, and the firm even had a special service group, called "Energy Trading and Marketing," comprised of partners and managers who audited only those types of clients. Auditing energy companies and utilities, in fact, was a legacy of the firm's midwestern industrial roots in Chicago. Former Andersen senior partner Leonard Spacek, for example, had worked at a utility before joining Andersen. As of 2001, Andersen audited more electric and gas utilities, oil companies, and energy trading companies than any other global firm.[1]

The rewards in the energy trading business in 2001 seemed enormous; and Houston-based Enron, an Andersen client, had already gotten a head start. Enron was an amazing, Texas-sized success story. The company had made the strategic decision back in 1985 to leave the restrictive natural gas pipeline business behind to become a diversified energy business that built and operated natural gas facilities, produced natural gas and electricity, and delivered natural gas and electricity. For three years in a row in the mid-1990s, Enron had been named the most innovative company in the United States in a survey of Fortune 500 CEOs and board members.[2]

The architect of this success was Enron's founder and CEO, Ken Lay, who prided himself on rarely saying "no" to an idea that he at first thought might be "unreachable, undoable, or even unwise." Lay and his protégé, Enron president Jeffrey Skilling, were early believers in hiring talented people and not restricting them with written job descriptions or other nuisances. They also believed that their prized recruits would work harder with generous company benefits, on-site health care facilities with doctors on staff, 90 percent education reimbursement, and employee education programs, like "The Foundations of Finance and Accounting" course. Lay also believed that "soft" corporate values could guide an organization. In one moment of inspiration early in Enron's existence, Lay scribbled Enron's four core values—respect, integrity, communication, and excellence—on a piece of paper that was preserved for years by Enron senior vice president for communications Elizabeth Tilney, who must have believed it was an important corporate artifact. By early 1998, Enron had started calling itself the "world's leading integrated electricity and natural gas company."[3]

MARK-TO-MARKET ACCOUNTING

Enron's creative spirit extended to its accounting and controls. Stretching back into the early 1990s, in fact, Andersen had been involved in lengthy discussions with the SEC regarding Enron's mark-to-market accounting methods.[4] Andersen and Enron shared common ground in their enthusiasm for mark-to-market accounting, which can be used to account for revenues years before they actually reach company coffers. Mark-to-market accounting allowed energy companies like Enron to count as current earnings the profits they expected to earn in the future from energy-related contracts. In 1999 and 2000, in particular, Enron's profits were bloated with earnings that existed only when using this method of accounting. In 1999, fully one-third of Enron's pretax profits were accounted for by projected earnings estimated by mark-to-market accounting. It is amazing that in 2000, more than *one-half* of Enron's reported profits came from gains projected through mark-to-market accounting.[5] The justification for Enron's mark-to-market accounting was that the company could obtain a truer, more current valuation than it could by simply looking at actual sales.

Enron naturally liked this method of accounting because it could book profits more quickly. Andersen liked mark-to-market because the firm had staked out a competitive position within the global firms as an innovator that wanted to help managers present the most up-to-date valuation of their organizations. Andersen wanted accountants to be more than mere historians looking back at the last quarter; it believed accountants (or, at least, *its* accountants) could deliver more information to the user of the financial statements by helping a client reflect future potential on the balance sheet. Andersen CEO Joseph Berardino believed that "most investors are really interested in predicting the future, and we don't have an ability in our present financial reporting model—mark-to-market is an attempt to get there—to give investors more current information on a more timely basis."[6]

Besides using mark-to-market accounting to boost current earnings, Enron's accountants also looked for novel ways to hide debt and smooth out volatility in corporate results. Enron's growth in the late 1990s was spurred by businesses—wholesale and retail electricity marketing, infrastructure development, and renewables—that hadn't even existed a few years earlier. Along with their upside potential, these complex businesses brought great risk, and they could sustain losses based on fluctuating exchange rates and other factors. It was critical for Enron's core energy trading business that the company retain its credibility as the high-flying industry leader. To minimize financial statement losses, maximize profits, and avoid adding debt to its balance sheet, Enron began hedging investments by using nonconsolidated special purpose entities (SPEs). Here's how it worked: Enron would pay its own stock into an SPE in return for a cash payment; the SPE's function would be to hedge the value of various investments on Enron's balance sheet, using the Enron stock as the payment. As Steven Schwarcz, a law professor at Duke University, wrote: "Because of its historically rising stock price, Enron apparently judged the risk that it would have to pay on its guarantees as remote. But undue reliance on historical price information is, of course, precisely what got Long Term Capital Management into trouble."[7] To keep tabs on the increasingly complex methods of accounting used for these businesses, Enron employed an army of over 600 CPAs worldwide.[8]

A BATTLE OF WITS

The Andersen on-site audit team, led by 42-year-old David Duncan, would have expected from company management nothing less than a vigorous defense of Enron's accounting. Constant negotiations about what qualifies as revenue, when revenue should be recorded, where debt can be hidden, and so forth, is how the accounting game is played at the highest level. As Enron's accounting became more oblique, however, Andersen's team was experiencing increasing difficulty with the technical issues cropping up in relation to the SPEs. For example, Andersen had to judge whether each of hundreds of SPEs represented legitimate stand-alone entities, which would justify off-balance-sheet treatment.

Soon, Melinda Lawrence and her colleagues noticed that one of the most frequent callers to the professional standards group was the Enron engagement team. According to Lawrence, Enron was simply moving too fast and making too many transactions for Duncan and his team to handle the client on their own. "The Enron engagement team would call us and say, 'We've never seen anything like this. How do we account for it?'" Lawrence said. To Lawrence's group, in fact, the Duncan team was what was known as a good client. "Our audit team at Enron made a lot of calls to the group," Lawrence said. "They did everything right as far as calling the group for certain transactions." But as everyone would soon find out, inquiring about accounting transactions didn't mean that Duncan and his audit team on the Enron account were going to take the professional standards group's advice.

Duncan and his team were not only outnumbered, but also way over their heads, even with the backing of Andersen's best technical minds. Former KPMG CEO Jon Madonna portrays big-time auditing at a challenging client like Enron as a struggle of wits, with the auditor constantly having to do intellectual battle with a crack team of executives. According to Madonna, engagement partners should absolutely be required to adhere to the ruling of the technical gurus like those in the professional standards group. "I just can't believe they let guys like David Duncan loose at those clients," Madonna said. "That's the one thing I always felt confident about, our Department of Professional Practice—that we'd have a backup for the partner."

Todd Walker, the single practitioner in Tennessee who worked for KPMG for nearly 10 years, agreed with Madonna that KPMG brokered no deals at their Department of Professional Practice. "The

Peat Marwick people, their technical guys were like Mr. 'No,'" said Walker. "You'd always just accept their decision and move on."

At Deloitte & Touche, according to former CEO Mike Cook, there was an appeals process—to Cook himself or to whoever was sitting at the highest level of the firm at a particular time. Then, the decision was presented as a single decision from Deloitte, not from an individual partner. "Certainly there were some partners at our firm that would not have had the ability to stand up to management without the backing of the entire firm," Cook said. "I would never have sent my partners out without the complete involvement and support of the firm against these very tough characters."

Cook touches on an interesting point, because something that has not been focused on is the relative ability of the Andersen team versus the high-powered Enron management team. It was clear that Duncan and his team struggled to keep up with the complex transactions Enron had creatively conjured up. "Dave Duncan was obviously not a hard-nosed business leader, but someone who wanted to be everything to everybody," said former Price Waterhouse CEO Shaun O'Malley. "It seems like he was more of a business developer, admired and liked by everybody. My biggest fear admitting people into our partnership wasn't letting in guys that were dumb. What you worry about is people that want to please everyone." But an overeagerness to please the client—the characteristic in a partnership that O'Malley had feared most when he led Price Waterhouse—was, in fact, the defining trait of star partners like Duncan in the late 1990s.

Reviewing the work of colleagues who might be dumb, eager-to-please, or both would seem to be a cardinal rule of a partnership. In that way, Andersen's professional standards group or KPMG's Department of Professional Practice was the modern equivalent of an accountant poking his head into his business partner's office 50 or 100 years ago. These technical groups, in essence, embodied the wisest judgment of the entire partnership. That's why it's surprising that Andersen made it so easy to circumvent the rulings of the other partners. In a way, the Andersen system reflects the famous Andersen arrogance: The partners thought each other could do no wrong. According to Lawrence, the practice director appeals process was being amended just when Enron imploded. "It was about to be changed, but we never got the chance," Lawrence said.

According to Cook, the process that allowed Duncan to circumvent Andersen's technical gurus was just part of a larger Andersen culture of investing power in the lead partner on a job. "What happened at Andersen was a decision to unleash the individual partner as the decision maker," Cook said. "They were leaving Duncan to get the information and then go make the right decision. He's out there making the ultimate decision, which would have been better left to a more senior partner not facing that client pressure every single day."

If Enron had been operating in good faith, according to Cook, there would have been no reason for Duncan and his team to have such a hard time with the Enron audit. "There is nothing about energy companies that is particularly challenging or complicated from an accounting standpoint," maintained Cook. But, in fact, Enron's accounting contained the grotesque distortions of a funhouse mirror—nothing was as it seemed. This wasn't Shell or BP Amoco, either in terms of complexity or, as it turns out, integrity. Partly because of the volume of transactions, partly because of the savvy of their internal accountants, partly because they were on the cutting edge of use of derivatives and other financial instruments, and partly because—allegedly—key Enron executives seemed to be mostly interested in enriching themselves, it became very difficult to keep up with Enron.

To make matters even worse for Andersen's Duncan, the Enron senior executive whom he, no doubt, viewed as his ultimate client (CFO Andrew Fastow) was receiving enormous compensation serving as general manager of the SPEs, a fact that created a massive conflict of interest for both Fastow and Andersen. After all, how could Andersen question the legality of a certain SPE if its primary client—the person who could fire Andersen in an instant—was earning millions managing that SPE?

NO HELP FROM STANDARD SETTERS

Meanwhile, the Andersen team was getting little help from the standard-setting bodies because they could not issue pronouncements fast enough to give the Andersen team any legitimate backing. According to Lawrence, the FASB's notoriously deliberate pronouncement method, in which the board issues its proposed rule and then gathers responses to it, was much too slow to be relevant to Enron. The FASB's speedier and spunkier little brother, the Emerging Issues Task Force (EITF), formed in 1984 to make faster judgments than FASB could, did issue many rulings based on Enron's corporate reporting activity. "Enron always had Emerging Issues Task Force issues," Lawrence said. "A lot of their innovations had to be addressed by the EITF."

According to one Big Four partner, the experience of Duncan and his team wasn't unique. Auditors out in the field typically receive precious little support in their quest to get some help understanding the potential Enrons of the world. The profession has complained many times, to little avail, that accounting reporting requirements have not kept pace with corporate innovation. The SEC has typically responded by saying curtly that auditors had independence problems. The FASB has issued even more complicated technical rules. The American Institute of Certified Public Accountants (AICPA), the accounting industry's professional association, has been interested in fluffier issues like public relations and marketing initiatives. "Investment banks, venture capitalists, and others are coming up with financial instruments so creative that it's very difficult to keep up with them," said the Big Four partner. "In the last couple of years, I've seen capital structures and financial vehicles I've never seen before."

Each year, according to this partner, accountants are inundated with 15 or so new pronouncements from the FASB and 30 or 40 pronouncements from the EITF. "Trying to keep up on all this stuff is my nighttime reading," she said.

Joseph Wells is a former FBI agent, a CPA, and a certified fraud examiner (CFE) who founded a national association for CFEs. Wells has a saying: "Complexity is the killing fields of fraud." What he means is that as businesses get more complex, fraud is easier to hide. But even absent criminal intent on management's part, Wells said that the way the financial reporting is structured places the burden of proof on the wrong party—the auditor, not the corporate officer. "There is wiggle room in GAAP so that a client can forcefully argue a very questionable transaction," Wells said. "Unless an auditor has a specific way of overturning the transaction, it usually stands. It really ought to be the other way around. You should have to demonstrate the proof of why you can book a certain transaction; the auditor shouldn't have to prove why you can't."

NO LONGER CONFUSED

Just before Lawrence left the professional standards group for her new assignment in Paris, Lawrence's colleague Carl Bass started to lead a chorus of protest against Enron's accounting. One of Bass's main concerns was the way in which Enron executives were being allowed to invest in the various SPEs. Bass, a veteran Andersen partner and a technical purist who had served on Andersen's audit team at Enron before joining the professional standards group, began to have major reservations about Enron's accounting in late 1999. In December, Bass wrote an e-mail to the Andersen team at Enron with advice on how to account for a transaction by one of the partnerships managed by Enron CFO Andrew Fastow. If Enron had treated the transaction the way Bass recommended, it would have had to take a $30 million to $50 million charge.[9] The audit team played its trump card, appealing to the practice director in Houston, who overruled Bass.

The treatment of this specific transaction would later be called "wrong" in a special investigation by Enron's new board of directors looking into the company's collapse. Clearly, Duncan and the Andersen team—even armed with sound, unequivocal decisions by Andersen's best technical partners—were, at that point, looking for any reason to agree with Enron. One might wonder why they were even bothering to still go to the professional standards group. "They didn't set out to not follow the advice of the professional standards group," Lawrence said. But they became worn down. Ultimately, Andersen's audit team stopped trying to figure out Enron's accounting and, instead, became apologists for Enron's riskiest transactions.

The practice directors were not immune either. Partner for partner, Houston was Andersen's most productive office. That was because of Enron. The $52 million in fees that Andersen collected from Enron in 2000 embodied the business strategy taken by the global firms in the 1990s: Maximize the revenue from blue-chip clients. With the costs of marketing and the steep learning curve at a new client, it's much more cost-efficient, from the firm's point of view, to simply extract more money out of current clients. No one wanted to be the one to say "no."

Mark Cheffers, a former Price Waterhouse auditor, runs a web site for accountants called www.accountingmalpractice.com. Since Enron's bankruptcy, he has published a series of research papers on the accounting failures at the company. Cheffers said that at one point Andersen eventually decided to "not become confused" in a systematic way. "This isn't just about whether SPEs should be consolidated or not applying the 3 percent rule," Cheffers said. "I've seen 10 or 15 ways the accounting was manipulated at Enron. It had to be an abject giving away of their obligations."

Greg Neu, who worked as a consultant at Andersen in the early 1990s, said that the slippery slope toward seeing things Enron's way most likely began innocuously, even while Andersen was still fighting the good fight. "They structured something one year, and so they had to do it the same way again," said Neu. "Sometimes it's as simple as that. And they did it the first time that way because so-and-so guy wasn't around that day. The checks and balances didn't catch it, and things just slowly went out of control." One "check" was the professional standards group. Unfortunately for Andersen, the group's advice was just too easily bypassed.

One fascinating aspect of the pressure that Duncan and his team were under to endorse Enron's accounting was the complete absence of consulting as a factor. It doesn't mean that consulting is not a factor to other clients; but at Enron, Andersen's predicament stemmed primarily from trying to audit a highly complex, rogue, and lucrative client. Several accountants interviewed believed that the Andersen audit team never saw beyond the mountain of accounting issues it confronted to ever consider Andersen's consulting or tax work. "I think where you really want to look is at those audit fees," said Steve Blum, former partner at KPMG. "Those were the recurring fees that would have created a conflict."

After Melinda Lawrence left in 2000, an Andersen partner named Dorsey Baskin took over as head of the professional standards group. Baskin's job was about to get very difficult, because the impending divorce from Andersen Consulting would put enormous pressure on Andersen to increase revenues from its top clients.

DIVORCE

The transformation of the Andersen team at Enron from spirited adversaries to management apologists accelerated with the August 2000 divorce of Arthur Andersen from Andersen Consulting, a breakup that started off badly for the auditors and only got worse. Indeed, much overlooked in all the coverage of the Enron/Andersen scandal is how bad things were becoming at Andersen in the year before Enron's implosion.

In early 2000, just when the subject of Enron was starting to heat up in Houston and within the professional standards group, it looked like smooth sailing ahead for Arthur Andersen. The firm's consultants raked in more Y2K revenue than just about any other firm. On January 24, 2000, in anticipation of that year's coming final split from Andersen Consulting, which the accounting firm hoped would bring in a $15 billion arbiter's settlement, Arthur Andersen introduced its new brand in a series of webcasts and concurrent announcements. The mastermind of the new branding was marketing executive Matt

Gonring, whom Andersen had brought in in late 1997 to lead its global marketing group. Gonring had been a successful executive at United Airlines and U.S. Gypsum. But he soon ran into many of the same problems that hamper executives who go to work for one of the global accounting firms expecting a typical corporate environment. "Every partner is a CEO at a Big Four firm," said Mark Friedlander, a former Andersen marketing director in the Chicago office. "Gonring was a strong person, but he never really fit. He tried to implement new programs, proactive programs." Though the firm did launch Gonring's global marketing campaign, he tired of the incessant battles with partners and left in the middle of 2000 to go to a top marketing position at another company.

The firm held on to Gonring's crown jewel achievement: Arthur Andersen's 2002 global advertising campaign. "We spent millions on that campaign," said Friedlander. "Andersen has had national campaigns in the past, but that was going to be the first global advertising campaign."

Gonring's replacement was Dan Archibal, an Andersen audit partner who had spent most of his career in the Boston office. Friedlander said it was an odd choice, giving a top national marketing position to an audit partner. "His whole take on life in terms of marketing was do more with less: 'Let's be more effective but spend half the money we spent last year,'" Friedlander said. Andersen would eventually pay dearly for its lack of an experienced communications executive when the Enron crisis hit the next year.

In August 2000, the arbitration decision was announced, and it was shocking to both sides. Arthur Andersen was expecting something in the vicinity of $15 billion from Andersen Consulting, but was awarded $1 billion.[10] "It was nowhere near the money Arthur Andersen expected," said Friedlander. "Andersen Consulting basically got away scot-free." Not only was Arthur Andersen left as the smallest of the global accounting firms, but the accountants received virtually nothing in return for their support of the consultants in the 1960s, the lean years of the early 1970s, and again during the recession of the early 1980s. The financial impact of Andersen Consulting's departure coincided with the end of the Y2K consulting revenues and the burst of the dot-com bubble. According to Friedlander, the Arthur Andersen partners had only themselves to blame. He said that their decision to turn down several offers from the consulting division and to insist on going by the arbiter's decision perfectly illustrated the Arthur Andersen culture. "The 'We're right, we know what we're doing,' attitude had always been the philosophy at Arthur Andersen," said Friedlander. Soon after the arbitration decision came down, Arthur Andersen CEO Jim Wadia resigned.

ARTHUR ANDERSEN FLIES SOLO

On January 1, 2001, Andersen Consulting changed its name to Accenture.

Arthur Andersen started to pick up the pieces. On the strength of his performance brokering a deal between SEC chairman Arthur Levitt and the global firms on auditor independence in late 2000, Joseph Berardino was elected to the top spot at Arthur Andersen, with 90 percent of the partner's votes.[11] There were four divisions at Arthur Andersen—(1) audit, (2) tax, (3) business consulting, and (4) corporate finance (basically another name for mergers and acquisitions)—and Berardino's first priority was getting consulting back to a level worthy of an Arthur Andersen consulting practice. Arthur Andersen had its own consulting practice since the initial split with Andersen Consulting in 1989, of course; but now there would be absolutely no other consulting revenue coming in. Instead of the urgency expected, however, there was a palpable drift after the final divorce from Andersen Consulting, which quickly turned into deep alarm over the business as the technology-sector downturn hammered systems-consulting earnings.

The consultants who had been hired in 1999 and 2000, first in anticipation and then in reaction to the split from Andersen Consulting, didn't have much to do. Diane Healy was the first person hired in her group at Andersen, a new business consulting group intended to make its mark installing a brand of accounting software called Lawson. The group eventually consisted of four people. When Healy joined Andersen in October 2000, she was sent to North Carolina right away to work on a project at Sara Lee. She enjoyed the project and thought she had done a good job. Then she had her second and last project in Missouri that ended in mid-September 2001. Then she sat. And sat.

"I used every imaginable type of online training Andersen had, learning different software programs and things," Healy said. "The room where they kept all of us not on an assignment became crowded. If you didn't get there early, you didn't get a seat."

The firm began to cut costs all the way around in the late autumn of 2000 and early 2001. The global advertising campaign was still a go, but it would be delayed if the economy didn't turn around. "We saw a lot of changes after the break from Andersen Consulting," said Friedlander. "There was serious cost-cutting all the way around. Budgets were cut, and they started slashing people from the payroll." According to Friedlander, there was also increased pressure to bring in more consulting fees from the blue-chip clients of the firm. The snapshot is one of a firm in distress. Money was tight, and problem clients like Enron, while high-risk, were pumping in needed cash to the firm. It wouldn't have been a stretch to say that there was no reason to get tough on Enron—and every reason to try to make sense of its impenetrable accounting.

The near stoppage in business spending after the 9/11 terrorist attacks, according to several people, upped the ante and created a sense of desperation at the firm. Even the vaunted and legendary St. Charles training center stood empty because training sessions were deemed a luxury and too expensive to conduct. "There was a moratorium on travel unless it was to visit a client; there was no training; you weren't even allowed to order food for meetings," Friedlander said. "Things were definitely not looking good even before Enron."

STOP THE SHREDDING

By early 2001, Enron had become the seventh-largest corporation in the United States, based on revenues.[12] But the inflated earnings resulting from the off-balance-sheet debt came to light when the faltering economy slowed the energy giant's growth. On October 16, 2001, Enron announced a $638 million third-quarter loss and a $1.2 billion reduction in shareholder equity, and two weeks later said that it was the target of an SEC investigation.[13] On November 11, 2001, Enron announced that it was restating financial statements covering the previous five years to account for $586 million in losses.[14] Melinda Lawrence was back in the United States attending the annual SEC-AICPA conference in Washington, D.C., when Enron announced the restatements. "There had been some questions about Enron leading up to the conference because of the earlier news," Lawrence said. "Nobody ever dreamed it could end like it did."

What Lawrence didn't know was that the Houston office was already taking steps to ensure that this wouldn't be another case of Waste Management. The case against Andersen and the $7 million penalty that had been levied against it by the SEC in the Waste Management case (the largest ever against an accounting firm) for its missing $1.1 billion in overstatements would never have materialized had not certain incriminating documents been retained by Waste Management's Andersen engagement team. Duncan's team at Enron, backed by the firm's Chicago legal department, was about to put to use the firm's document "retention" policy that had been in place for only a few months.

Anyone who has worked in an accounting firm knows how much paper audits generate, even in this age of the supposed electronic audit. Therefore, it's perfectly reasonable that accounting firms dispose of earlier drafts of work papers, while retaining the final drafts as support for their audit judgment. In fact, it is seen as sound policy to destroy early drafts of documents recording a firm's evolving opinion on a particular audit, lest investors get their hands on random partner doodles predicting the imminent downfall of the Fortune 500.[15] Where Andersen crossed the line was in its timing. On October 17, 2001, just a day after Enron's announced restatement, the SEC requested information from Enron about its financial accounting and reporting. On October 23, Duncan called an urgent meeting of the Andersen audit team at which he told members of the team to destroy various documents faster than the document retention policy at Andersen allowed. On November 8, Andersen received a subpoena from the SEC, after which Duncan's secretary sent the infamous e-mail to other secretaries in Houston with the instructions, "No more shredding." During the same roughly two-week period, coordinated shredding escapades allegedly took place in several other Andersen offices in the United States and in the London office.[16]

Looked at in terms of Andersen's stated document retention policy—which calls for retaining all documents when litigation has "commenced or is threatened"—the Enron audit team's actions don't come close to passing the smell test. The problem with Andersen's document policy was that it allowed the engagement team the right to decide when litigation was "threatened." In their statement to the House Energy and Commerce Committee on January 24, 2002, Dorsey Baskin Jr., managing director of the professional standards group, and C. E. Andrews, managing partner for Andersen's global audit practice, conceded, "Looking at this policy now, in light of recent events and with the benefit of hindsight, we have to say that this is not a model of clarity."

After Enron restated its earnings in November, it went into a death spiral and couldn't get out of it. On December 2, 2001, Enron filed for Chapter 11 bankruptcy protection. On December 3, it announced more than 4,000 layoffs.[17] "Enron went out of business because they lost their clients, not because of the restatements," said Wayne Guay, accounting professor at Wharton. "They found it hard to do business after things started spiraling out of control."

The AICPA, the industry's professional association as well as its lobbying arm, knew right away that the disintegration of $67 billion[18] in market value meant trouble not only for Enron, but for all the global firms. On December 4, the AICPA announced proposals on audits related to SPEs and related entities.[19]

The collapse of Enron was a historic scandal in U.S. business in terms of its size and scope. The evaporation of nearly $70 billion in market capitalization and the ruined careers and the evaporated pensions of thousands of Enron employees reminded everyone that fraud, greed, imperiousness, and human error would never be absent from U.S. business—New Economy or Old, big company or small. It also reminded everyone why the SEC, the Department of Justice, and auditors exist. In this case, not only did Andersen not see, find, or report fraud on the part of Enron's senior executives, but the public would soon become outraged at Andersen's actions as Enron imploded.

THE BLAME SPREADS TO ANDERSEN

On Friday, January 4, 2002, Berardino was told about the document shredding by an internal team of Andersen partners investigating Andersen's role with Enron. Andersen notified the Department of Justice and the SEC that it had shredded some Enron-related documents. On January 10, Congress and the public learned of the document shredding—and the outcry was immediate and devastating. Andersen dismissed Duncan, and the firm placed three partners from the audit team on administrative leave. Many thought the Duncan firing a strange move. "Joe [Berardino] is a decent guy," said Mike Cook, former CEO of Deloitte & Touche. "I think he made some mistakes. I don't believe he should have fired the guy (Duncan) and made him an adversary." On January 24, Baskin and Andrews testified before the House Energy and Commerce Committee on the destruction of Enron documents, reminding the government that Andersen had stepped forward on its own.

The admission of shredding and the firing of Duncan didn't seem to worry the partners inside Andersen all that much, according to Friedlander. Friedlander said that throughout January, some Andersen partners in the Chicago office were discussing how much money it would take for Enron and its shareholders to go away. "The arrogance of the partners was really coming to the fore in this process," Friedlander said. "One of the senior partners at the firm said, 'Money will make this go away.'" The idea was to eventually settle litigation without admitting guilt. "They let it linger, linger, linger, because they wouldn't take a settlement where they admitted guilt."

Indeed, Andersen's penalties for such audit failures as Waste Management, Baptist Foundation of Arizona, and Sunbeam had previously represented the cost of doing business. The Andersen partners had no idea how high that price was about to get.

Diane Healy remembered sitting with lots of other young Andersen employees, hoping for a project but just hearing about the case. "They kept sending us these e-mails and voicemails, three or four every day, saying that we had plenty of money and that we weren't going out of business," Healy said. "Then you'd go home and see the news. That's when you'd hear about other cases Andersen had been involved in; they were good at keeping that quiet at the office."

Holly Thompson, an Andersen marketing director and regional proposal manager in the Memphis office, had been with the firm just over one year when she found herself in disbelief over what was happening. "I just could not believe how great the people were I was working with, and how much I respected the partners in Memphis," Thompson said. It seemed to her that every day there would be a voicemail message from Joe Berardino saying that the firm was innocent of any wrongdoing. Every Friday, the 12 Memphis partners and the various managers and staff members would have a meeting to go over the developments of the case that week.

To Coretta Robinson, a senior executive assistant in the global best practices group at Andersen, it didn't seem as if things were going so great, no matter how many encouraging voicemails she received. In her position, Robinson was responsible for paying the group's bills and making budgets. "Well, I saw a lot of red in our books, and I asked one of the partners in our group, 'I guess this red isn't good?' He said, 'Between you and me, no, it's not good.' That's when I began thinking that I'd hate to see what the whole firm was like if we couldn't even pay our group's bills."

Things started to get extra tight as time went on. Robinson was told that there would be no overtime, no matter what. The firm also started monitoring supplies and how many sandwiches Robinson ordered for meetings. "I got called a few times regarding my time, saying that if I did any more overtime it was grounds for termination," Robinson said. "So I told them I'd appreciate if they stopped giving me work at 4:30 P.M., then."

From a corporate communications point of view, the firm was in disarray during January and early February. Dan Archibal, who had taken over the global marketing position, left Andersen shortly after Enron filed for bankruptcy and never returned. Although there was a national spokesperson who addressed the media, there was no national program for coordinated communications. There was no one telling the local offices how to get the message out, how to enlist clients in the firm's defense, how to rally alumni. "The reaction was, 'It's a Houston problem,' and then, 'It's a Washington, D.C., problem,'" Friedlander said. "But the firm was founded here. It was a Chicago problem. We had reporters camped outside our building."

THE MAGNIFICENT SEVEN CAN'T
STOP AN INDICTMENT

In February 2002, things got worse as clients started leaving every day and as Andersen's international affiliates started to get nervous, with some of them even bolting for other global firms. Berardino, desperate, asked former Federal Reserve chairman Paul Volcker to come into the firm with a handpicked team, perform a review, and suggest reforms. Included on Volcker's team was Cook, who said that the team liked to call itself the Magnificent Seven.

Volcker brought a missionary's zeal to the task of saving Andersen. He felt that Andersen could be resurrected as an auditor's auditing firm. "Paul's notion was that the market needed an audit firm," said Cook. "A firm that would say, 'We're here to sell chocolate, and maybe a little vanilla. Not 28 flavors, not tutti-frutti or cookie dough, but chocolate. And it's the best chocolate you are going to find.'" Andersen, offering just chocolate—core audit services—would have been the firm of choice for companies that wanted the marketplace to reward them for going to the accounting firm that provided the most rigorous audits. For consulting services, these companies would simply go to one of the other global firms or even to a nonaccountant.

"The idea was to maintain the limited scope of auditing, believing that the marketplace would welcome such a firm," Cook said. "Companies would want to buy their audits from the new Andersen." But as the Magnificent Seven did their work, clients fled. "I told Paul, 'We need a cadre of partners going forward,'" Cook said. "And we had that. But we needed clients as well. The first wave of clients went early on, and the second wave couldn't stand the pressure from the audit committees."

Within the Andersen partnership, there wasn't much support for an audit-only firm. Partners knew what kind of hair-thin revenues that would mean. At the other global firms, the proposed limitations on Andersen weren't any more popular. If Andersen became an audit-only firm, there was a belief that regulators would push the whole industry that way.

The new Andersen that was going to offer an alternative to the modern, consulting-based global accounting firm never stood a chance. Even as Volcker finished up his report, the Department of Justice (DOJ) obtained a sealed indictment in Houston. When last-minute negotiations broke down, Andersen was indicted on March 14 on charges of obstruction of justice. On March 26, Berardino resigned in a last gambit to show the DOJ that the leaders of the firm were taking personal responsibility for what had happened.[20]

The decision to indict Andersen no doubt stemmed largely from the fact that the Enron debacle so closely followed on the Waste Management case, making Andersen a repeat offender. In addition to being hit with the $7 million SEC fine after the Waste Management debacle, Andersen had pledged to improve its auditing practices. If the DOJ had looked back a few years and totaled up the market capitalization squandered in Andersen-audited companies, total shareholder losses at Sunbeam, Waste Management, Enron, Global Crossing, Qwest, and WorldCom would have been almost $300 billion.[21]

"They were signing off on audits that should have been challenged," Friedlander said.

EXPLAINING THE INDICTMENT

Still, even given all of the foregoing, many people disagreed with the DOJ's decision to indict the entire firm and not just the individuals involved. Even kindred spirits like former SEC chairman Arthur Levitt and his one-time chief accountant, Lynn Turner, saw things differently when it came to Andersen's indictment. Levitt didn't support the move, whereas Turner did. Levitt believed that all of the Big Five accounting firms had abandoned their core mission to more or less the same degree. But Turner was convinced that the firm had to be held responsible for the culture that permeated it. "You've got 1,600 partners there responsible for their actions," Turner said. "If you have a partnership where a culture had been allowed to develop that people break the law and that leads to Qwest, Global Crossing, Baptist Foundation, Enron, and WorldCom, I have no problems with them going after the firm. They should have gone after individuals as well."

The DOJ's indictment of Andersen remains controversial because the Enron engagement involved so few people compared with the 26,000 U.S. members of the firm and the 80,000 employees worldwide. "Something had to happen after Enron, and we were the easy target because we gave the information to them," Lawrence said, referring to Andersen's notification of the DOJ that it shredded some Enron-related documents. "We were trying to be upfront and honest. To go after the people at Enron, they would have had a lot of digging to do." Greg Neu, the consultant who was with Andersen in the early 1990s, shared a belief held by many that it was Andersen's arrogance, not its auditing, that eventually brought the indictment. "The Andersen culture made enemies. The culture told them they were superior to others. Our way is the right way—that kind of stuff. Even when they'd fire a bunch of people, it'd be like: 'It's not an insult to get fired. We hired you, and that's the greatest of compliments.' There are a lot of people in this country who were insulted, somewhere and somehow, by Andersen," said Neu. "I would find it entirely believable that a heavyweight in the DOJ said, 'Just take 'em down.'"

ANGER AND BAFFLEMENT AT ANDERSEN

When the indictment hit, the general reaction in the Chicago office was that the firm was the victim of malicious prosecution. People wondered why an entire firm was getting indicted, when most of the people at the firm had never been remotely involved in the Enron engagement. "I have never seen so many grown men walking around with tears in their eyes," Coretta Robinson said. "One partner was due to retire in May, and he lost all the money he put into the firm."

For some people, it was a relief, given the level of anxiety and confusion reigning in the workplace. "It was really weird going in to work at that point," said Jonathan Goldsmith, who was in the mergers-and-acquisitions consulting group for three years at Andersen and now runs a web site for Andersen alumni, www.andersenalumni.com. "There'd be a circus outside the building, and then you'd go in and people would just be gone," Goldsmith said. "A lot of people were laid off or just not coming to the office because it was a depressing, stressful place to work. After the indictment, it was almost like, 'Okay, it's out of our hands now.'"

The Chicago office decided to rally the troops. On Friday, March 22, 2002, the firm held a rally in Chicago attended by thousands of employees, as well as by Senator Paul Simon and Reverend Jesse Jackson. Robinson attended the rally and said they were told that they could write what they wanted on the signs but "couldn't disrespect Ken Lay or Enron." As far as the politicians went, their support for Andersen appeared lukewarm as they "kept a low profile and didn't speak out too much," according to Robinson. Just days after the big rally in Chicago, 4,000 Andersen employees were laid off. Many partners fled if they could find a good exit strategy, such as forming their own smaller firms. The biggest company formed by former Andersen partners was Huron Consulting, started by Andersen partner Gary Holdrin, who bolted shortly after the indictment and took scores of partners with him.[22]

Some Andersen employees tried to keep a sense of humor to cheer up an increasingly desultory workplace. At one point, a PowerPoint presentation playing off a well-known Sprint television commercial was being e-mailed around the firm. In the commercial, one caller mishears another one because of a poor cell phone signal. In the Andersen satiric version, David Duncan is talking on his cell phone and misinterprets his secretary's reminder to "Submit timesheet paperwork" as "Shred Enron paperwork."[23]

In the outlying Andersen offices around the country, the reactions following the indictment ran from anger to bafflement. In Memphis, where Andersen had been the premier firm for years, many clients openly expressed a desire to stay with Andersen. Even during Andersen's darker hours, business went on. Holly Thompson, the Andersen marketing director and regional proposal manager in the Memphis office, was doing proposals for new work almost up until the very end. "So many of our clients wanted to stay with us; these companies really believed in us," Thompson said.

According to Thompson, at one particular Andersen client in Las Vegas, given all the adverse Andersen publicity, the audit committee demanded that company management send out a request for proposal (RFP). Thompson and her team flew out to Las Vegas to work on the presentation the partners would give at the client. "We won the proposal process even after everything was being said about us all over the national media," Thompson said. Soon, though, the word came down—the Nevada Gaming Commission wouldn't let Andersen keep the work after all.

A particularly painful day in the Memphis office was the day that its prized client, FedEx, announced that it was leaving Andersen for Andersen's bitter rivals in Memphis, Ernst & Young. "The two firms were like Coke and Pepsi," said Thompson, who worked at Ernst & Young before joining Andersen.

For people like Thompson, who landed a job four months after she left as a director of business development at NASCAR, the anger is still palpable. "I never even heard of Enron before all this happened," she said. "I never heard of David Duncan. I never even spoke to anyone at the Houston office. When it all happened, I just wish they could have sectioned off the Houston office with yellow tape, and we could have gone on with our business." Thompson left on May 20, 2002. "I was so sad about it," she said. "For a woman in the South, that kind of job is hard to get."

Diane Healy was let go in March after the indictment came down. "I defended Andersen up, down, every which way," she said. "I believed everything they said. But I think the checks and balances there were terrible. I noticed that on my own stuff. I didn't have people watching me. The partner never met with me; he didn't talk to my manager. Maybe that's part of the whole thing; it's part of no accountability."

Andersen, in a desperate move illustrating how feeble its outreach attempts were, eventually sent out talking points to alumni to try to enlist their help in defending the firm. Once Neu received his set of talking points from Andersen, he knew it was over. "Even though I hadn't been an insider for 10 years, they were sending me talking points," Neu said. "The problem at Andersen was that their culture forbid them a mechanism to tell them when they were wrong. In retrospect, I'm sure you could go back and find that the right answers were there for Andersen. They just couldn't see them."

GUILTY

On June 15, 2002, Andersen was found guilty of obstruction of justice in a Houston federal district court. The verdict rested not on shredding but on the actions of Andersen attorney Nancy Temple, who had advised Duncan to delete words from an e-mail that might make it look like they had been trying to hide incriminating evidence. Several former Andersen partners and managers believe that the verdict was wrongheaded.

A major schism divides former employees of Andersen. Many hold steadfastly to the notion that Andersen did outstanding work but was punished for the actions of a renegade office and engagement team. Others believe they were duped—striving to do things the "Andersen way" while entire engagement teams were being overpowered by their corporate counterparts at the client.

After the deathblow of conviction, Andersen just had to wait until state regulators revoked its license to audit public companies. Former Andersen clients had to find another firm to go to. Because firms with international operations believe that midtier firms do not have the ability to audit them around the world, most of Andersen's Fortune 1000 clients went to the four remaining global firms. One Big Four partner said she never had a clue to the extent of Andersen's problem until she started doing work with Andersen clients after it went defunct. "Around [this geographic area], they had experienced much more than their share of problem clients," she said. At first, this partner didn't know if that was because of something going on at Andersen or simply bad luck. But when she started reviewing the work papers of former Andersen clients, she saw problems. "All the firms have litigation issues, so you wouldn't know the extent of the problem with Andersen," she said. "I certainly would not have thought it was a national problem. But I have had a couple of situations with audits from former Andersen clients, and Andersen clearly should have done more work on these engagements."

In retrospect, this partner believed that the excellence that Andersen traditionally demanded of its employees sowed the seeds of its demise. "This may be going out on a limb, but Andersen ingrained its people with this notion that they were the best, that if you worked at Andersen you were superior, and that the other firms were second-rate," she said. "At the same time, you have a lot of Andersen partners going to work for their clients. So you have a situation where Andersen auditors [are] looking at numbers prepared by former Andersen partners who are supposedly the best of the best. So when the CFO says, 'Oh, I've done this right. You don't need to follow that audit procedure,' you just might not do enough audit procedures."

Andersen had such a high opinion of itself that not even the humiliation of being convicted for obstruction of justice could alter the dim view many Andersen people had of the other global firms. "We needed some more people on a certain ex-Andersen client," said the Big Four partner. "We were trying to hire some people from Andersen, and a colleague told us that having to go to another Big Five firm was going to be a step down for them. We were told that, 'You are really going to have to massage their egos.'"

Most of Andersen's former Houston staff was picked up by KPMG. At Deloitte, which picked up most of Andersen's Chicago, Cleveland, Detroit, and Cincinnati offices, the Andersen and the Deloitte partners clashed right away. The problem, according to Friedlander, was—here's that word again—arrogance. "The way the partners acted, you always got the sense that they felt they were the best of the best," Friedlander said. "You have to understand, they are used to being in leadership roles. I think most of them feel the firm got screwed and they did nothing wrong."

Healy, the Andersen software consultant, said there are still a lot of Andersen people out there who still believe that the firm was done wrong and that continued denial says something about how the culture at Andersen grew so insular. "It's unfortunate for all of us," Healy said, who added that in several job interviews she has had, all anyone wanted to talk about was Andersen and the shredding. "It's the truth. You worked for a place that did stuff wrong." Said Friedlander, "Now you see WorldCom, Global Crossing, Qwest. The cases are lining up like flights at O'Hare. It took a while for a lot of Andersen people to realize it. This affected me greatly, my family, my lifestyle. At the same time, I can't blame the government. They took a drastic step because we were a repeat offender."

Lawrence, for one, does not believe that Andersen's fate impugns the global firms' 1990s push to sell consulting services. Lawrence said, "You had to grow. To grow, you have to put out new products. Clients expect you to be more of an auditor. As an auditor, part of your job is to evaluate the internal audit controls. Clients don't want you to just say, 'This is broken.' They want it fixed. They want you to be able to bring a consultant in who can do it."

Instead, Lawrence drew another lesson from Enron. She made

the point that Duncan's engagement team needed to better understand Enron's transactions, which meant that they needed more information from management—not more distance. "You always have to work with management, or you're never going to be productive," Lawrence said. "You have to be friendly with management, you have to respect them. With Enron, the engagement team didn't know certain things. If auditors didn't try to work with management and know things about them and their business, you'd have *more* Enrons, not fewer."

CHAPTER 9

ACCOUNTING 101

I N THE THREE MONTHS BETWEEN ARTHUR ANDERSEN'S MARCH indictment and its June conviction, the United States channeled its collective ire over corporate financial reporting scandals at the disgraced and doomed accounting firm. After all, Andersen had been the auditor at some of the biggest transgressors: Enron, Global Crossing, Sunbeam, Adelphia, and the Baptist Foundation. The fact that Andersen didn't actually have the responsibility of preparing the financial statements for these companies did not bother anyone—with the exception of Andersen employees. The public found catharsis through Andersen's travails. Andersen jokes making the rounds ranged from Andersen night at a minor league ballpark—where patrons' ticket stubs were shredded— to an Albuquerque disc jockey who peppered his morning show with Andersen barbs.

Even though much of the vitriole was unfair to thousands of former Andersen employees, that does not change the fact that Andersen made itself a perfect target. Meanwhile, as they always did, the other global accounting firms got back on their feet, dusted themselves off, starting picking up Andersen clients, and went about their business. When Andersen was convicted and put out of business, the outcry for strong antifraud legislation faded. At the beginning of June 2002, corporate governance and audit reform legislation proposed by Senator Paul Sarbanes, Democrat of Maryland, seemed dead in the water.

Then, from beyond the grave, Arthur Andersen struck again.

WORLDCOM: EVERYTHING CHANGES

Even before Enron restated earnings for the previous five years in November 2001, WorldCom, the Mississippi-based long distance and local carrier that in 1998 had become the world's second biggest telecommunications company, had been plagued by rumors of accounting wheeling and dealing. WorldCom and Andersen, in fact, had been accused in a shareholder suit in 2001 of overvaluing the company's fiber optic assets. Indeed, the entire telecommunications industry was suspect in mid-2002, as industry leaders' dubious business models seemed surpassed only by their "creative" accounting.

In an episode that now seems an eerie foreshadowing of what was to come, WorldCom's general counsel, Michael Salsbury, testified on March 21, 2002, at a House Financial Services Committee hearing on Global Crossing's bankruptcy. Salsbury spent much of his time saying that WorldCom didn't use any of the "swap" tactics that Global Crossing had used, in which a carrier records revenue from "selling" unused capacity to another carrier for their unused capacity, thus allowing each company to capitalize its unused capacity. Salsbury went on to blame the telecommunications sector's problems not on such false internal accounting or on poor decisions to overinvest in fiber optic capacity, but on the failure of the Department of Justice (DOJ) and the Federal Communications Commission (FCC) to enforce provisions of the Telecommunications Act of 1996 and break up the monopoly of the Baby Bells. Salsbury said, "[T]hose failures have destroyed far more capitalization and robbed far more value from shareholders' investments than any accounting issues."[1]

Even as Salsbury defended the industry's and WorldCom's accounting practices, however, WorldCom's internal audit department was starting a laborious review of its own accounting practices. WorldCom's plunging stock price had forced founder and CEO Bernie Ebbers to resign in April 2002, with John Sidgmore replacing him.

One of Sidgmore's first moves was to order the accounting review. That job fell not to the accounting or the finance department, any effort of which would have been led by CFO Scott Sullivan, but to the internal audit department together with KPMG, WorldCom's replacement for the defunct Andersen. Internal auditors have skills similar to those of public accountants at big firms. Just take away the charisma, and an internal auditor is born. Internal auditors had been for much of the 1990s unceremoniously tossed out the back door at many of Corporate America's biggest companies as it was cheaper and more efficient to outsource the internal audit to the accounting firm already doing the external auditing. By doing so, companies created situations where the outside auditors were auditing their own work.

WorldCom did have internal auditors in its employ, however; and they started on their review. The vice president of audit at WorldCom, Cynthia Cooper, along with Glyn Smith, a senior manager in the internal audit department, soon found something so startlingly off base in mid-June that it made the perpetrators of Global Crossing's swap tricks and Enron's SPE manipulation look like geniuses of deception. For five quarters, WorldCom had been booking millions of dollars in day-to-day expenses as capital investments. The difference is paramount: Costs associated with capital investments can be spread out over the projected life of the investment, whereas expenses have to be recorded in the quarter in which they occur. Most of these expenses were payments to third-party vendors for the much vaunted "capacity" that general counsel Salsbury had been defending in Congress three months earlier. It appeared that fully $3.8 billion worth of costs had been wrongly classified as capital expenses over five quarters stretching from 2001 to the first quarter of 2002 (several months later, that number would be revised to $7.1 billion in overstated earnings).

Cooper and Smith confronted CFO Scott Sullivan, who asked that they delay their report, insisting that any accounting issues would be taken care of in the second-quarter statements of 2002 as a one-time charge. Cooper and Smith then appealed to board member Max

Bobbitt. Bobbitt directed Cooper and Smith to next confront David Myers, WorldCom's controller. Over that weekend, Sullivan and Myers put together a last-ditch memo that justified the classification on the grounds that the Financial Accounting Standards Board (FASB), in certain narrow cases, had defined marketing costs as capital investments.[2] It was entirely inapplicable to WorldCom's capacity leasing, however, and Sullivan's presentation illustrated that he was not exactly in the class of George May or Leonard Spacek as a theoretician. On June 25, Sullivan and Myers were told to resign. Myers did; Sullivan refused and was fired.

The SEC investigation came down full-bore on WorldCom and eventually charged five employees: Sullivan, the director of general accounting, the controller, and two accountants. Sullivan, for his part, was indicted by a federal grand jury in New York on August 27, 2002, charged with seven counts of securities fraud, conspiracy to commit fraud, and filing false statements with the SEC, and faced up to 30 years in prison. Andersen, then in the process of closing its doors for good, came out with a statement that information had been withheld from the firm and that it, like WorldCom's investors, had been deceived and lied to by WorldCom senior management. This was not all bluster, as one of the federal criminal complaints against WorldCom's employees did charge the company with withholding crucial information from their outside auditors. Andersen's assertion that its work complied with generally accepted accounting principles (GAAP) was a last, bitter gasp from the firm. If Andersen was correct that it had done everything right—and yet WorldCom was still able to carry out this massive deception—then the value of a Big Five audit would have been demonstrated to be worthless.

Former FBI agent and certified fraud examiner (CFE) Joe Wells believes that finding such obvious cases of fraud as WorldCom is critical to the future relevance of accountants. "I've seen hundreds of cases of corporate fraud," said Wells, a CPA. "Most of them are not that complicated. Take a look at WorldCom. Auditors are just not trained to see how the system can be abused." WorldCom's fraud was the *definition* of "not complicated." The fact that Andersen overlooked the misplaced expenses was stunning to everyone, including former

CEO Joseph Berardino, who expressed shock and disbelief at Andersen's performance.[3] Everyone—from Wells, to former CEOs like KPMG's Jon Madonna and Deloitte & Touche's Mike Cook, to Arthur Levitt—characterized the skills that could have prevented the WorldCom debacle as second nature to anyone who had ever taken Accounting 101.

INTERNAL AUDIT HEROES

The clumsiness of WorldCom's accounting manipulation begs the question of why Andersen missed it. According to accounting experts, any accountant paying attention never would have. The obvious point to make is that Andersen's auditors were so busy helping the client—an underreported fact is that WorldCom had paid Andersen millions of dollars in consulting fees in 2000 and 2001—that they had essentially stopped auditing.

"There was clearly something broken at Andersen," said Shaun O'Malley, former CEO of Price Waterhouse. "You don't have four or five of these [failures] in the space of a few years without there being a major problem."

The performance of Cooper and Smith in tracking down WorldCom's fraud illustrates the value of internal auditors and is one reason that the external auditors should not be allowed to co-opt the internal audit function (under Sarbanes-Oxley, the internal audit cannot be outsourced to the external auditor). Internal auditors have been severely underrated as effective checks on management, and many people—including Smith, one of the internal auditors at WorldCom—believe that internal auditors should report directly to the audit committee, bypassing the controller, the CFO, and the CEO.

Florie Munroe, now an internal auditor at Greenwich (Connecticut) Hospital, worked at Price Waterhouse for nearly 10 years, where she rose to senior manager (one rung below partner). Companies that wanted to outsource their internal audit work would hire Munroe's group at Price Waterhouse. Munroe is one person who has always believed that the unique position of the internal auditor to detect management team wrongdoing has been overlooked. But for internal auditors to fulfill their promise as effective watchdogs over management, Munroe believes that they need access to the board. "If you wanted a picture of the ideal situation for an internal auditor, it would be independence within the company, and there'd be a direct line to the audit committee," said Munroe. "I know that many internal auditors are blocked from reporting to the board of directors or the board of trustees."

Munroe, who said that the disasters at Enron and WorldCom have clearly marked a watershed for internal auditors, has herself been blocked from performing her internal audit duties in the past. "In one of my jobs, the only way the CFO could handle internal audit was to control the information. Even where management is supportive, an audit committee that doesn't want to hear certain information can bury it. If you look at Enron, Sherron Watkins was talking to internal audit before she leapt over the pyramid and went to the CEO."

SAUSAGE MAKING

The WorldCom debacle had immediate ramifications in Washington. Both major political parties had assumed in early June 2002 that corporate fraud and audit reform legislation would be a topic next discussed when, say, Al Gore ran for president again. After WorldCom announced that it had overstated its earnings to the tune of $3.8 billion, however, the Democrats and the Republicans wasted no time in commissioning polls to see how the public was reacting. Within a week, the polls showed a 10 percent swing among the electorate toward Democrats. "Until WorldCom announced their restatements, any major corporate fraud legislation was facing defeat in Congress," Lynn Turner said. "It was only after the Republicans thought they were going to be unemployed that they went against what the [accounting] firms wanted."

The Senate approved the Sarbanes bill by a 97-to-3 vote. But the accounting firms' friends in the House, including House Republican leader Dennis Hastert from the Arthur Andersen hometown of Chicago, weren't finished yet. The following scenario is a good civics lesson in how things really work on Capitol Hill.

Hastert decided he was going to "blue-slip" the Sarbanes bill, intending to block the bill from even being debated and voted on. Blue-slipping is a device that House members use to delay or permanently shelve legislation coming over from the Senate. The Constitution specifically names the House of Representatives as the authoritative body on all revenue-raising measures. When the Senate crafts a bill that would result in an increase in fees or taxes, any House member has the privilege to object to the bill by "blue-slipping" it, which actually entails sending over a blue slip of paper to the Senate from the House member objecting to the bill. In this instance, however, Hastert went to his trusty Big Four talking points one too many times, because his impending move was leaked by Senate Republicans, and Hastert incurred the wrath of the White House.[4]

President Bush and his advisers, who knew they had to make a strong statement on corporate fraud, sent Hastert and the rest of the Republican House leadership a message of perfect clarity: Any attempt to blue-slip the bill would result in the White House calling for an immediate vote on the Sarbanes bill as it stood. Bush was not going to risk his popularity by letting the House play games with a bill that well more than half of the United States now believed was needed. An immediate vote would give the House Republicans two unpalatable choices: (1) Vote against a now-popular corporate fraud bill and risk censure on election night; or (2) vote for a bill that would completely hand Democrats every regulation they'd ever wanted to place on the accounting industry.

Bowing to White House pressure, Hastert didn't blue-slip the bill. Instead, on Friday, July 22, Oxley introduced 52 new amendments, many of them from the accounting industry. The Democrats knew they held all the cards and refused to consider most of Oxley's amendments, as well as those sent to the Hill by SEC chief Harvey Pitt. "From what I've heard, Sarbanes-Oxley was written in a hurry by a lot of junior staffers," said Shaun O'Malley. "The SEC tried to send a couple hundred amendments up, but no one would even listen." Oxley was successful in watering down just a few proposals, including a provision calling for mandatory rotation of auditors every five years. That particular provision was changed to mandatory rotation not for the firm every five years, but for the lead audit partner. Although much ridiculed since, this clause could actually do some good, as witnessed by the slow wearing away over the years of David Duncan's backbone. A new Andersen lead partner, particularly from another office within the firm, would have provided a fresh (if not wholly critical) look at Enron's accounting. Also, a not so technically inclined partner, knowing that a future audit partner would no doubt look back at his or her work, might redouble his or her efforts to get the numbers right.

On the following Wednesday, Oxley decided to join the Democrats, rather than try to beat them on the issue, and endorsed the legislation. There may be no greater irony in the wars of accounting reform than Oxley's name being attached to the legislation, as it endorses essentially what Arthur Levitt wanted in 2000, which is just about everything Oxley had fought against on this issue. On July 31, 2002, President Bush signed the bill into law. Just like that, corporate governance reform was a reality.

With Sarbanes-Oxley providing cover, the New York Stock Exchange (NYSE) also took the opportunity to get more aggressive, recalling the days of its partnership with George May and the committee on stock lists. The NYSE passed rules that banned former employees and auditors of listed companies from joining the boards of those companies until the end of a three-year "cooling off" period.

BITTER DEBATES

After the passage of Sarbanes-Oxley, in the summer and early fall of 2002, typical garden-variety, deadly dull accounting panel discussions became must-see events. In August 2002, at the American Accounting Association meeting in San Antonio, Kathleen Schipper of the FASB and Michael Sutton, a former SEC commissioner, exchanged heated words on whether the FASB and/or the SEC were doing enough to prevent fraudulent corporate reporting. In October,

Baruch College accounting professor Douglas Carmichael, long a critic of the profession and a supporter of Arthur Levitt's 2000 crusade to separate auditing and consulting, got into an argument with a senior PricewaterhouseCoopers partner at an NYU panel discussion on the state of the industry. The two clashed over whether anyone has ever linked audit failure to consulting at audit clients. Carmichael not only disagreed with the PricewaterhouseCoopers representative, but also brought up PwC's well-publicized problems with client Microstrategy. Carmichael said that Microstrategy had restated its earnings and that PwC missed the inflated earnings on the financial statement while selling software to Microstrategy, installing the software, and providing various other systems implementation related to the software. Carmichael also pointed out that PwC had announced a strategic partnership with Microstrategy. During a break in the panel, the partner confronted Carmichael, saying that he "would bet his house against Carmichael's house" that Carmichael was wrong.

"Unless you have the partner come into the courtroom and admit that he made this decision and was consciously thinking about the consulting, and that it impaired his independence, you're not going to get proof," Carmichael said. "I told the guy that it doesn't have to be a conscious decision. People don't consciously say, 'I'm going to abandon my integrity.' Very seldom."

Another charged event in a strange autumn of high-profile accounting events and announcements was a speech at the Yale Club in New York given by Barry Melancon, head of the American Institute of Certified Public Accountants (AICPA), just after Labor Day. Melancon used the speech to call for a "rejuvenation" of the accounting profession and to pledge that the AICPA would work to make Sarbanes-Oxley a reality. Melancon did not mention Arthur Andersen, Enron, Arthur Levitt, or any other flashpoints during the speech. He did concede that part of the accounting profession problem "is an inclination among many auditors to assume good intent." In retrospect, Melancon's speech was significant because it issued a warning of sorts that the AICPA would not be deterred in its pursuit of remaining a major player in accounting standard setting. While Melancon acknowledged that the Public Company Accounting Oversight Board "has broad responsibilities," he went on to say that CPAs, like doctors and architects, have a right to set their own standards: "To ensure that our standard-setting capacity is as robust as possible, the AICPA will make it a priority to obtain greater involvement of the users of financial statements in setting auditing standards."

REFORM: A MIRAGE?

The degree to which Melancon and the accounting profession would uphold the commitment to accounting reform that he made at the Yale Club came greatly into question over the next few months. Melancon's words were eloquent; but in fact at that moment there were factions within the accounting profession working to destroy the new Public Company Accounting Oversight Board.

The first deadline laid out by Sarbanes-Oxley was August 14, when CEOs and CFOs of companies with more than $1.2 billion in 2001 revenues were required to personally certify their companies' books. As Joe Wells, the former FBI agent and critic of the accounting profession, said with more than a chuckle, "Just because someone is a criminal, it doesn't mean he or she is not a liar as well. So that doesn't buy you much."

While many investors worried the requirement could trigger massive restatements, the exercise of CEOs giving their personal imprimatur on their company's books ended up having an undercurrent of farce about it, which in the summer of 2002 marked the corporate world's stance toward the new legislation. It was almost as if everyone gave each other a collective wink, saying, "Okay, John Q. Public wanted us to do this, but let's get back to business." Then, debate about a possible war on Iraq took center stage in the summer and into the early fall. The second half of 2002 was a paradoxical time for Big Four accountants. Even as they became the targets of ridicule, the audit market shares of the four remaining global firms grew as they divvied up Andersen's former clients, and the price of audits rose.

In late fall, Lynn Turner, for one, was sure that the Democrats' failure to stay focused on corporate fraud had led to another empty victory and that Sarbanes-Oxley's mandate of a strong accounting oversight body would go unfulfilled. "The Democrats have just blown it," said Turner two weeks before the elections that gave both houses of Congress to the Republicans. "They got caught up in Iraq and didn't get the public to focus on putting any strength into the bill. The public thought that after Sarbanes-Oxley passed, everything was done; wham bam, we had corporate reform. And the bottom line is that none of it is going to go in place. The Democrats let the public's attention stray off this. What they have to do is come back and say, 'Sarbanes is a start; now we've all got to go do it.'" Turner's fear would prove to be well-founded. During the fall, the accounting profession would wage a stealth campaign to take the teeth out of Sarbanes-Oxley. The most important step in defanging the legislation was stopping John Biggs.

PEEKABOO

The most important reform in Sarbanes-Oxley was the call for a new Public Company Accounting Oversight Board, nicknamed "Peekaboo" by accounting industry insiders. The oversight board was designed as a souped-up version of the old Public Oversight Board (POB), which had dissolved itself in early 2002 after the SEC disregarded the body in making several important decisions. For example, after the Enron scandal broke, Harvey Pitt proposed an independent body to oversee the accounting industry. Pitt didn't bother to notify Charles Bowsher, head of the POB, which was a . . . well, an independent body set up to oversee the accounting industry. The differences between the two boards were that the new body has enormous power to negate all other auditing standards, whereas the old POB had no real standard-setting or disciplinary authority.

The Public Company Accounting Oversight Board was designed to be attractive to potential candidates for positions on the board. The five directors of Peekaboo would each be paid nearly three times as much as an SEC commissioner. The head of the board would receive $500,000. The proposed budget was an extremely healthy $100 million, though the real boon wasn't the actual amount budgeted, but the fact that Peekaboo's funding came from a compulsory charge on the accounting industry, not from Congress. This meant that Peekaboo's eventual chairman could avoid the congressional hoops through which Arthur Levitt was forced to jump to secure funding for the SEC. Sarbanes-Oxley also mandated that no members of the accounting industry sit on the oversight board. "I don't know how they expect to monitor a highly technical industry with no one on the board that has ever done an audit," said one Big Four partner.

The early favorite for the lead position was John Biggs, the retiring chairman of TIAA-CREF, the national teachers' pension fund, which managed $300 billion in investments. Biggs started at TIAA-CREF in 1989 and became chairman in 1993. Since 1996, Biggs instituted a rule that TIAA-CREF would not buy consulting services from its auditor. Biggs would frequently say that because of this stance, his company's board never had to worry whether the auditor was influenced by consulting projects when reporting on management's prepared financial statements. TIAA-CREF's outside auditors, of course, never liked Biggs's rule. They tried to convince Biggs and the board that they could provide more value than other firms or other nonaccountants because they knew TIAA-CREF so well. The accounting firm would occasionally pitch services to TIAA-CREF through the years, but Biggs never bit.

One reason Biggs decided on this manner of corporate governance was because he'd been burned before by the auditors of some of the companies in which TIAA-CREF invested. One of these companies reported as an asset a new warehouse that was 90 percent completed. The auditors never looked at the site, which contained nothing but a massive hole in the ground where the building of the new warehouse had been abandoned. Biggs had always wondered to himself whether the auditor was negligent or just going lightly on the company out of awe, friendship, or misplaced respect. Biggs was even more perplexed when, in TIAA-CREF's suit against the auditors, the jury found that the auditor had been negligent but hadn't intended to defraud TIAA-CREF. As Biggs put it when he testified on auditor independence before the Senate in September 2000: "This is simply one more example of financial loss to investors due to audit error. But like all the others, it raises in the most direct way the suspicion that the auditor was not sufficiently independent of management. It seems the old concept of 'independence' no longer fits the practices and culture of today's accounting firms."[5]

Biggs had also insisted on retaining the wall between TIAA-CREF's auditors and consultants because, years before, he'd been on the board of a major industrial company where the consulting fees of approximately $12 million dwarfed the audit fees of approximately $3 million.[6] On the audit committee was a former chairman of one of the global accounting firms, who, according to Biggs, didn't have a problem with the situation. But when the company later hired a new CEO, the CEO said the relationship with the firm was untenable. Biggs admired this and thought that it was a principled stand. Thereafter, he always held himself and his company to a similarly high standard.

At TIAA-CREF, Biggs didn't stop with the ban on hiring his audit firm for consulting. TIAA-CREF, under Biggs, also had the largest corporate governance staff of any company in the United States, with eight people working on issues related to financial statement transparency and board of director performance.[7] All in all, Biggs seemed a perfect choice to lead the new oversight body of the accounting profession.

STOPPING JOHN BIGGS

On September 11, 2002, Biggs had lunch with Pitt and Harvey Goldschmid, a Democratic-leaning SEC commissioner. At the lunch, Pitt allegedly told Biggs that Biggs had his support. With Goldschmid's support and the support of the other Democrat on the five-member SEC board, the job would belong to Biggs. But the four global accounting firms were adamant that it would not be Biggs when they heard that Biggs actually might want the Public Company Accounting Oversight Board to write some new rules.

When the *New York Times* reported that Biggs was the likely choice, it was already apparent that the accounting firms had made serious headway in their objections to Biggs. Pitt insisted that the job hadn't been offered to Biggs and said that although Biggs was a fine candidate, there were plenty of fine candidates. In fact, it was reported that over 400 people had been considered in the first cut.[8] In October, Biggs confirmed Goldschmid's assertion that the job had been offered to him. Biggs even arranged to leave his job early;[9] obviously he was leaving to do something. When a firestorm broke out accusing Pitt of carrying water for the accounting industry and backing off his selection of Biggs, Pitt said in a statement, "At no time since this process began has any member of the accounting industry . . . or any member of the Republican party sought to influence my judgment."[10] On September 26, 2002, however, Pitt met Representative Michael Oxley, the Ohio Republican and close ally of the accounting industry, fueling speculation that the accounting firms were operating through the House Republican caucus.[11]

"I don't know if the rumors are true," said Don Kirk, former partner at Price Waterhouse and one-time chairman of the FASB. "But if the firms had anything to do with Pitt backing off Biggs, it's just unbelievable to me that they would do so after everything that has gone on."

In early October, the job was offered to former CIA director and FBI director William Webster, 78. At this point, Webster's leadership as head of the audit committee of U.S. Technologies was only known to Pitt, who hadn't seen fit to inform the other SEC commissioners who had voted to approve Webster.

Webster's appointment was met with mixed reaction. Some viewed it as just another example of the Bush administration turning back the clock to find trusted statesmen from yesteryear. Turner said in early October that the choice not only was a blatant case of using someone who had contributed much to his country,[12] but was also more evidence that very little of Sarbanes-Oxley would ever get implemented as envisioned. "The chances of anything being put in are zero," Turner said in October, while Pitt was still at the SEC. "All the rules and procedures will be approved by Pitt. People who could have been good on the Public Oversight Board have been blacklisted. That's why Biggs isn't there today."

WILLIAM WEBSTER AND U.S. TECHNOLOGIES

Pitt seems to have made a calculated gamble that no one would take the time to notice that Webster—even as he was being selected for the post—was a central figure in a major accounting scandal. What Webster and Pitt thought they could get by everyone in this climate is simply unbelievable. Documents filed by U.S. Technologies and its auditor at the time, BDO Seidman, tell a story of a company that was audit shopping in the worst sense of the phrase.

The auditor for U.S. Technologies in 1995 gave the company a qualified opinion on the company's financial statements because of "going-concern" issues, which means the auditor was not convinced U.S. Technologies could stay in business. U.S. Technologies decided to switch auditors to BDO Seidman in 1997. Webster's association with U.S. Technologies began in February 2000, when the company offered Webster a position as head of its audit committee. Within three months, Webster had been given a total of 650,000 options to purchase shares at significantly below the market price. That same year, however, BDO issued its own going-concern opinion on U.S. Technologies, citing two reasons: (1) financial accounting control weaknesses and (2) concerns over the competence of the CFO. A going-concern assessment is a politically difficult one for an auditor to make because investors are apt to flee from a company where the auditors, tinkering around under the hood, warn that there's a good chance that the company is a lemon.

"If you make a going-concern judgment, two things happen," said Patty Lobingier, an assistant accounting professor at George Mason University. "One is that the company is going to be very affected in its ability to do business. Two is that they very well might find another auditor. So you don't make that judgment unless you're really, really sure that something is coming up."

The company being audited is bound to try everything to convince auditors not to issue a going-concern opinion. But BDO went through with its going-concern qualification—and the U.S. Technologies audit committee, led by Webster, fired BDO. Every company that changes auditors has to file an 8-K report with the SEC. The U.S. Technology report said: "During the years ended December 31, 1999 and 2000, and through August 16, 2001, the Company believes it had no disagreements with its independent certified public accountants on any matter of accounting principles or practices, financial statement disclosure, or auditing scope or procedure."

But BDO's required letter to the SEC did not arrive at the same conclusion: "[T]he former accountant has advised the registrant that the internal controls necessary for the registrant to develop reliable financial statements do not exist."

In a nutshell, Pitt decided that instead of Biggs, he would nominate Webster, the head of an audit committee that just fired its audit firm in a very controversial manner for ostensibly doing its job. This company had also just filed an 8-K report that never mentioned the devastating evaluation of its internal controls by its auditor (if U.S. Technologies didn't disclose the disagreement, by the way, it meant that it *agreed* that its financial accounting was a mess).

In short, whoever led the effort to torpedo John Biggs and replace him with the elder statesman William Webster had no respect for either of them. Webster, to his credit, did bring up his U.S. Technologies baggage to Pitt, who was shortsighted enough to go ahead with Webster's nomination. Webster was elected to the post by a 3-to-2 vote of the SEC commissioners. When Webster's involvement with U.S. Technologies became front-page news in late October, it sealed the fate of both Pitt and Webster, and each would soon resign.

The elephant in the corner office at the accounting firms throughout the 1990s was the dreaded f-word: fraud. One reason the firms fought so hard behind the scenes against Biggs and for Webster was fear that a new board led by Biggs would make new rules that would reintroduce the search for fraud as a prime duty of auditors. Shaun O'Malley's Panel on Audit Effectiveness, for example, said that the fraud-searching standards for auditors did not go nearly far enough.

ELECTION NIGHT

On November 5, 2002, Norm Coleman won the late Paul Wellstone's Minnesota Senate seat over Walter Mondale. Jeb Bush won reelection as governor of Florida. Elizabeth Dole won a Senate seat in North Carolina. And Pitt resigned, removing a major political headache for the White House.

Just as the SEC was ready to write 27 new laws mandated by Sarbanes-Oxley, Pitt's election-night resignation threw the agency into turmoil. Some of the external—and more likely—candidates mentioned for the SEC post at the time included Assistant Attorney General Michael Chertoff, who spearheaded the Arthur Andersen prosecution; former federal judge Stanley Sporkin; former National Association of Securities Dealers (NASD) chairman Frank Zarb; and James Doty, SEC general counsel under the first President Bush. But the real issue as 2002 closed was that, while the execution of their plan was even clumsier than usual, the accounting firms did avoid the appointment of a real reformer to lead the Public Company Accounting Oversight Board. Nipping the Biggs appointment in the bud is exactly the kind of move the accounting firms have always made when a new regulatory body has been proposed or enacted. It's useful to remember how Joe Kennedy backed down on demanding harsher audits in those fateful first months of the SEC's existence. Back then, in 1934, the profession said it already had a plan and would take care of it. In essence, it took the same tactic with Sarbanes-Oxley. The legislation passed—and the accounting profession simply worked to make the legislation toothless.

Many wondered, however, if the firms hadn't overplayed a fairly weak hand, depending on who eventually got named head of the board. For example, one of the issues with the Public Company Accounting Oversight Board was whether the board would introduce forensic auditing techniques into the standard audit. "The real question is still how much teeth this board is going to put into the standards," said Joe Wells at the end of 2002. "Are they going to take the boilerplate from the AICPA, or are they going to write their own rules and make some forensic accounting techniques mandatory? That's going to be interesting to see."

SARBANES-OXLEY EARLY EFFECTS

The Sarbanes-Oxley legislation had a tough start. In many places, its careless and too-broad provisions adversely affect those far removed from the battles of Corporate America—disbarring European-based lawyers?—while letting U.S. scofflaws off the hook too easily. By November 2002, people had actually read the tome, and a rising chorus was already saying that Sarbanes-Oxley was a disaster. "I think it's clear that Sarbanes-Oxley is one of the worst pieces of legislation that's come out in a long time," said Shaun O'Malley, former CEO of Price Waterhouse. And he was one of the legislation's supporters! One possibility is that Sarbanes-Oxley may be amended in the same manner as the Securities Act of 1933. That law was passed quickly in a tsunami of New Deal legislation and then protested against because of its many unintended consequences, like the monstrous company prospectuses its detailed requirements produced. In 1934, the Securities Exchange Act corrected many of the original legislation's flaws while remaining true to the intent of the original legislation. In the same way, there is a chance that the Sarbanes-Oxley legislation could be amended, though leaders of both houses of Congress have said they don't anticipate any further fraud legislation on the horizon.[13]

Steve Blum, a former corporate finance partner at KPMG, said that Sarbanes-Oxley should get a chance to work. "If not for the legislation that created the SEC, you wouldn't have markets as good as they are today. The legislation can change things. Legislation in the 1930s helped us get out of the Great Depression. I think it's important to let this thing do what it was designed to do."

Indeed, Sarbanes-Oxley fulfilled some of its promise even before many of its provisions had been enacted. It's common parlance among accounting firm insiders to describe auditing as a form of "diagnosis" and consulting services as a form of "cure." Before Sarbanes-Oxley, accounting firms could diagnose *and* cure. With the consulting restrictions in Sarbanes-Oxley, however, if an auditor diagnoses an information systems or internal audit problem, he or she won't be able to cure it.[14] By late fall 2002, this new dynamic between companies and their auditors was already taking form. For example, audit committees were much more wary of hiring their accounting firms as consultants for even those services that were allowed under Sarbanes-Oxley. "Audit committees are actually going overboard," said one Big Four partner. "We're often the ones with the most knowledge and the best people for the job. But the audit committees are basically afraid to hire us. We keep saying we're allowed to do it, but it's tough to get hired."

Why can't accounting firms just be satisfied with selling consulting services to nonaudit clients? "It's very difficult to market those services when you don't know the people and you don't have insight into the operations," the Big Four partner said. "It's not as easy as just deciding to do it. We don't really have much of an apparatus for getting into those nonaudit clients." Also, while attention has been focused mostly on the increasing cost of audits, consulting will eventually go up in price. One reason for this is that it takes time and money to run a bidding process, and before Sarbanes-Oxley, the auditor was such a natural that the job was "sole-sourced"—no competition was sought for the consulting job. The bottom line is that it's difficult for accounting firms to get consulting jobs at nonaudit clients.

This same Big Four partner said that audit prices were going up so fast in late 2002, due to extra audit hours helping clients implement aspects of Sarbanes-Oxley, that she had to "fire" some of her smaller clients. "It was good for me, and it was good for them," she said. "They couldn't afford the new prices, and they really didn't need the kind of experience and range of knowledge you get from a Big Four accountant."

Already, Sarbanes-Oxley is rewriting some of the old rules on fraud. Oddly enough, when it came to fraud, Sarbanes-Oxley chose to get tough on lawyers as well as accountants. The legislation says that external law firms must make a "noisy withdrawal" from clients who refuse to act when lawyers report "material violations" by company officers. In the almost 70 years of the SEC's existence, there was never a rule saying that auditors had to make a "noisy withdrawal" from a client where they found fraud.

The Sarbanes-Oxley bill isn't all bad for the Big Four auditor, specifically in its mandate that company management state that it has reviewed the company's controls and believes that they are adequate. "Companies are putting in some pretty good processes that we didn't see before," said another Big Four partner. "People have to remember we're just the auditors. I'm glad to see management stepping up to the plate."

SARBANES-OXLEY AROUND THE WORLD

One consequence of Sarbanes-Oxley that seems to have been very poorly planned for is its effect on foreign companies listed on U.S. stock exchanges. Eno Inanga, an accounting professor and researcher at the University of Maastricht in the Netherlands, said that not only is Sarbanes-Oxley too onerous on Europeans, but it's not right for U.S. companies either. "Accounting has been overregulated in the United States; they should leave it on its own," Inanga said. "The problem is education. Many people are using audited accounts for purposes they are not intended. The auditor is simply saying the accounts have been presented in accordance with GAAP. This is not enough information to make any kind of informed investment decision." In Europe, Inanga said, investors are much more skeptical than they are in the United States. A generation ago, the Institute of Chartered Accountants, the equivalent of the AICPA in commonwealth countries, published a caveat that published financial statements were purely historical and could not enable users to make investment decisions. "Published accounts should be looked at very skeptically," Inanga said. "In Europe, they are regarded not as a result of science, but as an art."

Swept up in the Sarbanes-Oxley legislation are all manner of innocent international bystanders with no idea what hit them. For example, draft proposals issued on November 6 by the SEC (yes, work was going on at the SEC the day after Harvey Pitt resigned) designed to fulfill provisions of Sarbanes-Oxley would "require both in-house and external lawyers to U.S. listed companies—including foreign law-yers—to report 'material violations' to senior company officers." Onerous complications like this one have produced commentary in Europe that companies should think twice before attempting to list on U.S. exchanges.

There is a certain irony to the European angst over Sarbanes-Oxley. After Enron declared bankruptcy, WorldCom announced it had overstated earnings by over $4 billion, and other U.S. companies lined up to announce their accounting problems, there was an initial sense of restrained glee as U.S. capitalism was taken down a peg. "I think the Europeans were laughing at us," former KPMG chairman Jon Madonna said in June.

They weren't laughing in August when they received their copies of the Sarbanes-Oxley legislation.

LIFE GOES ON AT THE SEC

On December 10, 2002, President Bush nominated William Donald-son, one of the founders of the firm DLJ, to serve the remainder of Pitt's five-year term, which expires in June 2007. Like Arthur Levitt, Donaldson had served as the head of a U.S. stock exchange—he was head of the NYSE from 1990 through 1996. As of the end of February 2003, Donaldson's confirmation hearings had not started, and Pitt was still listed on the SEC's web site as SEC Commissioner.

The SEC had a full plate after passage of Sarbanes-Oxley, which is why the money allocated for the SEC in President Bush's proposed budget, 20 percent lower than promised in Sarbanes-Oxley, caused such a firestorm. On Wednesday, January 8, 2003, Peekaboo board member Charles Niemeir was named interim chairman of the over-sight body. The following day, the board unveiled its $36.6 million budget for 2003, which included salaries higher than those originally envisioned in Sarbanes-Oxley: $560,000 for the chairman and $452,000 for each of the four board members. The not-for-profit board was scheduled to begin operating on April 25, 2003, with a staff of about 200. Although the relatively huge budget and generous salaries drew fire from some quarters, the Public Company Accounting Oversight Board had an enormously challenging task ahead of it, and it needed all the resources it could get to attract the best people to do the job—people who, no doubt, could attract large private-sector salaries.

Some of the things the SEC had to accomplish within six months of the passage of Sarbanes-Oxley, but that it couldn't accomplish because of the distractions surrounding Pitt's resignation, included a study of the civil penalties and disgorgements still owed the SEC in the previous five years; a study of the number of accountants, investment bankers, brokers, attorneys, and other professionals who were convicted between January 1, 1998, and December 31, 2001, of violating federal law; and a review and analysis of all SEC enforcement actions over the previous five years.

One of the interesting things about the SEC is that in most respects it is a typical government agency and real veterans could care less who is in charge. "That's the way it is," said Turner, the former chief accountant at the SEC. "The work gets done no matter who is in charge, particularly after a case has been brought." For example, after Pitt resigned, there were still a record number of investigations into corporate fraud going on.

There's no doubt about it: The SEC is overworked. From 1996 through 2002, the workload of the SEC grew four times as fast as did its staff. About 40 percent of the SEC's staff left between 1998 and 2001,[15] a turnover rate comparable with that of the global accounting firms. At the end of 2002, the SEC had a total of approximately 3,000 ongoing investigations.[16]

IN SEARCH OF FRAUD

In late 2002, the nature of auditing in the United States changed forever. But it wasn't just Sarbanes-Oxley that caused a fundamental change. It wasn't the resignation of Pitt and the permanent padlocking of the doors of Arthur Andersen. It was SAS 99, and it went virtually unnoticed.

SAS 99, a rule proposed by the AICPA, was a white flag of sorts issued by the accounting profession. With SAS 99, the AICPA (and with it the global accounting firms) agreed that auditors had to pursue fraud more vigorously than they had been. According to SAS 99, all frauds are material because they indicate a lack of management integrity. This is bound to change the relationship between a lead partner—a David Duncan—and his or her client. With the penalties, both criminal and civil, that will now be meted out, the accounting profession will be looking at, perhaps, a more adversarial relationship between auditors and management. With the loss of systems consulting and other lucrative consulting services, together with SAS 99, the big accounting firms' incentives will be more aligned with the role envisioned by the Securities Acts.

Statistics support the need for auditors to look beyond GAAP to areas of typical fraud. The number of announcements of financial restatements has increased significantly each year, rising from 92 in 1997 to 225 in 2001 to approximately 250 in 2002.[17] For companies listed on the New York Stock Exchange, the Nasdaq, or the American Stock Exchange, the number of restatements has increased 165 percent, even while the total number of listed companies on these exchanges went down by 20 percent in the same time period, from 9,275 in 1997 to 7,446 in 2002.

2002 LEGACY

On the Arthur Andersen web site at the end of 2002, a single press release headline stood out, maintaining that the June 15 conviction was based on faulty instructions to the jury. It is ironic that of all the accountants charged with crimes in 2002, none was from Arthur Andersen.

Whether Arthur Andersen partners are ever charged with crimes over their deeds at Enron, 2002 was still the most important year for accounting since the Securities Acts were passed in 1933 and 1934.

The Sarbanes-Oxley legislation, the reintroduction of fraud responsibility for auditors, and the demise of Andersen irrevocably changed the financial reporting landscape.

Something else remarkable happened in 2002: Accountants became the story. In early November, in fact, debate over the botched hiring process for Peekaboo joined the U.S. congressional elections and a looming war on Iraq as the top stories. The attitude of the accounting profession to the events of 2002 can be summed up with this quote from Barry Melancon at his September 4, 2002, speech at the Yale Club: "We will not look back at 2002 fondly." As groundbreaking as 2002 was, however, the most fundamental changes to public accounting will come in the next few years.

CHAPTER 10

THE FUTURE OF ACCOUNTING

FOR ALMOST 70 YEARS FOLLOWING THE PASSAGE OF THE SECURI-ties Acts of 1933 and 1934, accounting developments occurred at a glacial pace. Standards evolved in fits and starts. Public accountants took almost 30 years to stop investing directly in their clients and 40 years to start naming women partners. For decades, accounting firms wouldn't get near another firm's client, even if that client had initiated the contact. The Financial Accounting Standards Board (FASB) and the American Institute of Certified Public Accountants (AICPA) mused for years over new accounting and auditing pronouncements (the FASB, in fact, has been looking at various incarnations of special purpose entities, Enron's off-balance vehicle of choice, for nearly 20 years). Most tellingly, after the passage of the Securities Acts, there had never been another piece of legislation that affected the nature of accounting oversight.

Then came Enron, and the accounting world went from being stuck in a time warp to being stuck at warp speed.

Enron was one of the most successful corporations in the world one day and bankrupt the next. Andersen was a respected industry leader one day and a punch line of jokes the next. WorldCom had revenues of over $300 million for fiscal year 2001 and was suddenly in the red for 2002. Audit reform legislation was dead in the water one day and a sure thing the next.

Most important, the accounting profession had the respect of the public one day and the derision of the public the next. That's where the accounting profession stood in early 2003. All CPAs—those auditing public companies, those employed by public companies, those who just did tax work, single practitioners, big firms, small firms—were caught in a profession changing too fast for them to keep up.

Before 2002, the global accounting firms could set any kinds of standards they wanted for two reasons: (1) There were no limits on accounting industry concentration, and (2) they had a virtual lock on the market. By buying up or merging with any firms that could have competed with them, Arthur Andersen, Deloitte & Touche, Ernst & Young, KPMG, and PricewaterhouseCoopers had become five complacent, all-powerful behemoths, selling anything to anybody and dividing up the audits of the entire roster of Fortune 500 companies. Now there are only four global firms, and each one has more audit clients but far more restrictions on the scope of services it sells.

But above and beyond the global accounting firms, there are a couple hundred thousand more CPAs toiling away. The two overriding issues for the entire profession in the next five years are whether CPAs will:

1. Accept the fraud-detection duties that the United States wants them to fulfill.
2. Bounce back to become stewards of a respected profession that talented young people want to enter.

These two issues depend on how accountants, the Fortune 500, Congress, and the Securities and Exchange Commission go about tackling several different issues. Here are some informed predictions of some of the likely trends of the next few years.

TOUGHER OVERSIGHT OF THE PROFESSION

There seems little, if any, doubt that the accounting profession will attempt to marginalize the Public Company Accounting Oversight

Board scheduled to start working in April 2003. AICPA president Barry Melancon so much as admitted it when he said in September 2002 that the AICPA will retain its standard-setting ability. It's difficult to see how the trade organization can do so, however. Peekaboo has the power to supersede any AICPA rule. The most likely scenario is that the AICPA's relevance will recede quickly, and the AICPA will settle into a role of fighting for the interest of its members and will not retain credibility as a standard-setting body. The big question, of course, is who will get the job as chairman of the oversight board. The aggressiveness and tenaciousness of the board will depend on whether the new chairman is a friend or a foe of the global accounting firms, which is why the firms feared a reformer like John Biggs so much.

Following the John Biggs fiasco, the next chairman of the SEC must nominate someone to the oversight board with solid accounting credentials (William Webster's were extremely shaky). Peekaboo will face many challenges besides fighting the AICPA over standards. There is already an extreme skepticism among public accountants over the ability of the oversight board to understand the technical, practical, and political realities of accounting at the global firms, because none of its members can have a simultaneous connection to any accounting firm. "The Board already has very little credibility with the big firms," said Shaun O'Malley, former CEO of Price Waterhouse. "It's very difficult to establish a commission to monitor one industry. How is this Board going to monitor accountants doing derivative work, tax work, auditors on big multinationals?" The only response to that admittedly persuasive argument is that people who know the technical aspects of financial reporting and auditing have proven unfit for the job.

Besides specific auditing concerns, the oversight board will no doubt become embroiled in the major corporate financial reporting issues of the day. For example, according to the vast majority of accounting experts both in academia and in public accounting practice, the standard of not accounting for stock options as an expense in the balance sheet is just plain wrong.

A RETURN TO AUDITING BASICS

Enron prompted Congress to wonder if accountants were corrupt. WorldCom prompted Congress to wonder if accountants were incompetent. All the reform in the world will not help accountants if they cannot manage to be both straightlaced and highly competent, particularly with their blue-chip clients. "We can fight all day about auditor independence," said Lynn Turner, former chief accountant of the SEC. "Right now, we're just not getting the numbers right. We're not looking at them hard enough." When it begins work in April 2003, the Public Company Accounting Oversight Board must emphasize a return to more detailed audit testing in the field. For too long, the global firms have been emphasizing the risk-based auditing techniques that lead to consulting contracts.

As an example of the global firms' inattention to audits, Turner pointed to the fact that several years ago a $1.6 billion earnings overstatement by Rite Aid was not caught by its auditors, KPMG, yet it was noticed by an accountant on Arthur Levitt's Earnings Management Task Force in Washington.[1]

"As we ramped up all this consulting, we actually cut down on the audit work," Turner said. "At this point, we couldn't find something if it hit us between the eyeballs."

This basic auditing incompetence has discredited the value of the outside audit for all public companies. Given the Enron and WorldCom debacles, the public believes that auditors are either rubber stamping financial statements in hopes of gaining lucrative consulting business or not looking with a critical eye at all.

In fact, an accounting firm's stamp of approval on a financial report, for the first time, offers in the public's mind very little assurance that the accounting was done properly. It doesn't matter which auditor has certified the financial statements; the auditor's opinion has become part of the boilerplate that investors brush over.

The much-maligned Sarbanes-Oxley Act may be already helping in this area, however. The fact that auditors are now banned from selling many consulting services to audit clients ought to improve the credibility of an auditor's opinion on the financial statements. Also, as part of its mandate to implement Sarbanes-Oxley, the SEC proposed rules in November 2000 that prohibit auditors from advocating for clients in court, although they can still provide advice on tax matters. The more accountants are barred from advocating for their clients, the more investors will trust their seal of approval.

Regarding tax services, another major step that must be taken by the new oversight board is to bar accounting firms from providing highly lucrative tax-planning projects to their audit clients. Tax compliance—basically just completing corporate and personal tax returns—is one thing; but large-scale tax planning, in which the auditor assists the client in reducing its worldwide tax rate, is bound to have a negative impact on auditor independence. In late January 2003, the global firms and the AICPA feared that the SEC might ban these services under its mandate to implement Sarbanes-Oxley. One of three basic principles underlying Sarbanes-Oxley—that an accounting firm was not to act as an advocate for the client—would appear to preclude these tax-minimization services. The SEC, however, backed off its threat to ban tax planning. Perhaps when Peekaboo is in place, the issue will be reconsidered.

All in all, a return to valuing the basic audit shouldn't be too hard: 2002, if anything, illustrated that the "public watchdog" role that Supreme Court Justice Warren Burger affirmed in 1984 is more important than ever.

TOUGHER CONTROLS IN CORPORATE AMERICA

CPAs do not issue a client's financial statements; they give an opinion on the company's adherence to generally accepted accounting principles (GAAP), according to generally accepted auditing standards (GAAS). That means it's not just accounting firms that need to do a better job; it's all of Corporate America.

And that includes the CPAs in Corporate America. In-house accountants at corporations—even if their work is being audited by their pals back at their old firm—are about to become much more severely tested by their public accounting firm brethren, and that is a good thing. The big accounting firms simply have too much to lose to rubber stamp complicated and nontransparent accounting. It follows that auditors, if they know what's good for them, will spend more time on the audit and return to rigorous sampling and fraud-detection procedures. In turn, corporate accountants, because their work will be more closely checked, must become more accurate and more precise if they are to avoid huge audit firm fees. The internal auditors who caught the alleged WorldCom accounting fraud should serve as a model for tough internal accounting departments that will ensure that the goals of financial reporting accuracy and transparency are fulfilled.

G. A. Swanson, accounting professor at Tennessee Tech, believes that public companies need to provide investors with more original, unvarnished information. "It's time for more disclosure," Swanson said. "For investors to trust the numbers, we have to give them a little more background about where they're coming from. I'm talking about showing the full flow in the audit report, from process, to GAAP, to the balance sheet."

Accounting professor Joshua Ronen of NYU's Stern School of Business believes that taking the radical step of disallowing stock options would remove the incentive for CEOs to inflate earnings. "Options give them an intent to maximize short-term growth and to hide any slipup," Ronen said. "The 1990s boom magnified any reward and any penalty." Another accounting professor, S. P. Kothari of MIT, has a different solution for controlling the effects of stock options expenses on the behavior of corporate managers. "We should have the managers announce they are going to sell shares a day or two before they do it," Kothari said. "If you are going to sell a million shares, announce a day or two before. That way everyone knows it."

The impetus for any of the aforementioned solutions must come from corporate boards. There is every reason for directors to want their corporate accountants and internal auditors to be committed to financial statements that are as transparent as possible.

A CHANGE IN LEADERSHIP AT THE AICPA

One likely development in 2003 is a change in leadership at the AICPA, the trade organization for accountants. Once the Public Company Accounting Oversight Board begins work in April, there is a good chance of a confrontation between the two organizations, especially if Peekaboo is aggressive about proposing new fraud-searching standards for auditors.

Barry Melancon retained some support as leader of the AICPA's 330,000 members throughout 2002, but judging from the trouncing that his initiative to introduce a new designation for accountants (certified business adviser) received several years ago in a vote (it lost by more than a 60–40 percentage), that support is very soft. "A large body of members think the AICPA leadership is leading the membership down the wrong road," said Robert Fox, an accountant in Rochester, New York, who sits on the state Board of Accountancy.

THE AUDIT COMMITTEE: THE LAST LINE OF DEFENSE

If the recommendations of the Blue Ribbon Report on Audit Committee Effectiveness in 1999 had been adopted by Enron's board of directors, Enron's audit committee would have been getting much better information from Arthur Andersen, Enron's external auditors. The Blue Ribbon Report called on audit committees to, among other things, ascertain from the auditors whether the company was using "just" GAAP or whether the company used superior, best-practice auditing principles. It's hard to believe that even Andersen would have characterized Enron as using best-practice accounting, and that vote of no-confidence might have raised more of a question in the minds of Enron's directors. But then, one never knows, given the track records of all involved in Enron.

Even since Sarbanes-Oxley was passed, the nature of being on an audit committee has changed. Audit committee members today have to spend much more time on their duties—double the time, in some cases—and many are afraid that with their increased responsibility will come increased exposure to litigation. "Now you have to have an audit committee meeting before a press release, an audit committee meeting before the 10-K is released," said Shaun O'Malley. "There is a question whether people are going to be bolting from audit committees."

But higher standards, longer hours, and a more demanding workload are the new standards for the post–Sarbanes-Oxley audit committee; and as of January 2003, there were few reports of Fortune 500 companies that couldn't find audit committee candidates.

A RESURGENCE OF LEADERSHIP AT THE BIG FOUR

Not one person interviewed for this book could name someone as a serious contender for "leader of, or spokesman for, the accounting profession." The CEO positions at the big firms have all changed since the bruising battles with Arthur Levitt in 2000. But so far, none of them has been getting very good reviews. "Today, all you get from the firms is, 'No, no, no,'" said Mike Cook. "I think there is a leadership void, and I don't think it can be filled from within the profession. No one from within the profession has the credibility or the voice to do it."

Although men like Price Waterhouse's George May and Arthur Andersen's Leonard Spacek disagreed about almost every important accounting debate of their time, each of them contributed positively to the public discourse in the United States.

The profession *is* sorely lacking in the kind of strong leadership it had from the 1920s through the 1980s. Accountants, even more so than attorneys, were trusted professionals who were key players in the economic life of the country. The profession can return to those proud roots again. But it will be a difficult process, and more radical change is needed than is currently being seriously debated.

But there is still a good chance of stronger leadership at the Big Four in the next few years. One result of the demise of Enron, WorldCom, and Andersen is that the Big Four will be more careful about who represents them in the future, both at big clients and in national jobs within the firms. It's apparent from interviews that he gave not long after his resignation that former Andersen CEO Joseph Berardino barely knew David Duncan and the members of the Enron engagement team.[2] In addition, within the global accounting firms during the 1990s, it seemed that every partner was a "national director" of something or other. Promotions and tough assignments were often made with no real vetting process. Some bad apples are bound to sneak through; after all, thousands of partners can't all personally know each other. But one of the first places the firms will look to avoid future litigation is the process by which they promote and hand out choice assignments.

AN INCREASE IN ETHICS EDUCATION
AND FRAUD EDUCATION

There is one aspect of this debate on which the leaders of the global accounting firms, professors, regulators, and corporate CEOs all agree: The future of accounting depends on the caliber of students who join the profession. Now, if everyone could just agree on what these students should be taught.

Two decades ago marked the last great crisis in accounting education, as educators and practitioners were at great odds. The academics were teaching plenty of theory, but the practitioners wanted students better prepared in the practical aspects of auditing. Something had to be done to get the colleges and the firms on the same page. "The Big Eight poured money into redoing accounting education," said accounting professor G. A. Swanson. The result was that theory and other "soft" topics such as ethics were essentially expunged from the curriculum.

"We need to integrate ethics back into the courses," said John Koepel, a Jesuit priest and accounting professor at the University of San Francisco. "There is a pervasive ethical problem out there. What's happening now is that firms are looking at the probability of suffering a loss if they take the client's position on a specific issue. They might say, 'Hey, if we take the client's position, there's only a 20 percent chance of getting caught.' So you get a rationalization of just a few small shortcuts here and there. It's a slippery slope, and I don't know that there is a line that some people out there won't cross right now."

A major emphasis on fraud detection must, sooner or later, make its way back into the undergraduate and continuing education curriculums. Joe Wells, the former FBI agent who started the nation's largest certified fraud examiners' association, believes that as auditors get punished in the courtroom, it's only a matter of time before they start emphasizing ethics—for practical purposes, if nothing else.

"The accounting profession, and auditors specifically, have always been against being mandated to seek out fraud," said Wells. But reporting issues are of little interest to the public. "The reality is that auditors have been brought kicking and screaming into the fraud business." Accountants realize that to keep insisting they can't find fraud will do nothing to reclaim their credibility. For one thing, most people have now heard of "forensic audits," which are done by CPAs who've taken just a few courses to become a CFE. Wells believes that investors will now demand sophisticated fraud detection from auditors and that accounting students—indeed, accounting professionals at any point in their careers—can be educated to find fraud. It just takes the right frame of mind. "If the auditor had a modicum of education, he could detect a lot more fraud. . . . It starts with professional skepticism, which has been lost," Wells said. In this regard, the AICPA announced in 2002 that it will provide eight hours of antifraud education to every CPA in the United States.

NYU accounting professor Joshua Ronen, however, cautioned, "You can teach auditors as much fraud detection as you want, but it will only help if they have the right incentives." Auditor incentives, though, appear to have been radically realigned over the past few months. Audits have already gotten more lucrative. Thousands of Andersen clients on the market got the big firms talking about their audit prowess again, in order to attract the best of these potential clients. Also, the penalties for not finding fraud have obviously become much more severe, as Andersen's litany of audit failures illustrates.

One educational device that could be used to help train accountants to find fraud is the use of case studies, a staple of MBA programs. Case studies could show accounting students the ramifications of an auditor's decision not to question dubious numbers on a balance sheet. But some within the industry worry that a job description that reads "searching for fraud" will scare off prized recruits. Jon Madonna, former CEO of KPMG, worries that the kind of people attracted to straightforward auditing will not be able to compete with savvy financial managers intent on the auditors seeing things their way.[3] Mike Cook, though, remains an optimist. "There could be a Renaissance period coming up, a time when our stature gets restored," he said. "Maybe we'll see a whole new level of quality and a correspondingly high level of respect for the public accountant."

A SHRINKING CONSULTING MARKET

Sometimes people forget under Sarbanes-Oxley that accounting firms can still provide all kinds of consulting services. They're simply restricted from providing certain consulting services to audit clients, such as installing accounting systems. The consulting practices at the accounting firms will most likely shrink because demand for consulting will most likely go down. That's because many consulting projects are started as a result of an auditor finding a problem. "Companies go to their accountants for these services because we're in there every year," said Robert Fox of the New York State Board of Accountancy. "The auditor says, 'I told you about this problem in the management letter. I have the expertise. You already have a relationship with me.' Also, a lot of CEOs and CFOs are from the big firms. They're basically working with their buddies."

The auditor isn't likely to tell company management that it needs to hire Accenture or McKinsey or Bain Consulting to take care of that system problem. In that way, barring accountants from providing consulting services may end up hurting disclosure because accountants were good at finding issues. What accounting firms might do, however, is try to steer the issues they do come across under the tent of "audit-related services" that they wouldn't be barred from providing. For example, a few years before Sarbanes-Oxley was passed,

KPMG had developed a group of services called advisory-based audit services, which are consulting services deemed to arise directly out of the audit work. Thus, there may be an attempt by the firms to frame their service offerings into the three or four consulting options that are still allowed.

THE NEXT BATTLEGROUND: ACCOUNTANTS AND ATTORNEYS

There are likely to be further backlashes on the accounting profession. For example, for years the big firms have been hiring lawyers who then claim to not be practicing law. Unlike those in France and the United Kingdom, U.S. accounting firms are not allowed to share fees with attorneys. That hasn't stopped them, however, from doing it. In a way, the accountants are doing exactly what they did in the late 1990s with the unallowed investments in their clients. When a tip from a disgruntled ex-employee led the SEC to PricewaterhouseCoopers's thousands of ethics violations, the reaction from the profession was: "Hey, these are bad rules." Once the public realizes that accountants are still pushing the edges of the law in terms of the services they provide, the SEC might have to act to force the Big Four to stop providing these legal services, which Sarbanes-Oxley specifically outlaws. If accounting firms shouldn't be providing systems consulting, they also shouldn't be providing legal services.

An example from France illustrates the chaos that joint accounting firms/law firms would produce. In France, Ernst & Young can practice law. In mid-2000, two lawyers from Ernst & Young agreed to be expert witnesses in a case the French government was bringing against IBM. When IBM learned of this, it became upset that Ernst & Young, also its auditor, had been working against the company in its case with the government. When the French government learned of the situation, it also was upset and decided not to let Ernst & Young help it *or* IBM. This web of entanglements and conflicts is exactly where the profession is heading.

Another structural issue at the firms is alternative practice structures, in which an accounting firm tries to address the problem of being undercapitalized by becoming part of a bigger corporate entity. American Express and H&R Block each purchased accounting firms in the past several years. "The problem is firms have no way to get capital," said Steve Blum, formerly a KPMG corporate finance partner. "All they have is partner revenue. The firms are seriously undercapitalized. All these other arrangements you see are attempts by the firms to get capital." When the brokerage industry was in this situation in the early 1970s, industry maverick DLJ simply charged ahead and went public. Other brokerages soon followed, and the New York Stock Exchange had to accept the changes.

FINANCIAL STATEMENT INSURANCE

One of the most revolutionary and thought-provoking ideas is to hand audits over to the insurance industry. This solution would solve the structural flow of the company paying the independent auditor. The proposal floated by Joshua Ronen and others is to require corporations to buy financial-statement insurance. Payouts would go to investors who suffered losses as a result of misrepresentations on financial statements. The reason it would solve so many conflicts is that insurance companies would be the ones to hire the auditors, who would have a clear incentive to find errors and fraud. "Auditors are typically biased because they are paid by the company they audit, and their incentives are not aligned," Ronen said. He thinks that would go a lot further than simply training auditors to find fraud. "Auditors are good enough to detect whatever needs to be detected—if they have the right incentives."

The amount each company pays in premiums could be disclosed, and investors could factor accounting risk into their investment decisions. Ronen said the cost of the insurance would roughly equal the amount companies now pay for audits. This private-sector solution has merit over anything regulators have come up with. After every spasm of audit failures in the United States—which seems to occur every 15 years or so—there is a flood of new rules and pronounce-ments by the SEC and the FASB and the inevitable panel and committee reports. But in each case, another cycle of audit failures occurs, typically following a slowdown in economic growth (where there are business failures, there will always be audit failures under the current system). Under Ronen's plan, there wouldn't be a need for more band-aids because the source of the wound—misaligned auditor incentives—would have been addressed.

PUBLIC WATCHDOGS AND THE SEARCH FOR FRAUD

Although many accountants interviewed at the end of 2002 insisted that public accounting isn't about finding fraud, the truth is that fraud detection is exactly what most members of Congress, the SEC, and the public believe it should be about. The most interesting aspect of auditors' insistence that finding fraud is not part of their job is how good they are at other types of complex diagnosis. For example, the full range of consulting services provided for so long to audit clients (now mostly banned by Sarbanes-Oxley) was mostly initiated by the audit teams and their astute observations of their clients' operations. Those were the famous synergies between auditing and consulting that the accounting firms said were so important to good service. So, why are accountants so good at finding problems that need consult-ing solutions, yet not good enough to detect WorldCom-like fraud? The obvious answer is that accountants could find operational ineffi-ciencies because that's exactly what they are looking for. They didn't see fraud because that's *not* what they were looking for.

Take the Continental Vending case from the 1960s and the Enron scandal, both of which involved executives setting up related-party entities. Both companies told their auditors point blank that they were essentially using these entities in a borderline illegal way. Harold Ross at Continental was borrowing millions of dollars from a shell subsidiary, and Enron's Jeffrey Skilling was allegedly reaping millions from SPEs set up mainly for hiding debt and pumping up Enron's stock price. All the auditors had to do was look, instead of keeping their heads down. The truth is that auditors dig all the time—they simply dig for consulting projects.

"During part of the audit, you have to suspend neutrality," said Shaun O'Malley, former CEO of Price Waterhouse. "You have to say to yourself, 'Okay, if these guys wanted to play around, how would they do it?' You then attack those areas that you know are most susceptible. You can't do it across the board, of course, because no one would pay for that; but it can be a deterrent because it does increase the chances for detection."

Accountants' investigative energy in the late 1990s became overwhelmed by a desire to be indispensable business advisers to management. The focus of auditors needs to be recentered on the audit; and Sarbanes-Oxley, while a problematic piece of legislation, does attempt to accomplish this. Auditing can be interesting still to those undergraduates seeking a job requiring backbone, rigor, and business savvy.

Auditors need to be rewarded for finding fraud and for becoming technical gurus in certain areas. This can happen by changing compensation standards. As it is now, the best-paid partners are the rainmakers, just as in big law firms. While AICPA and SEC rules ban firms from rewarding auditors with contingency fees for bringing in consulting business, those efforts do get reflected in compensation. "It's not like you get a cut of what you bring in," said one Big Four partner. "But if you are really good at bringing in consulting projects, it certainly is factored into your compensation." That is as it should be; but there's no reason that other skills—such as being a great detector of fraud—can't be rewarded.

THE FUTURE OF THE PROFESSION

If young professionals like Suzette Lopez are any indication of the profession's future, then there is hope for auditing yet. Lopez, a native of Kingston, Jamaica, worked at PricewaterhouseCoopers for several years in her home city before coming to the United States with her husband, who is also an accountant. Lopez is a chartered accountant and hopes to pass the CPA exam in 2003. "The chartered accountant test is very difficult; it's done at three different levels," she said. "The CPA exam is pretty tough in terms of volume. The content here is a little wider, but at least it's multiple choice."

Here in the United States, Lopez is with Watson Rice, a minority-owned firm in Manhattan. Because Watson Rice does so many government contracts, several firms usually handle the jobs, so Lopez works alongside partners and managers of the global firms. She believes her skills—particularly her ability to stand up for the correct accounting treatment—rival those of any of her colleagues at the bigger firms. "The Big Five firms use a more risk-based approach than smaller firms do," Lopez said. "This has resulted in many positive changes, such as being less of a historian and looking at more current issues. But the downside of the risk-based approach is that you might not detect errors until they hit the million dollar area."

Lopez, however, believes that with more auditors like her coming up, the pendulum can swing back to doing more detailed work again. "I tend to be more aggressive," she said. "One client said to me, 'You don't let go, do you?' I need to verify what the client is talking about. I may go a little further, and that has helped me. Once I see something that seems strange, I follow my gut feeling, and I've identified things that way."

Lopez believes that her "sixth sense" is nothing other auditors can't obtain. "It's partly my training. In Jamaica, the clients were a little smaller than Big Four clients in New York, so I used a detailed audit approach," she said. "My opinion is that as a profession, whereas we need to use the risk-based approach, we also should get back to the basics. I think it might improve the likelihood of identifying errors that the public and shareholders are concerned about, like with Andersen at Enron."

It would be nice for all of us to go back in time and, for just a few days, see what Suzette Lopez could come up with at Enron. Maybe someday she and others like her will go a long way toward preventing the Enrons of the future.

NOTES

MY INTRODUCTION TO ACCOUNTING

1. Price Waterhouse, internal memo, December 14, 1909, PwC collection, Columbia University Rare Book and Manuscript Library.
2. Price Waterhouse, New York metro region newsletter, July 1993, Arthur Levitt Jr. papers, Columbia University Rare Book and Manuscript Library.
3. James Mahon, donated papers, *Mini-History of C&L*, draft, 1986, PwC collection, Columbia University Rare Book and Manuscript Library.
4. Arthur Levitt, speech to Financial Reporting Institute, June 6, 1996, text sourced from SEC.gov.
5. Arthur A. Carter, Senate testimony, April 1, 1933.
6. Leonard Spacek, *An Address by Leonard Spacek*, pamphlet of speech given August 27, 1957, PwC collection, Columbia University Rare Book and Manuscript Library.
7. Arthur Andersen partner, telephone interview with author, October 2002.
8. Jane Mayer, "The Accountant's War," *The New Yorker*, April 22, 2002, 64.
9. KPMG, internal presentation, May 2002.
10. Thomas W. Morris, *The International Dictionary of Accounting Acronyms* (Chicago: Glen Lake Publishing, 1998), vii.

11. AICPA, annual report, 2001–2002, 22.
12. Arthur Levitt, speech at New York University Center for Law and Business, September 28, 1998, text sourced from SEC.gov.

CHAPTER 1: THE FIRST ACCOUNTANTS

1. Ada Calhoun, "Count Her In," *Austin Chronicle* (online version), December 10, 1999.
2. John Farmer, "President's Working Vacation Defies Logic," *Star-Ledger*, August 12, 2002, 15.
3. Heather Pringle, "The Cradle of Cash," *Discover,* October 1998 (www.discover.com/oct_issue/cradle.html).
4. Michael Chatfield and Richard Vangermeersch, *The History of Accounting* (New York and London: Garland, 1996), 223.
5. Ibid., 506.
6. R. Hussey, *Dictionary of Accounting* (Oxford and New York: Oxford University Publishing, 1995), 132.
7. Chatfield and Vangermeersch, *The History of Accounting,* 506.
8. Hussey, *Dictionary of Accounting,* 132.
9. Edward III, account books, Montgomery collection, Columbia University Rare Book and Manuscript Library.
10. Ibid.
11. Commissioner of accounts, letter to William Legge, August 1668, Montgomery collection, Columbia University Rare Book and Manuscript Library.
12. Alexander Stanhope, expense report, Montgomery collection, Columbia University Rare Book and Manuscript Library.
13. Chatfield and Vangermeersch, *The History of Accounting,* 221.
14. East India Company, account books, Montgomery collection, Columbia University Rare Book and Manuscript Library.
15. George May, speech at Indiana University, March 29, 1950, PwC collection, Columbia University Rare Book and Manuscript Library.
16. Robert Fox Tavern, accounts, Montgomery collection, Columbia University Rare Book and Manuscript Library.

17. Ibid.
18. Gary John Previts and Barbara Dubis Merino, *A History of Accountancy in the United States* (Columbus: Ohio State University Press, 1998), 16.
19. Ibid.
20. Ibid.
21. *An Essay upon the Italian Method of Bookkeeping*, Montgomery collection, Columbia University Rare Book and Manuscript Library.
22. John Selnyn, papers, Montgomery collection, Columbia University Rare Book and Manuscript Library.
23. British government, report on public revenue of the Crown, 1740, Montgomery collection, Columbia University Rare Book and Manuscript Library.

CHAPTER 2: THE BIRTH OF AN AMERICAN PROFESSION

1. *General George Washington's Accounts of Expenses, 1775–1783* (New York: Houghton Mifflin, 1917), vii; PwC collection, Columbia University Rare Book and Manuscript Library.
2. Ibid., 52.
3. Ibid., 142.
4. Oliver Wolcott (U.S. comptroller), correspondence, Columbia University Rare Book and Manuscript Library.
5. John Cassidy, "The Greed Cycle," *The New Yorker*, September 23, 2002, 64.
6. Mill Creek Marsh Company, account books, 1820–1870, Montgomery collection, Columbia University Rare Book and Manuscript Library.
7. Ibid.
8. Ibid.
9. Mounthope Plantation, waste book, 1800–1820, Montgomery collection, Columbia University Rare Book and Manuscript Library.
10. Pajaro and Salinas Ranch, account books, Montgomery collection, Columbia University Rare Book and Manuscript Library.

11. Continental Railroad, account books, Montgomery collection, Columbia University Rare Book and Manuscript Library.
12. New York Stock Exchange web site, text sourced from NYSE.org, "About the NYSE"—Historical Perspective.
13. Gary John Previts and Barbara Dubis Merino, *A History of Accountancy in the United States* (Columbus: Ohio State University Press, 1998), 80.
14. Ibid., 84.
15. Ibid., 86.
16. Oscar Berry & Carr, records, 1883, Montgomery collection, Columbia University Rare Book and Manuscript Library.
17. Joseph Klein, oral history, Columbia University Oral History Research Office.
18. George May, articles of clerkship certificate, PwC collection, Columbia University Rare Book and Manuscript Library.
19. George May, dinner remarks at Union League Club, April 13, 1914, PwC collection, Columbia University Rare Book and Manuscript Library.
20. Price Waterhouse, internal railroad document, PwC collection, Columbia University Rare Book and Manuscript Library.
21. Price Waterhouse, audit report of Louisville & Nashville, PwC collection, Columbia University Rare Book and Manuscript Library.
22. World Congress of Accountants pamphlet, PwC collection, Columbia University Rare Book and Manuscript Library, iii.
23. Walter Staub, letter to George May, July 28, 1944, PwC collection, Columbia University Rare Book and Manuscript Library.
24. World Congress of Accountants, pamphlet.
25. Price Waterhouse, internal sales call document, 1905, PwC collection, Columbia University Rare Book and Manuscript Library.
26. Arthur Andersen, *Behind the Figures: Addresses and Articles by Arthur Andersen, 1913–1941* (Chicago: Arthur Andersen, 1970).
27. Ibid.
28. Ibid.
29. Jean Strouse, *Morgan: American Financier* (New York: Perennial, 2000), 564.
30. Ibid., 565.

31. George May, *Twenty-five Years of Accounting Responsibility, 1911–1936* (New York: Price Waterhouse, 1936), 173.
32. Klein, oral history.
33. Robert H. Montgomery, "What Have We Done and How?" 1937 speech, quoted in Lybrand, Ross Bros. & Montgomery newsletter, August 1953.
34. Klein, oral history.
35. Ibid.

CHAPTER 3: ACCOUNTANTS EARN A PUBLIC TRUST

1. George May, letter to J. M. B. Hoxsey, January 22, 1934, PwC collection, Columbia University Rare Book and Manuscript Library.
2. George May, letter to T. K. McClelland, PwC collection, Columbia University Rare Book and Manuscript Library.
3. Mary Murphy, *Britain in an Opulent Age* (unpublished Price Waterhouse history), 55, PwC collection, Columbia University Rare Book and Manuscript Library.
4. George May, letter to accounting firm Arthur Young confirming American Radiator and Standard Sanitary Company opinion, March 27, 1934, PwC collection, Columbia University Rare Book and Manuscript Library.
5. Joseph Klein, oral history, Columbia University Oral History Research Office.
6. Federal Securities Act of 1933, testimony insert, "A Study of the Economic and Legal Aspects of the Proposed Federal Securities Act," U.S. Senate Committee Hearings on Banking and Currency, March 4, 1933.
7. Ibid.
8. Gary John Previts and Barbara Dubis Merino, *A History of Accountancy in the United States* (Columbus: Ohio State University Press, 1998), 250.
9. Ibid., 148.
10. Michael Chatfield and Richard Vangermeersch, *The History of Accounting* (New York and London: Garland, 1996), 302.
11. Price Waterhouse, New York metro region newsletter, July 1991,

PwC collection, Columbia University Rare Book and Manuscript Library.

12. George May, letter to Arthur Wiesenberger, April 4, 1961, PwC collection, Columbia University Rare Book and Manuscript Library.

13. "To Have Outside Audit," *New York Times*, October 11, 1934, 7 (no byline).

14. Ibid.

15. Chatfield and Vangermeersch, *The History of Accounting*, 409–410.

16. George May, Senate testimony on Securities Act, March 1, 1934.

17. George May, *Twenty-five Years of Accounting Responsibility, 1911–1936* (New York: Price Waterhouse, 1936), 119.

18. George May, correspondence, PwC collection, Columbia University Rare Book and Manuscript Library.

19. George May, letter to Frank Altschul, April 19, 1950, PwC collection, Columbia University Rare Book and Manuscript Library.

20. "To Have Outside Audit."

21. May, *Twenty-five Years of Accounting Responsibility*, 211.

22. Arthur A. Carter, Senate testimony, April 1, 1933.

23. Ibid.

24. Lewis Ashman, letter to George May, January 22, 1934, PwC collection, Columbia University Rare Book and Manuscript Library.

25. George May, letter to Lewis Ashman, January 24, 1934, PwC collection, Columbia University Rare Book and Manuscript Library.

26. George May, letter to W. A. Paton, August 20, 1934, PwC collection, Columbia University Rare Book and Manuscript Library.

27. Ibid.

28. Ibid.

29. Felix Frankfurter, letter to George Brownell, December 1, 1933, PwC collection, Columbia University Rare Book and Manuscript Library.

30. Ibid.

31. May, Senate testimony.

32. George May, letter to Arthur Goodhar, September 26, 1944, PwC collection, Columbia University Rare Book and Manuscript Library.

33. George May, letter to Louis H. Renn, July 23, 1934, PwC collection, Columbia University Rare Book and Manuscript Library.

34. George May, letter to Judge John Burns, October 16, 1934, PwC collection, Columbia University Rare Book and Manuscript Library.

35. George May, letter to George Armistead, December 26, 1934, PwC collection, Columbia University Rare Book and Manuscript Library.

36. George May, letter to Edwin F. Gay, October 18, 1934, PwC collection, Columbia University Rare Book and Manuscript Library.

37. Minutes of July 18, 1934, SEC meeting, PwC collection, Columbia University Rare Book and Manuscript Library.

38. Ibid.

39. George May, letter to H. C. Clifford-Turner, January 4, 1935, PwC collection, Columbia University Rare Book and Manuscript Library.

40. Joseph P. Kennedy, letter to Price Waterhouse, June 28, 1935, PwC collection, Columbia University Rare Book and Manuscript Library.

41. Business Advisory Council, letter to Sidney J. Weinberg, May 5, 1936, PwC collection, Columbia University Rare Book and Manuscript Library.

42. George May, letter to John Landis, December 6, 1936, PwC collection; Columbia University Rare Book and Manuscript Library.

43. George May, letter to William B. Franke, April 20, 1936, PwC collection, Columbia University Rare Book and Manuscript Library.

44. George May, letter to Professor Bishop E. Hunt, September 10, 1959, PwC collection, Columbia University Rare Book and Manuscript Library.

45. A. A. Berle Jr., speech to American Association of Accounting, Atlantic City, N.J., December 27, 1937, PwC collection, Columbia University Rare Book and Manuscript Library.

46. A. A. Berle Jr., speech to American Institute of Accountants, Atlantic City, N.J., June 4, 1936.

47. May, letter to Goodhar.

48. Ibid.
49. George May, letter to J. M. B. Hoxsey, February 3, 1939, PwC collection, Columbia University Rare Book and Manuscript Library
50. Chatfield and Vangermeersch, *The History of Accounting*, 409–410.
51. Previts and Merino, *A History of Accountancy*, 295.
52. May, letter to J. M. B. Hoxsey, January 22, 1934.
53. Chatfield and Vangermeersch, *The History of Accounting*, 409–410.
54. Dorothy Wilkerson Bertine Questionaire, 1997, PwC collection, Columbia University Rare Book and Manuscript Library.
55. F. W. Thorton, letter to George May, August 1, 1944, PwC collection, Columbia University Rare Book and Manuscript Library.

CHAPTER 4:   THE QUEST FOR GROWTH

1. George May, letter to Sir Frederick Alban, July 6, 1949, Society of Incorporated Accountants & Auditors, PwC collection, Columbia University Rare Book and Manuscript Library.
2. Editorial, *Controller Magazine*, October 1948, 506.
3. George May, letter to A. R. Prest, January 10, 1951, PwC collection, Columbia University Rare Book and Manuscript Library.
4. Summary of Price Waterhouse MAS 1957 national meeting, PwC collection, Columbia University Rare Book and Manuscript Library.
5. Ibid.
6. Ibid.
7. Herman Bevis, oral history, PwC collection, Columbia University Rare Book and Manuscript Library.
8. Ibid.
9. Ibid.
10. Ibid.
11. Leonard Spacek, letter to George May, October 6, 1955, PwC collection, Columbia University Rare Book and Manuscript Library.
12. George May, letter to Jack Inglis, December 5, 1955, PwC collection, Columbia University Rare Book and Manuscript Library.

13. Bevis, oral history.
14. Ibid.
15. Ibid.
16. Ibid.
17. Ibid.
18. Ibid.
19. Lee Berton, "Auditors' Critics Seek Wider, Faster Action," *Wall Street Journal*, November 15, 1966, A1.
20. Andy Barr, speech to American Institute of Accountants, 1955, PwC collection, Columbia University Rare Book and Manuscript Library.
21. Ibid.
22. Maurice Stans, speech at Stanford University, PwC collection, Columbia University Rare Book and Manuscript Library.
23. Bevis, oral history.
24. "Grand Jury Indicts Four Men for Fraud in Continental Vending's '62 Report," *Wall Street Journal*, October 18, 1966, 32 (no byline).
25. James A. Largay III, "Lessons from Enron," *Accounting Horizons*, June 2002, 153.
26. "Grand Jury Indicts Four Men for Fraud in Continental Vending's '62 Report."
27. Ibid.
28. Ibid.
29. Morris Kaplan, "3 Lybrand Aides Are Found Guilty," *New York Times*, June 22, 1968, 43.

CHAPTER 5:   CRACKS IN THE FACADE

1. Mike Cook, testimony before U.S. House of Representatives Committee on Energy and Commerce, April 17, 1985.
2. "ZZZZ Best Denial Issue," *New York Times*, February 2, 1988, D22 (no byline).
3. Coopers & Lybrand, unpublished history, PwC collection, Columbia University Rare Book and Manuscript Library.
4. Ibid.

5. Amey Stone and Mike Brewster, *King of Capital* (New York: Wiley, 2002), 74.
6. Henry Gunders, oral history, PwC collection, Columbia University Rare Book and Manuscript Library.
7. John Biegler, oral history, PwC collection, Columbia University Rare Book and Manuscript Library.
8. Ibid.
9. Ibid.
10. Gunders, oral history.
11. Bill Miller, oral history, PwC collection, Columbia University Rare Book and Manuscript Library.
12. Biegler, oral history.
13. Ibid.
14. Gary John Previts, "Accounting History and Public Policy," *Accounting Historians Journal*, fall 1984, 1–17.
15. Biegler, oral history.
16. Ibid.
17. Ibid.
18. Gunders, oral history.
19. Miller, oral history.
20. Wallace E. Olson, *The Accounting Profession, Years of Trial: 1969–1980* (New York: American Institute of Certified Public Accountants, 1982), 215.
21. Biegler, oral history.
22. Gunders, oral history.
23. H. Erich Heinemann, "Accounting Role Undergoing Tests," *New York Times*, March 27, 1966, 1.
24. G. Christian Hill, "Close, Accountants Brought Equity Funds Fraud Almost to Surface in '71. Long Before Case Broke, Peat Marwick Was Hot on Firm's Trail," *Wall Street Journal*, February 20, 1976, 1.
25. Olson, *The Accounting Profession*, 88–90.
26. Harvey Kapnick, *In the Public Interest* (Chicago: Arthur Andersen, 1974), 18.
27. Ibid., 16.
28. Gunders, oral history.

29. Biegler, oral history.

30. Olson, *The Accounting Profession*, 51–52.

31. Gunders, oral history.

32. Biegler, oral history.

33. Gunders, oral history.

CHAPTER 6: THE END OF THE AUDIT

1. Jeff Baily, "Continental Illinois Dismisses Ernst & Whinney," *Wall Street Journal*, November 2, 1984, D1.

2. Ibid.

3. John Biegler, oral history, PwC collection, Columbia University Rare Book and Manuscript Library.

4. Division for CPA firms Practice Section Peer Review Manual, 1981, PwC collection, Columbia University Rare Book and Manuscript Library.

5. Baily, "Continental Illinois."

6. Lee Berton, "Big Accounting Firms Face Ban in S&L Bailouts—Six of Top 10 U.S. Concerns May Miss Out on Work Totaling $100 Million," *Wall Street Journal*, March 14, 1990, A3.

7. Ibid.

8. Ibid.

9. Price Waterhouse, partner newsletter, "Executive Letter," September 5, 1986, PwC collection, Columbia University Rare Book and Manuscript Library.

10. Alison Leigh Cowan, "Bankruptcy Filing by Laventhol," *New York Times*, November 22, 1990, D1.

11. Edward Clifford, "AM International Follows Parent by Seeking Reorganization Plan," *The Globe and Mail*, April 15, 1982, B2.

12. Price Waterhouse, partner newsletter, "Executive Letter."

13. "Judge Says SEC Lacks Proof in Price Waterhouse Case," *Portland Oregonian*, August 1, 1992, E1 (no byline).

14. Price Waterhouse, partner newsletter, March 2, 1986, PwC collection, Columbia University Rare Book and Manuscript Library.

15. AICPA, *Big Eight Valuation by Fortune 1000 Executives 1990* (New York: AICPA, 1990), 3.
16. Price Waterhouse, New York metro region newsletter, July 1993, PwC collection, Columbia University Rare Book and Manuscript Library.
17. Ibid.
18. Dana Hermanson (co-author), Committee of Sponsoring Organizations of the Treadway Commission (COS), 1999 report.
19. *O'Dwyer's PR Services Report,* October 1995, 1 (no byline).
20. Michael Quint, "Peat Marwick Moves to Garner Some Deal Fees," *New York Times,* September 1, 1995, D1.
21. Judith Burns, "Court Rejects KPMG Appeal," Dow Jones News Service, May 15, 2002.

CHAPTER 7:   THE FIGHT OF HIS LIFE

1. Michael Daly, "Success Story Beyond Belief," *New York Daily News,* February 6, 2002, 8.
2. Amey Stone and Mike Brewster, *King of Capital* (New York: Wiley, 2002), 10.
3. Arthur Levitt, *Take on the Street* (New York: Pantheon, 2002), 25.
4. Arthur Levitt, speech at Columbia University Business School, December 5, 1972, Arthur Levitt Jr. collection, Columbia University Rare Book and Manuscript Library.
5. Arthur Levitt, speech at *Business Week* conference on personal financial planning, May 22, 1978, Arthur Levitt Jr. collection, Columbia University Rare Book and Manuscript Library.
6. Arthur Levitt, speech at Securities Regulation Institute, January 17, 1979, Arthur Levitt Jr. collection, Columbia University Rare Book and Manuscript Library.
7. Arthur Levitt, speech at Citizen's Union, April 17, 1979, Arthur Levitt Jr. collection, Columbia University Rare Book and Manuscript Library.
8. Levitt, *Take on the Street,* 165.
9. Ibid., 152.
10. Arthur Levitt, speech at 24th annual national conference on SEC

developments, AICPA, Washington, D.C., December 10, 1996, text sourced from SEC.gov.

11. Arthur Levitt, speech at New York University Center for Law and Business, September 28, 1998, text sourced from SEC.gov.

12. Michael Porter, letter to Arthur Levitt, December 12, 1998, Arthur Levitt Jr. collection, Columbia University Rare Book and Manuscript Library.

13. James E. Wheeler, letter to Arthur Levitt, November 23, 1998, Arthur Levitt Jr. collection, Columbia University Rare Book and Manuscript Library.

14. Report and Recommendations of the Blue Ribbon Committee on Improving the Effectiveness of Corporate Audit Committees, February 1999.

15. James Taranto, letter to Arthur Levitt, May 11, 1999, Arthur Levitt Jr. collection, Columbia University Rare Book and Manuscript Library.

16. Lynn Turner, letter to ISB chairman William Allen, Arthur Levitt Jr. collection, Columbia University Rare Book and Manuscript Library.

17. Eli Mason, letter to Charles Schumer, July 8, 2000, Arthur Levitt Jr. collection, Columbia University Rare Book and Manuscript Library.

18. Levitt, *Take on the Street,* 128.

19. Lynn Turner, interview with author.

20. KPMG source, interview with author.

21. Arthur Levitt, letter to Bevis Longstreth, November 15, 2000, Arthur Levitt Jr. collection, Columbia University Rare Book and Manuscript Library.

22. "War of Independence," *The Economist,* August 12, 2000 (online).

23. Editorial, "Unbiased Accounting," *New York Times,* July 18, 2000, A20.

24. Arthur Levitt, letter to Ken Lay, June 13, 2000, Arthur Levitt Jr. collection, Columbia University Rare Book and Manuscript Library.

25. Joseph Lieberman, letter to Arthur Levitt, March 21, 2000, Arthur Levitt Jr. collection, Columbia University Rare Book and Manuscript Library.

26. Spencer Abraham and Robert Bennett, letter to Arthur Levitt,

December 16, 1999, Arthur Levitt Jr. collection, Columbia University Rare Book and Manuscript Library.

27. Financial Executives Institute, letter to Arthur Levitt, May 20, 1999, Arthur Levitt Jr. collection, Columbia University Rare Book and Manuscript Library.
28. Barry K. Rogstad, letter to Arthur Levitt, July 14, 2000, Arthur Levitt Jr. collection, Columbia University Rare Book and Manuscript Library
29. Shaun F. O'Malley, prepared testimony before U.S. Senate Committee on Banking, Housing, and Urban Affairs, September 28, 2000.
30. Phil Laskaway, testimony at SEC Hearing on Auditor Independence, September 20, 2000, text sourced from SEC.gov.
31. Bevis Longstreth, testimony at SEC Hearing on Auditor Independence, September 9, 2000, text sourced from SEC.gov.
32. Terry Strange, testimony at SEC Hearing on Auditor Independence, July 26, 2000, text sourced from SEC.gov.
33. Arthur Levitt, testimony at SEC Hearing on Auditor Independence, September 26, 2000.
34. Laskaway, testimony at SEC hearing.
35. Levitt, *Take on the Street*, 133.
36. Arthur Levitt, letter to Jim Morhard, October 19, 2000, Arthur Levitt Jr. collection, Columbia University Rare Book and Manuscript Library.

CHAPTER 8:   ENRON AND THE FALL OF ANDERSEN

1. Arthur Andersen web site, Energy and Utilities Industry page.
2. Elizabeth A. Tilney, testimony before House Subcommittee on Oversight and Investigations Committee on Education and Workforce, May 20, 1998.
3. Ibid.
4. Joseph Berardino, Senate testimony, December 12, 2001.
5. Stephen Taub, "Question Mark-to-Market: Energy Accounting Scrutinized," CFO.com, December 4, 2001 (www.CFO.com, site archive).

6. Berardino, testimony before House Subcommittee.
7. Steven L. Schwarcz, *Enron and the Use and Abuse of Special Purpose Entities in Corporate Structures,* unpublished paper, Duke University School of Law, 2002.
8. Tilney, testimony before House Subcommittee.
9. John A. Byrne, "Fall from Grace," *Business Week,* August 12, 2002, 52.
10. Ibid.
11. Ibid.
12. Berardino, Senate testimony.
13. AICPA, annual report, 2001–2002.
14. Ibid.
15. C. E. Andrews and Dorsey L. Baskin, statement to House Energy and Commerce Committee, Destruction of Enron Audit Documents, January 24, 2002.
16. U.S. Department of Justice indictment of Arthur Andersen LLP, unsealed March 14, 2002.
17. AICPA, annual report, 2001–2002.
18. Ibid.
19. Ibid.
20. Byrne, "Fall from Grace," 50.
21. Ibid., 50.
22. Mark Friedlander, interview with author.
23. Coretta Robinson, interview with author.

CHAPTER 9:   ACCOUNTING 101

1. Michael Salsbury, testimony at House Financial Services Committee hearings on Global Crossing, March 21, 2002.
2. "Another Cowboy Bites the Dust," *The Economist,* June 29, 2002 (no byline).
3. John A. Byrne, "Fall from Grace," *Business Week,* August 12, 2002, 50.
4. Lynn Turner, telephone interview with author.
5. John Biggs, testimony before Senate Banking, Housing and Urban Affairs Committee, September 28, 2000.

6. Ibid.
7. Spencer Stuart, press release, "How to Fund Corporate Governance," October 30, 2002.
8. "The Pitt and Webster Show," *The Economist*, November 2, 2002 (online).
9. Sebastian Mallaby, "The Chairman Joins the Lobbyist," *Washington Post*, October 28, 2002, A19.
10. Biggs, testimony.
11. Ibid.
12. Robert Trigaux, "Despite Fixes, Corporate System Still Broken," *St. Petersburg Times*, October 25, 2002, E1.
13. Ibid.
14. "Independence vs. Advocacy," accountingmalpractice.com.
15. "Pitt and the Pendulum," *CFO Magazine*, October 2002, 55 (no byline).
16. SEC.gov.
17. Report of the United States General Accounting Office, October 4, 2002 (2002 totals are projected).

CHAPTER 10: THE FUTURE OF ACCOUNTING

1. Lynn Turner, telephone interview with author.
2. John A. Byrne, "Fall from Grace," *Business Week*, August 12, 2002, 52.
3. Jon Madonna, telephone interview with author.

BIBLIOGRAPHY

Anderson, Arthur, *Behind the Figures: Addresses and Articles, 1913–1941* (Chicago: Arthur Anderson, 1970).

DiPiazza, Samuel A., Jr., and Robert G. Eccles, *Building Public Trust: The Future of Corporate Reporting* (New York: Wiley, 2002).

Hanson, Walter E., *Peat, Marwick, Mitchell & Co.: 80 Years of Professional Growth* (Atlantic City, N.J.: Peat, Marwick, Mitchell, 1978).

Kapnick, Harvey, *In the Public Interest* (Chicago: Arthur Anderson, 1974).

McMickle, Peter L., and Richard G. Vangermeersch, *The Origins of a Great Profession* (Memphis, Tenn.: McMickle & Vangermeersch, 1987).

Olson, Wallace E., *The Accounting Profession, Years of Trial: 1969–1980* (New York: American Institute of Certified Public Accountants, 1982).

O'Malley, Shaun F., *Price Waterhouse: 100 Years of Service in the United States* (Atlantic City, N.J.: Price Waterhouse, 1990).

Previts, Gary John, and Barbara Dubis Merino, *A History of Accountancy in the United States: The Cultural Significance of Accounting* (Columbus: Ohio State University Press, 1998).

Stevens, Mark, *The Accounting Wars* (New York: Macmillan, 1985).

INDEX

auditor independence *(continued)*
  consulting's effect on, 126–127, 145, 154
  financial interests in clients, 116, 127, 208
  for watchdog function, 164
auditor independence proposals (and SEC), 188, 190, 196–198
  accounting firms' reactions, 208–218
  consulting-auditing separation, 208–218
  hearings on, 218–221
  opponents of SEC proposals, 213–218
auditor shopping, 132, 269
auditors, 15, 19, 30, 33, 125. *See also* accountants
  audits of, 80
  changing, 114, 132, 140
  conflict with consultants, 176. *See also* consulting
  government, 43, 64, 79
  incentives for, 291, 294
  internal, 258, 260–261
  relationship with client's management, 73, 114, 253, 278. *See also* auditor independence
  responsibilities of, 50, 54, 62, 119–121, 132
  rotation of, 156–157, 181, 263
audits, 5–7, 11, 178
  British methods, 75, 95
  certainty in, 68–69, 83
  certifications, 53
  charges for, 19, 139–140, 162–163, 179, 236–237, 287, 291
  consulting and. *See* consulting
  as consulting tool, 177–179
  content, 103
  cost, 94, 213, 265, 274
  detailed field testing, 29, 49, 285, 297
  difficult, 169–170
  focus change away from, 10–11, 124, 138, 182, 285
  forensic, 272–273, 291

fraud detection during. *See* fraud detection
by government, 9
independence of, 4, 14. *See also* independent audits
by insurance companies, 294–295
internal. *See* internal audits
large firms' domination, 115
mandatory, 44, 50
neutrality in, 296
opinions, 73
preparation for, 97
pressure for, 53
product differentiation in, 155–156
quality of. *See* quality of audit
quarterly, 76, 85–86
report format model, 82
rigor of, 4, 155. *See also* auditor independence
risk-based, 179, 297
risk in, 11, 119, 145
scope of, 50
standards. *See* accounting rules and standards
time allowed for, 12
uses of, 51–52, 275
value of, 120, 124, 259, 285

balance sheet, 47, 284
Balmuth, Miriam, 25
banking, 36, 144, 211. *See also* savings and loan crisis
  investment, 169, 183–185, 191
Barkley, Alben, 79–80
Barr, Andy, 116, 131, 133
Baskin, Dorsey, 237, 242, 243
Bass, Carl, 235
Bayh, Evan, 205
Belmont, August, 53
Bennett, Robert, 205, 206, 215, 222
Berardino, Joseph, 229–230, 260, 289–290
  as Andersen leader, 190, 239, 243–246
  as negotiator, 222–223

INDEX